D1489988

PRAISE F
THE SPIRITUALITY OF WORK AND LEADERSHIP

"Among the deepest and most important management thinkers of our age - someone whose ideas help us reexamine the role business plays in society and our lives. His latest book, *The Spirituality of Work & Leadership*, is among his most thought-provoking."

DAVID BENNETT, CHAIRMAN, VIRGIN MONEY PLC,
AND CHAIRMAN ASHMORE PLC

"Gibbons towers above business thinkers in the way that Drucker did in an earlier era. Even Drucker did not bring to business thinking the breadth of scholarship and originality of thought that Gibbons does."

ROBERT ENTENMANN, EVP AND GLOBAL HEAD OF E-COMMERCE
AT UNICREDIT, FORMER GLOBAL HEAD OF MARKETS AT ABN-AMRO

"An incredible dive into the intersection of spirituality and business. Gibbons wrote the book that needed to be written for our world — showing us how our spirituality is the key to our humanity in business."

MARSHALL GOLDSMITH IS THE NEW YORK TIMES #1 BESTSELLING AUTHOR
OF TRIGGERS, MOJO, AND WHAT GOT YOU HERE WON'T GET YOU THERE.

"Paul Gibbons' excellent book on spirituality at work suggests gaps and weaknesses in the definitions of workplace spirituality, as well as gaps and weaknesses in the evidence that it helps workers and workplaces. His integration with other disciplines, particularly the psychology of religion, business ethics, and organizational science, produced unique and groundbreaking insights."

JUDI NEAL — FOUNDER OF THE TYSON CENTER FOR FAITH AND
SPIRITUALITY

"A comprehensive and unflinching look at the conflict between humans as material cogs in the economic machine and the human potential for spiritual thriving. Gibbons' work also gives good guidance for functioning as a spiritual person in businesses driven by the bottom line."

DON MAYER, PROFESSOR OF BUSINESS ETHICS AND LEGAL STUDIES, UNIVERSITY OF DENVER

Paul Gibbons' new book examines the pros and cons of the many different approaches to bringing spirituality to leadership and the workplace. To this end, leaders, scholars and those involved in the world of organisations will resonate with much of what he has to say and be guided to be more thoughtful in their tendency to blindly follow the latest fads in the world of leadership and organizations.

DR. ROBIN LINCOLN WOOD, AUTHOR OF 8 AWARD-WINNING BOOKS ON TRANSFORMING ORGANIZATIONS AND LEADERS IN THE 21ST CENTURY

"Paul Gibbons has spent a large part of his life in the biggest and most admired global corporations and has thought deeply about spirituality, and broad intellectual disciplines such as philosophy, psychology, sociology, religion, management, leadership, and performance. His book, *The Spirituality of Work & Leadership*, is a valuable treatise for those wanting to bring greater spirituality into their workplaces as well as those interested in developing a broader and deeper understanding of spirituality in their lives generally."

DANIEL J. SWEENEY, PH.D. - DIRECTOR OF THE INSTITUTE FOR ENTERPRISE ETHICS, THE UNIVERSITY OF DENVER

"Paul has done it again! This time he explores spirituality through a comprehensive analysis of its evolution and the impact it has in our world today as well as how it informs our future. This is a must-read book for anyone who wants to learn more about how spirituality evolved and how it informs our world."

MAUREEN METCALF – CEO INNOVATIVE LEADERSHIP INSTITUTE

"Gibbons' exploration into the relationship between work and purpose embraces the diversity of spiritual experience while envisioning a common starting point of shared human values. His arguments are clear and passionate, resonating a pearl of practical wisdom and a new vision for the role of spirituality in the workplace."

TYLER MONGAN, PRESIDENT HA:KU GLOBAL

"In his new book, Paul has once again decided to face the big existential issues of our era. In a time of great divisiveness, he finds common ground in the worlds of religion and spirituality and from there into the challenge of humanizing business and reshaping capitalism. His ambitious thinking is never constrained, and he is undaunted by seemingly intractable problems. This is a compelling read and for anyone who is seeking answers to some of the biggest issues of the day!"

CHRIS MAJER, CEO HUMAN POTENTIAL PROJECT, AUTHOR OF POWER TO TRANSFORM

Cover image: The Carina Nebula seen from the Hubble Telescope – a "stellar nursery," 8,500 light-years from Earth, in Sagittarius, containing a "hyper-giant" star 150 times more massive than our Sun.

Publisher: Phronesis Media

Senior developmental editor: Kelli Collins
Diagrams: Andrés Goldstein
Cover: Dania Zafar
Interior: Dania Zafar
Proofing and indexing: Cory Emberson
Publicity: Jo Detavernier

Phronesis Media is the publishing company owned by the author Paul Gibbons. For rights, foreign language translations, and bulk orders, please contact the author directly: paul@paulgibbons.net

Printed in the United States of America First Printing October 2020

ISBN – 13: 978-0-997-6512-7-0 (paperback)
ISBN – 13: 978-0-9976512-6-3 (ebook)

Library of Congress Control Number: 2020946798

The
SPIRITUALITY
of WORK *and*
LEADERSHIP

Finding Meaning, Joy, and Purpose in What You Do

PAUL GIBBONS

DEDICATION
TO THE "PALE BLUE DOT"

(On seeing the first images of Earth from Voyager, a pixel-sized dot on the fringe of a myriad of Milky Way stars.)

"Look again at that dot. That's here. That's home. That's us. On it everyone you love, everyone you know, everyone you ever heard of, every human being who ever was, lived out their lives. The aggregate of our joy and suffering, thousands of confident religions, ideologies, and economic doctrines, every hunter and forager, every hero and coward, every creator and destroyer of civilization, every king and peasant, every young couple in love, every mother and father, hopeful child, inventor and explorer, every teacher of morals, every corrupt politician, every "superstar," every "supreme leader," every saint and sinner in the history of our species lived there—on a mote of dust suspended in a sunbeam.

The Earth is a very small stage in a vast cosmic arena. Think of the rivers of blood spilled by all those generals and emperors so that, in glory and triumph, they could become the momentary masters of a fraction of a dot. Think of the endless cruelties visited by the inhabitants of one corner of this pixel on the scarcely distinguishable inhabitants of some other corner, how frequent their misunderstandings, how eager they are to kill one another, how fervent their hatreds.

Our posturings, our imagined self-importance, the delusion that we have some privileged position in the Universe, are challenged by this point of pale light. Our planet is a lonely speck in the great enveloping cosmic dark. In our obscurity, in all this vastness, there is no hint that help will come from elsewhere to save us from ourselves.

The Earth is the only world known so far to harbor life. There is nowhere else, at least in the near future, to which our species could migrate. Visit, yes. Settle, not yet. Like it or not, for the moment the Earth is where we make our stand.

It has been said that astronomy is a humbling and character-building experience. There is perhaps no better demonstration of the folly of human conceits than this distant image of our tiny world. To me, it underscores our responsibility to deal more kindly with one another, and to preserve and cherish the pale blue dot, the only home we've ever known."

Carl Sagan (1994)

ABOUT THE AUTHOR

Paul Gibbons keynotes on five con-
tinents on the future of business,
particularly on humanizing business,
culture change, ethics, and the future
of work.

He has authored five books, most
prominently *The Science of Successful
Organizational Change* and *Impact,* and
he runs the popular philosophy podcast, *Think Bigger Think Better.* Those
books are category best-sellers on Amazon in organizational change,
decision-making, and leadership.

After eight years as a consultant at PwC, Gibbons founded Future
Considerations, a consulting firm that advises major corporations,
including Shell, BP, Barclays, and HSBC, on leadership, strategy, and
culture change. From 2015 to 2018, he was an adjunct professor of
business ethics at the University of Denver.

Paul is also a Fellow of the Royal Society of Arts, a hyperpolyglot,
has been named a "top-20 culture guru," and one of the UK's top
two CEO "super coaches" by CEO magazine. He is a member of the
American Philosophical Association, and the American Association
for the Advancement of Science and lives in the Denver area with
his two sons and enjoys competing internationally at mindsports
such as poker, bridge, MOBA, and chess.

*"True glory consists in doing what deserves to be written,
in writing what deserves to be read, and in so living as to
make the world happier and better for our living in it."*

PLINY THE ELDER

A special thanks

As this writing began, a youthful stranger reached out on LinkedIn saying she was a fan of one of my earlier books. No author that I know can resist flattery and I asked whether she would like an advance chapter of this book. What came back was the finest piece of editing I've ever received including from major magazines and the largest publishing firm in the world. **Kelli Collins** provides a level of insight and challenge at the highest conceptual level while never missing a comma. She has since immeasurably strengthened every chapter, although the errors that remain are mine. This is a much better book for her contribution – thank you, Kelli!

CONTENTS

LIST OF FIGURES

PREFACE

This is a book on spirituality and the human side of business. Within, I suggest that spirituality touches on every aspect of the human experience at work, on every aspect of human capital, and on the purpose of business and the capitalist economic system. The book explores how we can recruit spiritual ideas to help humans find greater meaning and purpose in their work and to improve business practices – that is, to make business more human. **Spirituality, human capital, purpose, business, and capitalism** – each is a vast topic so when this manuscript hit 700 pages, I did us both a favor and split it into two volumes.

The first volume covers individual-level topics only; by that, I mean meaning, work, workaholism, vocation and purpose, happiness, mindfulness, altruism, motivation, engagement, and leadership. The second volume (tentatively called *Culture, Capitalism, Sustainability*) turns first to talent, employer brand, ethics, service, culture, values, and profitability. Then it turns to 21st-century capitalism with its great triumphs and some of its limitations, exploring how spirituality might help us create a more human-centered version of capitalism fitter for the 21st century.

To that discussion, I bring two decades of scholarship in philosophy, psychology, and spirituality and four decades in business from the perspective of an investment banker, consultant, and adjunct professor of business. I also bring my perspective as (former) CEO of a start-up founded to bring spiritual principles to the development of senior business leaders and their teams.

TOUCHY TOPICS

We start by talking broadly about spirituality to capture what people mean by that term in the 21st century. Why? Because the word "spirituality" conjures up different meanings. People tend to equate the term with their cherished beliefs, so we cannot talk about spirituality as it applies to work, nor business, nor to society without giving ourselves some common ground.

There are many good books on specific spiritual traditions and their relationship to work, for example on Christian leadership. This book has a much broader target. My goal in the first part of this book is to help people from across the spectrum of spiritual beliefs and practices better understand each other – (dare we say even love each other?) – perhaps through understanding their tradition in the context of other traditions. The goal is not to help a Christian better understand Christianity nor to help a Humanist deepen their appreciation for Humanism, and it is certainly not to persuade someone to switch horses, but rather to encourage us to treat each other as humans who seek similar goals in different ways.

Inside these volumes, we tread on cherished topics of religion, values, beliefs, culture, and capitalism – some of the things that you are supposed to avoid discussing during Thanksgiving dinner. It is axiomatic about touchy topics that the touchier they are, the more important they are to our shared future. We need to talk about those topics, forthrightly and without platitudes, because they matter – so we will. Some people will therefore take offense – even putting religious, mystical, and secular spirituality next to each other in a common framework will offend people who think their brand of spirituality has a special claim on spiritual ideas.

While I treat all spiritual traditions with reverence and respect, I am sometimes critical of some aspects of some traditions. Humanists can be poor at building community when compared to churches and faith traditions that build strong local and global communities. Mystics enjoy a sense of peace and well-being, but they are often less active in the world (and are certainly disorganized politically, compared to Humanists and the religious.) Certain New Age beliefs fly in the face of science, and some of those unorthodox beliefs are harmful. Some of the faithful use their faith to divide and justify violence. Environmentalists, although mostly right about the plight of the Earth and climate, can be self-righteous toward people who don't yet "get it." (Don't get me started on plastics pollution unless you have an hour to spare.)

Spirituality touches on touchy topics. There are great challenges in writing a book that an Evangelical Christian, a Secular Humanist, and a New Age seeker will each find valuable and enjoy, without avoiding controversy at all costs. It is possible that the religious will find the book too Humanistic, the mystics will find the book too religious, and Humanists will find too much mysticism and religious thought – although that is precisely the aim!

This book's ethos is that we must learn from each other, embrace what unites us, and extract synergy from what divides us.

FROM TOLERATION TO LOVE

"Agree to disagree doesn't work when your liberation and thriving is bound up with mine and vice versa."
CHELSEA ROBINSON

Spirituality, ardently practiced, "comes from a deep place" and people of all traditions have a passion for their own path. That, in my view, is a good thing and empirical research reveals that this depth is linked to numerous outcomes, not least happiness, and well-being. However, that passion for one's own views can lead to lack of toleration of others'.

English philosopher John Locke's 1689 essay, *A Letter Concerning Toleration,* argued for the first time that different religions should tolerate one another. To some extent, that has become the "bar" for inter-spiritual relationships. But we should pause. Toleration – putting up with difference – is an extremely low bar for how citizens and co-workers should interact. Certainly, mere toleration does not seem to be solid ground for forming pluralistic communities. Furthermore, if I merely tolerate your path, that does not necessarily accord me the opportunity to learn from it.

Our time, the third decade of the 21st century, has seen a deepening of moral and ideological conflict. Partly this is because the internet amplifies extreme voices and the media prefers the sensationalism of conflict to reasoned dialog and reasonable moderation. An alternative view, advanced by the late political philosopher Jerry Gaus, suggests this moral disagreement is a feature and not a bug. Moral difference, he argues, is an important form of diversity, a "critical resource for free societies to discover better ways of living together." Morality, Gaus continues[1], is "the crowning achievement of humanity: in our evolutionary development, it made us into the co-operative, fair-minded, and deeply social species that we are – what an incredible species to have invented this way of living together!"

As citizens of pluralistic communities and in a globalized world, we need to evolve our perceptions of other beliefs and perspectives from mere tolerance to reverence. This may be the greatest spiritual challenge of our time.

---

[1] Gaus, J., *The Order of Public Reason: A Theory of Freedom and Morality in a Diverse and Bounded World.* Cambridge: Cambridge University Press, 2011.

LESS TOUCHY, JUST AS CONTROVERSIAL

When we switch gears to talk about how spirituality relates to work and business, we should be in less controversial territory. However in business circles, I'm known as an *agent provocateur* – known for debunking some of the canonical ideas emanating from top business schools, especially those that start with "H." That makes me about as popular as Daenerys Targaryen at the Red Keep.

But to progress our ideas on business, I maintain that we need to take a hard look at cherished assumptions. For example, we fight tooth and nail for democratic rights as citizens, but when we enter a workplace, we sign away all say over decisions that affect our lives and livelihoods along with those of our colleagues. The only rights that remain, apart from the right to quit, are skimpy. So, must democracy end at the door to the corporate lobby?

We cannot challenge the current business paradigm without being willing to painstakingly examine the history and assumptions that got us to where we are. The process of doing so will not be free of controversy.

MORE QUESTIONS THAN ANSWERS

A book on spirituality and business is a poor place to pretend to have definitive answers, and a lengthy book on spirituality and business **without** controversial ideas on complex issues would be a terrible book. **I hope you will find within these chapters much with which to disagree.** In this book, I try to say novel, non-trivial and challenging things, some of which will inevitably be wrong. Proposing new ideas, even if they are shot down, is the way to progress human knowledge. So shoot away!

To that end, this two-volume series is largely written as a dialog or a conversation, prompted by questions. Throughout the two books, I invite you to think along with me on topics interesting and complex.

Here are some of the questions we will explore together in book one:

- What do we mean by "spirituality"? How is it different from religion?
- What is the relationship between religion and science?
- Is the world becoming more or less spiritual?
- What is the historical relationship between spirituality and work? Where does that leave us today?
- Can we prove workplace spirituality is of value? What is the evidence?
- What are the benefits of private prayer or meditation at work?
- What insight does spirituality give us into human motivation?
- What is the purpose of purpose?
- How do we create purposeful lives and organizations?
- What is the link between leadership and spirituality?
- Can spiritual experiences at work be cultivated?
- What would a spiritual consulting firm look like?

In book two, *Culture, Capitalism, Sustainability*, the questions[2] we explore together are:

- What is the relationship between money, consumerism, and spirituality?
- What new conflicts might a spiritual organization face?
- Does spirituality make you a more ethical person? Could spirituality make businesses more ethical?
- Why do culture change efforts usually fail?
- Do values statements add any value?
- Might spirituality enhance external or employer brand?
- What is the link between personal purpose and corporate purpose?
- Is there such a thing as a spiritual culture?

---

[2] Book two is in draft and the title and contents will almost certainly change between now and publication.

- Do spiritual values conflict with capitalist ones?
- Might spirituality guide corporate social responsibility (CSR) and sustainability?
- What have been recent attempts to reform capitalism and create a new vision of it?
- What is the difference between conscious capitalism and human-centered capitalism?
- Could businesses use spirituality for illegitimate aims (to make tolerable the intolerable, among other things?)

A SPIRITUAL AND INTELLECTUAL DILETTANTE

"Siempre imaginé que el Paraíso sería algún tipo de biblioteca." (I have always imagined heaven to be some kind of library.)

JORGE LUIS BORGES

There is a pretense in formal and academic writing that the author writes objectively, in the third person, and without perspective. Not only does it make for dull writing, but, as philosopher Thomas Nagel reminds us, there is no "view from nowhere." We cannot, as writers and thinkers, stand outside of reality and observe from "on high." In my writing, I often write in the first-person to avoid such a pretense.

Since the early 1990s, I've explored widely in contemporary spirituality. This stemmed from curiosity and perhaps also some weakness of character – there is much to be said for sticking to one thing and doing it well. On this journey, I've had daily practices from across the spectrum, from Bible study, to daily yoga, to daily meditation, to journaling, and many, many more. I've been on 10-day monastic retreats and every kind of "Californian" weekend workshop that you might care to imagine.

Intellectually, my dilettantism is much worse. My passions have included electronics, computer science, math, biochemistry, medicine, neuroscience, and economics. Those subjects were my first loves, but after I turned 30, I switched to the humanities and social sciences: psychology, organizational behavior, leadership, sustainability, culture, philosophy, behavioral science, and evolutionary biology. Today, I read mostly history and philosophy.

My mission when it comes to business writing is to turn that dilettantism from weakness into strength and to harvest ideas from the sciences and philosophy that can be useful to business leaders. In this book, you will get a bit of everything. I think I've even managed to weave in some ideas from mathematics. There are two consequences to this. First, almost everything you read is novel—my own research on business and spirituality—and second, the risk of novelty is that new ideas need testing.

Finally, I try to have fun. Sadly, I do not think I've ever chuckled while reading a book on spirituality—we do-gooders are so earnest. To add to the fun, I'm very fond of quotes and have included hundreds within—from scholars, poets, philosophers, Tyrion Lannister, Inigo Montoya, Notorious B.I.G, and more. There is too little beauty in business books, so I've added a few images and diagrams that break up the walls of text. I use slang throughout and cuss a bit more than Mother Teresa but less than Tony Soprano. While this book is neither funny nor beautiful nor poetic, I hope to add some humor, some beauty, and some poetry to make it more fun to read.

This is an ambitious and maybe foolish project. A book that tries to capture too many things – spirituality, talent, business, and capitalism – risks capturing nothing at all. A book that tries to welcome readers of all spiritual stripes risks welcoming no one. But we proceed.

INTRODUCTION

Workplace spirituality for skeptics

WORKPLACE SPIRITUALITY FOR SKEPTICS

DEAR SKEPTIC

You are reading a book with "spirituality" in the title, so either 1) spirituality is important to you, or 2) you're curious about what spirituality might have to do with business, or 3) you're a skeptic-agnostic who had this book thrust in your hands by an annoying but well-intentioned friend.

That super-spiritual friend thought you needed some spirituality, so long ago persuaded you to spend a weekend at a sweat lodge, and the only thing you took away was a dry-cleaning bill to remove the scent of sage and patchouli from your clothes. A few years later, that friend dragged you to a yoga class where you fell asleep during the opening *savasana* and flatulated non-stop during *Adho Mukha Shvanasana* (downward dog). She assured you there is science behind mindfulness, but repeatedly chanting "*om mani padme hum*" didn't seem very scientific. Never again – no more spirituality!

Even if you are committed to a naturalist worldview and secular values, this book is still for you – perhaps particularly so. In this book, I'll argue that everyone, regardless of their spiritual beliefs – even the hardest-nosed businessperson and the most stridently atheistic – can use ideas from spirituality for the betterment of their working lives and the world without having to (so to speak) eat the whole metaphysical enchilada. There are universals from the world of spirituality, grounded in philosophy and evolutionary biology, that will resonate with you, dear non-believer, even if you disdain the word "spirituality" and finally decided to ghost that friend who "helpfully" bought you this book.

Those universals come from the definition of spirituality that I later suggest: **growing and striving for meaning, purpose, goodness, and connectedness.** That definition connects not just religious but also secular approaches to the good life. We all want meaning in our lives, are inspired by purpose, have and pursue our conceptions of the good, and yearn to be connected. Growing and striving, I propose, are part of what makes us distinctively human.

That journey toward becoming more human is one that inspires me and what inspired this book series (although the quick-witted skeptic may wonder what else a human could become other than human!) Becoming more human is doing more of what makes us uniquely so – developing and using our superpowers as a species such as imagining more perfect worlds, using science to understand the world we live in, and collaborating for the greater good. Humans are the only animals who do those things (to my knowledge), but we can certainly do them better. **Humanizing workplaces** means creating an environment where such "superpowers" can flourish. **Humanizing capitalism**, in the next volume, considers how capitalism might reshape itself toward more human goals.

Spirituality, for skeptics, mystics, and the faithful, can help guide your personal development and vocation choice. It touches on topics such as mindfulness, human flourishing, and our relationship with work. Along with helping us become more fully ourselves (so to speak), spirituality can provide insight and guidance for businesses to help them become more fit for humans – influencing topics such as culture, values, brand, engagement, and profitability. Finally, ideas from spirituality can help us reorient our economic system toward one that is more focused on human need and less on human greed.

"Spirituality matters, but in business?"

Even the ardently spiritual might find themselves skeptical. Could not meaning and purpose be saved "for Sundays?" Psychologists tell us, as we explore later, that people compartmentalize, perhaps having resigned themselves to the drudgery of a working life bereft of meaning and purpose. "Work sucks, because, you know, it is work." You may practice your spirituality in your spiritual or faith community but find it understandably hard to put those principles into practice at work. Within this book, there are ideas in every chapter on how to do that.

Perhaps you think that business "all 'bout the Benjamins."[3] True – that is society's current paradigm, but the business paradigm was not handed to humans on tablets of stone. We designed it, and we can change it. **This is a truth worth remembering – the systems humans make, we can change; the systems we break, we can fix.**

As citizens, workers, and business leaders, **we have the power to reshape the culture of business and the laws that enable it** – but we must do so in a principled way. And from where, we should ask, might those principles come from? Here we should cast our net as widely as possible – those are complex human phenomena and restricting ourselves to just orthodox business writing would be a mistake. The areas I think we can learn from are:

- The **wisdom literatures,** but wisely used. For example, the Abrahamic religions' wisdom literature, though sometimes wise, has dysfunctional views on work (if you care about

---

[3] For non-Americans, Benjamin Franklin is on the hundred-dollar bill. Benjamins are good things.

happiness and joy and freedom, their views on work were pretty dark.)

- **Philosophy**, but again used wisely. Just because Plato said it, does not make it true. There is an apocryphal quote, perhaps from Richard Feynman, "I like to quote Einstein because nobody ever argues when you quote Einstein" – let us avoid that. However, we can ground our ideas on happiness, good life, ethics, flourishing in philosophical ethics.

- **Moral intuitions and reason** should balance the influence of older texts. Neither the Tao Te Ching, the Upanishads, nor the Book of Mormon anticipated artificial intelligence, human cloning, or robots replacing half of humanity's workers. Some wisdom depends on context and the 21st-century context is different.

- **Evolutionary biology and anthropology**. Our purpose must be grounded in what we are able to do and what is special about us – our superpowers. A purpose for dolphins should make use of echolocation; ours should align with what we have learned about ourselves from our biological and cultural heritage. Over millennia, we have risen above the instinctual to become more collaborative, more creative, and more altruistic.

- **Systems theory** helps us understand not just the Interdependence of the biosphere and humankind, but the realization that outcomes and behaviors result from systemic effects, not just culture, values, and beliefs. The experience of COVID-19 in 2020 showed us how politics, medicine, economics, business, and personal health are intertwined and that pulling on just a single lever results in devastating error.

"Sure, but I have a business to run!"

You may also think, "None of this is practical; I have a business to run. I don't have time to care." There are **practical reasons** to care – here is just one example. You probably know that employee engagement numbers tell a terrifying story – only 30 percent of US workers are fully engaged. Research suggests that the effect of money on engagement is tiny – that is, leaders cannot "buy" engagement, and the marginal cost of increasing it through financial means is exceptionally high. This applies moreso to highly paid knowledge workers, many of whom earn six figures. Buying engagement through significant percentage increases in compensation gets expensive and is ineffective.

So, what is effective? Humans engage when work is meaningful and purposeful – but how many jobs or workplaces are designed with meaning and purpose in mind? In essence, the link between spirituality and business boils down to the need to make business more human, including ideas on what makes work meaningful and purpose-driven, what allows workplaces to nurture that, and much, much more.

One hundred years ago, making business more human meant five-day work weeks, safer workplaces, sick pay, and vacation time. (Thank you, union movement!) Over a century's time scale, our concepts of work, workplaces, business, and human flourishing have evolved. Today, that focus has shifted toward the concepts of meaning, purpose, wellness at work, mindfulness, community, and other human-centered phenomena. If you believe, as I do, that such conversations, coupled with policy and action, make our **businesses more fit for humans**, we have found ethical and practical grounds for our interest in spirituality and business.

The sea change in business is not just to the "soft" side of business, people, and culture, but it is also structural (the "hard" stuff.)

As I document in *Impact*,[4] gig working, global teams, and teleworking are important new species in the employment landscape. This has profound implications for how workers connect to their work and to its purpose. Remote workers and their leaders face challenges such as loneliness, feeling that they are "always-on," maintaining team spirit and creating company culture by virtual means. As I concluded in *Impact*:

> *When employees aren't tethered by hard, structural relationships, when they aren't physically connected, then company ethos (vision, values, purpose, meaning, ethics) becomes more important.*

The implications of these structural changes to business, accelerated by the 2020 pandemic, require that leaders understand purpose and meaning. But as we see when we talk about work in Chapter IV, many jobs still seem meaningless. Is that meaninglessness innate – a property of the work – or can one bring meaning and purpose to serving Chicken McNuggets? This jocular question is serious – what matters more for creating meaning and purpose: what you do, or which attitudes you bring to your work? And how do leaders facilitate and enable meaning-making – a deeply personal process?

Along with advances in business culture and structure, the last two decades have ushered in the advance of transformational ideas such as sustainability, net-zero businesses, organizational democracy, corporate social responsibility, and human rights. It seems to me that businesses are doing far greater good than they did 20 years ago. Now, being a "good business" is not just a hygiene factor or a greenwashing exercise, but a differentiator and an opportunity for innovation, better customer service, and cost reduction, all while reducing "footprint."

---

[4] *Impact: 21st Century Change Management, Behavioral Science, Digital Transformation, and the Future of Work*, Paul Gibbons, Phronesis Media, 2019.

While the moral center of gravity of business has changed for the better, and hopefully forever, the war is not yet won. We can further progress business by using insights from spirituality to inform today's ethical discussions about sustainability, corporate responsibility, emergence, presence, organizational democracy, whole-systems problem solving, multi-stakeholder dialogue, non-violent communication, and the purpose of business.

THE WORKPLACE SPIRITUALITY MOVEMENT

With our great power comes great responsibility. Our spiritual evolution and collective wisdom struggle to keep pace with the power granted by our technological evolution. But we can harness power of business for good, scaling science for the benefit of humanity, furthering human flourishing, and creating communities where people can learn and contribute more than they could alone. Those are the noblest aims business may pursue."[5]

If you have had a long working career, since the 1970s in my case, you will know that advocating "business responsibility" during the "greed-is-good" 1980s would have merited a chuckle or snide remark. If you had tried foolishly to place on the board's agenda the question of how to consider the needs of communities and the environment instead of only those of shareholders, you probably would have been laughed at. Much less might you have found a single book on the subjects of meaning, purpose, goodness, connectedness, or other spiritual concepts as they pertain to business. Even in the late 1990s, when I told people I was writing on business

---

[5] From *Impact: 21-century Change Management, Behavioral Science, Digital Transformation, and the Future of Work*, Phronesis Media, 2019.

and spirituality, they'd wisecrack, "that will be a short book." Little did they know.

In 2020, a plethora of business magazines including Forbes, Inc., Huffington Post, Entrepreneur, Fox Business, People Matters, and The Washington Post began to talk about "business meets spirituality" as a new theme for this decade. The New York Times talked about a new group of spiritual consultants for business who claim that spiritual advertising, ritual, and office design are opportunities to bring the sacred to work.[6]

They were twenty years too late. In the late 1990s, the "**workplace spirituality movement**" (WPSM) was born, quickly attaining fad-like status with many hundreds of books, conferences, or papers published per year. Dozens of consulting firms sprung up, including my own in 2001, although we were more reticent then about using the "s-word."

Given that there were several hundred books published on the topic in the 90s and early 00s, and now there are only a few per year, maybe it was a fad, and today's interest will end at a few magazine articles. Is the topic like an aging rockstar attempting a comeback?

Not so fast.

Talking about **purpose** or **mindfulness** in a 1990s business would have seemed very "out there," but today some of the world's most admired companies talk about those concepts constantly.

Many management and leadership terms and concepts that were birthed in the 1990s have spiritual roots. Although the WPSM fad may have faded, these concepts have become commonplace in the business world. Such concepts include **vision, values, community, meaning, purpose, calling, mindfulness, vocation, service, and servant leadership.**

For example, the word "vision" comes from Numbers 12:6 and Daniel 7:13. Today, creating shared **vision** is a standard leadership tool, but in 1993, it was too "woo." IBM's CEO Lou Gerstner decried

---

[6] Bowles, N.," God is Dead. So Is the Office. These People Want to Save Both", New York Times, August 28, 2020.

the importance of "vision" as a leadership tool in 1993 saying, "The last thing IBM needs right now is a vision." (Ironically, the statement was a kind of vision, demanding a focus on urgently needed improvements.) Similarly, the word "vocation" comes to us from the Latin *vocātiō*, meaning a call, or summons. Originally, vocation meant "called to spiritual work." Today it means "called to any occupation to which a person is spiritually drawn."

While the workplace spirituality movement has faded (today's mentions pale compared to twenty years ago,) it left an imprint on management ideas and books (shown in Figure 0-1) that do not explicitly refer to spirituality.

Some 21st-century spiritually oriented business topics that do not use the term "spirituality"

Topic	Author/ source
Theory U (book)	Otto Scharmer
Spiral Dynamics (book)	Don Beck, Christopher Cowan
Workplace democracy	Brian Robertson, Paul Gibbons
Non-violent Communication (book)	Arnold Mindell
Purpose and meaning at work	Multiple authors
Mindfulness and neuroscience	Dan Siegal
Finding your vocation or calling	Multiple authors
Developmental leadership frameworks	Robert Kegan
Conscious Capitalism	John Mackey, Raj Sisodia
Principles	Ray Dalio
Leadership and Self-deception	Arbinger Institute
Thriveability	Robin Wood
Natural Capitalism (book)	Amory Lovins, Paul Hawkins
Defining Moments (book)	Joseph Badaracco
Ecology of Commerce (book)	Paul Hawken
Integral theory in business	Ken Wilber, Paul Gibbons, Frederic Laloux
Holacracy (book)	Brian Robertson
Servant Leadership (book)	Robert Greenleaf

© PAUL GIBBONS — PAULGIBBONS.NET

Figure 0-1: List of spiritually oriented business topics that do not use the term "spirituality."

At various times during the last decades, I have written on these topics or used their tools in my consulting business – sometimes with great results and sometimes less so. I expect the earnest reader of this book to find some guidance on which to try and which to avoid.

Partying like 1999

In the mid-1990s, the business world was agog with a radical new concept called "emotional intelligence." That idea helped to broaden the way we think about humans at work (a nail in the coffin of the "machine" metaphor[7] so prevalent then) – and I wondered whether we might go further, whether bringing spiritual ideas to work might expand our understanding the way emotional intelligence had. I got lucky.

PricewaterhouseCoopers was willing to sponsor my research, so I turtled up in a tiny dorm room style apartment on sabbatical, stacked it with 100 thick academic books on theology, spirituality, and psychology and dug in to write a dissertation (downloaded 10,000 times) that became the first draft of this book.

That thesis was titled *Spirituality at Work: Definitions, measures, assumptions, and validity claims.* (Still awake?) It proposed that many worthwhile ideas about **humankind's relationship to work, to purpose, and to ethics have roots in spiritual writings**, and that scholars outside of management circles (theologians, philosophers, mystics, psychologists, and sociologists of religion) offered insights on topics we care about as business leaders and as business scholars. Some of this breadth of topics I discussed back in the day, and in this edition, are in the table below.

My zeal for this topic became evangelical in 2000. I taught a gradu-ate-level course in spirituality and change, was a contributor to a book

---

[7] There are eight metaphors, according to author Gareth Morgan, that guide organiza-tions (see his must-read Images of Organization.) The (now out of fashion) machine metaphor emphasizes control, systematization, hierarchy, and reproducibility.

Spirituality at Work topics

Individual	• Vocation choice – calling • Leadership – values-based, servant leadership • Meaning and purpose • Well-being, spiritual well-being • Creativity & innovation/ intuition • Work-life balance • Spiritual practices at work – meditation, prayer • Spiritual experiences at work – joy, epiphany
Organization	• Design of work • Team and community building • Poetry, storytelling, metaphor, ritual, myth • Systems thinking, emergence, unfoldment • Culture change • Spiritual organizing principles – democracy, anti-hierarchy • Transformation/ change • Interventions – e.g. EAP
Organizations and Society	• Business ethics • Sustainability • Post-capitalist organizations • Social responsibility

© PAUL GIBBONS   PAULGIBBONS.NET

Figure 0 –2: From the 1999 edition of Spirituality at Work – topics in workplace spirituality.

called *Work and Spirit*, joined the advisory council of the US Academy of Management and toured the world talking about spirituality at work. Then I started a firm with spiritual principles at its heart.

My mission was to make possible workplaces where people might bring their passions, values, spiritual practices, and "whole selves" to work. But the scientist in me worried. I felt that the subject needed a healthy dose of self-criticism and a whole lot more and better evidence. Even today I find too much of what I read **even in the academic literature** "hand waving,"[8] for example:

- "...it is about people who perceive themselves as spirited beings, whose spirit needs energizing at work."
- "...there are parallels between the roles of shamans in their communities and the roles which organizational change and development consultants can play in guiding organizational transformations."

---

[8] Hand waving is academic speak for making big claims that involve fallacies, no evidence, and lack of precision. I've kept the quotes' authors anonymous.

- "To survive in the 21st century, organizations need to be spiritually based. This, in turn, will lead to workers being satisfied with their entire work experience."
- "...when the organization is spiritual as well as its employees, value congruence might occur, which may imply even greater organizational outcomes, such as quality, productivity and profitability."
- "Spirituality has now become an effective tool to handle stress-related issues and for overcoming business problems."

The scientist in me worries about whether workplace spirituality need be restricted to spirited beings and shamans. (Indeed, there are people for whom those terms are fatally off-putting.) It worries whether organizations really **need** to be spiritually based (although that **might** be a good thing). I worry a great deal about the assumption that value congruence will necessarily happen in a spiritual organization and even more that "spiritual organization" is undefined – as if it were obvious what that meant. I worry that any moves toward more spiritual workplaces will be dashed on the rocks of the capitalist system, or worse – that spiritual ideas might be misused to make the intolerable tolerable – to soften up workers' resistance to an often oppressive system. Lastly, I worried whether there was any science to back up the claim that spiritual organizations are more profitable, or lead to more satisfied workers, or help overcome business problems.

There is also a kumbaya feel to writings on spirituality in business as if spirituality were always easy, always of the "feel good" variety, and as if different spiritual traditions – say in a workplace – could easily sit down and hammer out ideological differences. In this book, we also talk a lot about conflict. I never assume that the "wolves shall dwell with the lambs." The question of where the secular and the spiritual worldviews meet and what they might share, is one our world has wrestled with for at least several hundred years in hot conflict that shows no signs of abating. **Work is usually for**

someone else who has power over your life and livelihood – your spirituality may not be important to them. Nothing suggested herein is trivial or easy – but possibly worth the effort.

After the first publication, I found myself in the position of being both an evangelist and debunker-in-chief, failing tests of ideological purity on both sides, and sometimes offending both! Despite the number of downloads, the book was too evangelizing for academics and had too many correlation coefficients and p-tests for a popular book.

Writing that early edition of this book changed my life. You cannot spend nine months studying wisdom literature from three millennia and writing about vocation, corporate responsibility, values-based leadership, and purpose without it getting under your skin. I was first inspired with the life of Paul the Apostle, a teacher, evangelist, and "entrepreneur" of the day. That Paul inspired me to become **mission-driven,** that is to dedicate my life to something bigger than myself. (This was a humungous deal. I had spent a decade on Wall Street, the Mecca for self-interested people.) If I'm still Pauline in any sense of the word, it is that I'd like to evangelize business – my mission or "mantra," if you will forgive the word, became **"better leaders, for better businesses, for a better world**" as a result of my immersion in this topic. So much so that I tried to put those ideas to work in the world biggest companies.

Trying to apply these ideas in business was a moving target – the little firm I founded had some of the most passionately spiritual people I know. Every week (it seemed) there was a new approach or methodology we should try, although that weakness became our strength – big name clients tired of same-old, same-old, cookie-cutter solutions came to us rather than the biggest names in leadership development such as Duke and INSEAD. (Tip for entrepreneurs and branding, think about turning your weaknesses into strengths.)

WHY WRITE A 2020 EDITION?

The list in Figure 0-1 is only partial but includes some of the models and ideas we experimented with. That experience, combined with another twenty years of scholarship, means there is a new and exciting story that needs telling.

Tempus fugit and times and authors change. My aim in 1999 was to help workplaces use ideas from spiritual writing and to help people integrate their spirituality with their working lives – in the grossest terms, to "make business more spiritual." In 2020, my aim is to **make business more human.** That is, to create a human-centered capitalism with workplaces that serve and bring out the best in humanity.

The term "spirituality" perfectly "umbrellas" some vital human concerns – meaning, purpose, ethics, values, connection, and community. None of those terms is uniquely spiritual but spirituality is a term that appeals to the noblest of human aspirations. It embraces the "inner" work of personal development, and the "outer" work of what is needed in the world. Furthermore, some of the best writing on those human topics comes not from psychology, but from spirituality (and philosophy, evolutionary biology, sociology, and systems thinking.)

Much has changed since the turn of the millennium in spirituality, in the business landscape, and in our understanding of humankind (the so-called human sciences.) Alongside the emergence and reemergence of spirituality as a business subject over the last decades, there have been simultaneous shifts in the mosaic that is spirituality itself. The New Age movement that flowered during the *Celestine Prophecy* and *Alchemist* 1990s has receded but partly become utterly mainstream (thanks to Gwyneth and Oprah). There has been a rise in interest in philosophy and self-help style books based upon the Greeks, particularly the Stoics. Strange though it may seem (because many were agnostics), the Stoics gave us the "Serenity Prayer," the gratitude list, and ascetic rituals such as fasting, cleanses, and ice baths that are all the rage in Silicon Valley.

It would take another book to chronicle in detail the changes in the business world since the turn of the millennium, but what is called the 4th Industrial Revolution includes trends such as globalization, digital business, data and analytics, purpose, remote working, AI, and robotics. What do those have to do with **spirituality and human-centered businesses**? Let's take an "easy" example – by 2030, about one-third of all of today's jobs will be replaced by a robot or an AI. What is left for us to do? What is our competitive advantage as humans? We can't match a robot's sinew (or even its precision any longer), we can't outcrunch an AI. One answer, we shall see, is that our competitive advantage will come from human superpowers, what machines may never equal – some of those superpowers are spiritual.

That brings us to a question that is on nearly every page of this book. What makes we humans unique? Some of what makes us unique lies in the realm of purpose, vision, connectedness, compassion, and creativity – and spirituality has something to say on those topics. So, yes – we get to talk about spirituality and artificial intelligence.

Those changes, in me and in the world, prompted this second version that considers where our ideas about work and about human meaning come from and how business intersects with the **history of ideas,** ideas such as such as democracy, capitalism, freedom, equality, reason, rationality, and science. We then explore the links between those topics and mindfulness, motivation, leadership, values, values conflict, happiness, community, flow, culture, employer brand, and talent.

WHAT YOU MIGHT GET OUT OF READING THIS BOOK

"Philosophy needs vision and argument... there is something disappointing about a philosophical work that contains arguments which are not inspired by some genuine vision, and something disappointing about a philosophical work that contains a vision, however inspiring, which is unsupported by arguments."

HILARY PUTNAM, HARVARD PHILOSOPHER

One of my ongoing goals as a writer is to resolve the paradox articulated in the above quote– to be passionate in vision while reasoned in my beliefs. The Royal Society of Great Britain has as a motto, *nullius in verba*, which in New York-ese means "don't take nobody's word for it." In the world of spirituality, and excessively in the world of management and leadership, too much weight is attached to the speaker, and too little to the evidence for what they say. I'm fond of saying, "don't confuse inspiration with information" and so I hope you find *The Spirituality of Work & Leadership* balanced in that regard, sometimes inspirational, and sometimes analytical.

Business and entrepreneurship, to my mind, are divine expressions of human ingenuity, creativity, and intellect – different than art or science, but evoking the same *stupor mundi*[9] as the moon landing, the Hubble Telescope, the Sistine Chapel, Starry Night, and the Louvre. To dream up new ways of creating value for yourself others **and** to organize dozens or tens or hundreds or even hundreds of thousands of people toward common projects and purpose is a breathtaking feat. The inventiveness of business means we can scale technologies that would otherwise remain on a lab bench.

---

[9] A great expression from Catholic theology – the marvel of the world, an object of admiring bewilderment and wonder.

While they may not be the demi-gods represented by the media, entrepreneurs can create communities of purpose by harnessing talent while, if nobly inspired, virtuously creating value.

The **humanizing business** project gives us, as citizens and as business leaders, the opportunity to do great good by pointing business toward our most inspirational and noble aims and leading those changes with passion and reason. This book, I hope, is a tiny step in that direction. Here are my goals that I hope reflect what the reader may get out of my attempts to balance my vision and reason in this two-volume series:

- Articulate, reverently, the incredible diversity of contemporary spirituality, to explore common ground, and promote mutual understanding between the mystics, the religious, and the secular.
- Help the reader find their "sweet spot" combining passion and purpose through explorations of meaning, work, motivation, happiness, and values.
- Enable leaders to understand how to lead meaning and purpose through a more holistic understanding of human experience at work and insights on how to make workplaces more human.[10]
- Debunk some contemporary ideas on happiness, work, and wealth, and explore newer ideas on mindfulness, well-being, and human flourishing.
- Explore the notion of corporate purpose, how purpose drives organizational results, and how corporate purpose relates to individual purpose.
- Offer the reader practical insights into values-led organizations, creating values-oriented cultures and the potential for values conflict.

---

[10] "Making workplaces more human" is the kind of expression that can set me ablaze, what else might they be? There are humans in them. Do we mean human as opposed to bestial? Celestial?

- Detail what a human-centered capitalism might look like, one that meets human needs inside work and outside work, including sustainability, multi-capital systems, conscious capitalism, and the circular economy.

The first volume of the Humanizing Business series: *The Spirituality of Work & Leadership* is divided into two sections. The first section covers what spirituality has come to mean in the 21st century and the relationship of spirituality to vocation, work, and human development. Although there are thousands of books published annually on each specific tradition (say Christian leadership, or The Tao of Leadership, or Integral Leadership,) there are almost **no books that try to unite different approaches to spirituality under a single umbrella.** To borrow from a later chapter, "Do wisdom traditions really converge around certain values? What could unite the traditionally religious, mystics, pagans, New Agers, Buddhists, Humanists, and environmentalists?" We shall see.

Here is the way section one of the book, **Spirituality, Work, and Vocation**, is organized:

- **Chapter I, Human nature and the history of God**, tells the story of spirituality, human history, and human nature and how spirituality likely gave our species an evolutionary advantage and helped turn humankind into what it is today.
- **Chapter II, 21st-century spirituality**, shows the myriad of ways people pursue spirituality and shows how those converge upon some common themes including the universal hunger for growth and meaning. My hope is that you see your spirituality in the context of other spiritual paths, and in the context of human development.
- **Chapter III, Spiritual growth and development,** suggests that spirituality is about growth and effort, a mix of revelation and searching.

- **Chapter IV, The history and gospel of work**, discusses the history and future of work, how work and business went from being distasteful to revered and today's costs of "workification" of society.
- **Chapter V, Vocation and "spiritual fit,"** provides models and tools to help people of all spiritual and religious traditions better **integrate** their spirituality with their work, to balance the secular and the spiritual.

The second section, **Loving Your Work and Leading Others**, reviews the research on the relationship between spirituality and personal, individual outcomes such as mindfulness, motivation, leadership, happiness, flourishing, and personal purpose.

- **Chapter VI, The science of mindfulness in business**, is a hard look at the evidence for mindfulness practices that concludes that their benefits are too many and powerful to ignore.
- **Chapter VII, The science of happiness and flourishing**, asks the hard question whether spirituality makes you happier, but also whether happiness is a sufficient goal and offers some better ideas about the good life from ancient and modern thinkers.
- **Chapter VIII, The philosophy of purpose,** looks at purpose through the lens of altruism, mastery, and the Greek transcendentals – Truth, Beauty, Goodness.
- **Chapter IX, Leadership and spirituality,** summarizes the panoply of different ideas on spiritual leadership and adds a few new models to an already vast topic.
- **Chapter X, Love in the time of COVID,** uses 2020's once-in-a-century crisis as a case study asking which spiritual principles were in evidence, and whether we learned and grew spiritually as a result.

Spoiler alert - the second volume[11]

One of my "bumper stickers" as a business writer is current work-places do not do a sufficiently good job of engaging and developing human potential and today's workplaces are very poorly equipped to handle the 4th industrial revolution – 50% of today's jobs lost to AI and robotics. The second volume, perhaps titled *Culture, Capitalism, Sustainability,* uses that context as the backdrop for deeper conversations about humanizing business, still with philosophy and spirituality in mind. Here is a quick look at the topics covered.

The second book starts where this volume leaves off, with leadership and purpose, although the purpose we talk about is **organizational purpose** – which purposes for business ennoble them and inspire their workers. The leadership section looks at how values and how values-based decisions are made in business. It then turns to culture change, employer brand, talent, and profitability as factors that could be fostered by organizational spirituality.

From there, we turn to ethics, and why individual ethics, though **necessary,** is **insufficient** for ethical businesses and what to do about that. The "answer" is creating ethical cultures, but that seems glib – how do we do that? What are the challenges?

The last chapters turn to the enormous question of how the business/ government/ consumer/ worker ecosystem that we call capitalism can reform itself without bloody revolution, draconian state intervention, or loss of individual liberty. The chapters illustrate the weakness of old school capitalism, and the weakness of some "capitalism 2.0" ideas, and then examine other species on the landscape: conscious capitalism, purposeful capitalism, multi-capital capitalism, CSR, circular economies, and sustainability.

---

[11] An author gets to change his mind, but volume II is 75% finished and although me committing to topics now has my editor freaked out, this is a teaser.

Reading the first volume

If the reader is like the author, then the chances of reading the first third of a book are much higher than reading the last third. The last two-thirds of this volume has most of the practical goodies, happiness, motivation, mindfulness, flourishing, and purpose, while the first third is historical and philosophical groundwork.

I officially invite the reader to start where their interests lie and see where their reason, or perhaps their intuition, takes them.

Enjoy and challenge. Although I write confidently, I do not write from a place of certainty. I expect readers to digest, challenge, dislike as well as, fingers crossed, to praise. My earlier books spawned internet discussion groups and forums, if you feel moved to do so, I often make time to drop into one of those sessions, so let me know. Kindly connect on LinkedIn if you feel so moved or visit my website (paulgibbons.net) to get in contact more directly. I have a podcast, ranked top-20 in philosophy, called *Think Bigger Think Better* which has been on hold during this writing, but there are thirty episodes of which I'm very proud – give that a listen.

Finally, I don't advertise. Whatever success my books enjoy is through likes, shares, book reviews, and word of mouth recommendations. If you find this book valuable, kindly tell a friend, or let your LinkedIn community know. The images from this book and from my others can be downloaded free from paulggibons.imgur.com/all.

Warmest thanks!

Human nature and the history of God

Covered in this chapter:

The greatest story ever told

That spiritual feeling

Spirituality and science

Nietzsche and the "death of God"

Secularization and its discontents

The spiritual revolution

CHAPTER 1

HUMAN NATURE AND THE HISTORY OF GOD

"Deprived of meaningful work, men and women lose their reason for existence; they go stark, raving mad."

FYODOR DOSTOYEVSKY

THE GREATEST STORY EVER TOLD[12]

If you had looked at the African savannah 100,000 or so years ago, you would have seen a collection of animals, among which would have been a small, vulnerable, hairless biped – *homo sapiens* – not as fast or fanged as predators, nor as protected or camouflaged as most prey. From a distance, these frail bands of hunter-gatherers were unspecial in their appearance and accomplishments. Fewer than half a million in number, about the same as today's population of gibbons (no relation) monkeys. Today's non-human species live roughly in the same geographical, ecological niches as then – we don't find zebras in the rainforest. However, our hunter-gatherers were curious, relentless, and adaptable – by 10,000 years ago, they had settled the entire planet including its most inhospitable regions.

---

[12] If you want to read as good and beautifully written book as exists on the history of God, try the book by Karen Armstrong, *The History of God*. If you are interested in pre-history, try *Sapiens*, by Yuval Harari – one of the most stunningly written books I've read.

They traveled from Africa[13] to the farthest reaches of New Zealand and South America settling every habitable space on the planet. Then in a blink of an eye, they would transform those habitats into vast cities, and achieve technological feats that allowed them to send starships beyond their solar system.

History also marks us a playful species. Although other mammals play, human playfulness, curiosity, tinkering, and inventiveness are fanatical. Play, how children learn today, allowed us to leap forward technologically then to become sophisticated tool-users. When a lioness killed a gazelle, she didn't use the skin to keep her and her cubs warm, nor did she use the bones and antlers as weapons to hunt or defend herself. Mama bears didn't create sewing needles from fishbones to sew fishnets to more efficiently catch fish. *Homo sapiens* invented and collaborated and painted and made jewelry told stories that conveyed knowledge across generations in ways we are still discovering.

Nothing like this has happened before or since.

Spirituality became part of this story early on, allowing shared meaning and moral codes that strengthened communities. Some anthropologists even think that shamanism arose 500,000 years ago, in pre-*sapiens* species such as *Homo Erectus, Homo Neanderthalenis, and Homo Habilis* giving them a competitive advantage. Even today, the human story remains a story of religion and spirituality, constantly evolving when seen from a 10,000-year perspective **and** a ten-year perspective! Some claim that religion became peripheral to human history after the Enlightenment, but the facts say differently. Even in the world's least religious country, Sweden, nearly 50% of residents claim spirituality matters to them and the world religions still have six billion followers.

---

[13] As this book goes to press, late 2020, the "out of Africa" theory that we learned in school is being challenged by evidence that sapiens evolved simultaneously in many regions (China notably) – however, China to Chile is still a ways.

AN ESSENTIAL PART OF HUMAN NATURE?

"To seize and put into words, to describe directly,
the life of humanity... appears impossible."
LEO TOLSTOY

The human story is a spiritual story, but does that mean that there is a **spiritual dimension to human nature?** Are we **spiritually hardwired** metaphysically, neurobiologically, or anthropologically?

One argument is **metaphysical**: there is a non-material aspect of humankind – a soul, a spirit, or an immanent God. Not all spiritual people believe so – I can't build a case upon that. A second is **biological**. Neuroscientists of a religious bent have tried unsuccessfully (despite what appeared in the popular press) to find such a "God-spot," concluding mostly on the contrary that, "spirituality is a much more dynamic concept that uses many parts of the brain. Certain parts of the brain play more dominant roles, but they all work together to facilitate individuals' spiritual experiences."[14] Neither can I fall back upon biology to justify spirituality's importance.

If we cannot ground spirituality biologically, can we do it a third way – **anthropologically**? Yes, we can. Most persuasively, humans seem to search for **meaning**. That may be a cognitive phenomenon via our pattern recognition apparatus, a product of our unique capability for language, or a by-product of curiosity (also found in our ape ancestors).

It seems we are born to ask big questions. To quote Carl Sagan,

"When we recognize our place in an immensity of
light-years and in the passage of ages, when we
grasp the intricacy, beauty, and subtlety of life,

---

[14] Brick Johnstone, professor of health psychology at the University of Missouri, in International Journal of Psychology of Religion, 2012 https://www.sciencedaily.com/releases/2012/04/120419091223.htm.

*then that soaring feeling, that sense of elation
and humility combined, is surely spiritual[15]."*

That search for meaning is linked to our search for **purpose**. Our contemplative nature begins with toddlers' endless "whys" and reaches toward what Einstein called,"...our love for the mysteries of eternity, of life, and of the marvelous structure of reality seem to drive ceaseless enquiry." [16]

We want also to be **connected**. An anthropologist might point to our social nature: how we came to depend upon connectedness **for survival** and how that need for solidarity was made possible by shared beliefs, pro-social emotions such as love, caring, and loyalty, and by mitigating negative emotions. These factors might have led to the ubiquity of spiritual belief and practice which we see in our earliest cave paintings and oral traditions and which later became organized religion. Religion and the connectedness it provided may well have conferred a cultural evolutionary advantage, first for mutual protection, then for flourishing.

The anthropological case for hardwiring is strong. (Although hardwiring implies biology, after a hundred thousand years, cultural patterns become engrained cognitive patterns.) However, even though the case can be made, it isn't essential to our case that spirituality is part of human nature today and to make it relevant to workplaces and business.

---

[15] Sagan, Carl. *The Demon-Haunted World: Science as a Candle in the Dark*
[16] Hermanns, William, *Einstein and the Poet: In Search of the Cosmic Man*

THAT SPIRITUAL FEELING

"The future is uncertain... but this uncertainty
is at the very heart of human creativity."
ILYA PRIGOGINE – NOBEL PRIZE CHEMISTRY, COMPLEXITY THEORIST

Even if spirituality were not hardwired, there is the **fact** and ubiquity of spiritual experience and beliefs. (See Figure I – 1.) Spirituality is everywhere, in "endless forms," today.

Figure I – 1: Does the ubiquity and diversity of spirituality suggest it is part of human nature?

"Don't stop believin', hold onto that feeling..."

A demographer will tell us that the world contains 2.1 billion Christians, 1.5 billion Buddhists, and 1.8 billion Muslims. That is already a lot of believing. 54% of Americans consider themselves religious and 75% consider themselves spiritual. One can also contemplate the great cathedrals' glorious architecture (and the economic investment required to build them), 5,000 years of religious writing, centuries of art and musical works dedicated to worship, and all of the wars fought in religion's name to conclude people **feel** that spirituality (expressed through religion) matters superlatively.

39

The metaphysical, romantic, and nature poets have all pointed to the spiritual longing within man. Whitman reveals this spiritual awe in *Song of Myself*:

"Swiftly arose and spread around me the peace and
knowledge that pass all the argument of the earth,
And I know that the hand of God is the promise of my own,
And I know that the spirit of God is the brother of my own,
And that all the men ever born are also my brothers, and
the women my sisters and lovers,
And that a kelson of the creation is love,
And limitless are leaves stiff or drooping in the fields,
And brown ants in the little wells beneath them,
And mossy scabs of the worm fence, heap'd stones, elder,
mullein and poke-weed."

Or we can read great Humanists such as Sagan and Einstein whose writings on the universe move many people to tears, for example Einstein's famous outlook:

"The most beautiful experience we can have is the
mysterious. It is the fundamental emotion that stands at
the cradle of true art and true science."

Wonder, awe, reverence, and sacredness work their magic whether the object be science, the divine, art, or nature. This becomes an important point to return to. Is sacredness something "out there," or do humans sanctify the world through their attentions?

Despite the ubiquity of religion, there are thinkers who, although acknowledging religion's critical role in development of human society, think that its explanatory power has been replaced by science and its moral codes by reason. Although religion, they think, once helped us form tightly knit moral communities, it now divides us and causes more violence and conflict than benefit. They argue that religion is on the decline, and that that is a good thing. Before delving more deeply into spirituality, let's look briefly at religion's detractors.

SPIRITUALITY AND SCIENCE

"Science is wonderful at destroying metaphysical answers,
but incapable of providing substitute ones. Science takes
away foundations without providing a replacement."
HILARY PUTNAM, HARVARD PHILOSOPHER

There have always been doubters. Atheism has some roots in the East and some in the West appearing in Greek thought as early as 2500 years ago. By 1700 CE or so, believers had won: non-believers were less than 1% of the world population, and religion was everywhere. However, with the Scientific Revolution and the Enlightenment, some scholars began to foretell the **death of religion.**

Religion's death would be by the hand of science. French philosopher Auguste Comte, writing in 1822, believed that society would move from a theological stage to a metaphysical stage to a scientific/rational stage. The theological stage was dominated by supernatural beliefs and Divine Command ethics; the metaphysical was characterized by abstract principles (e.g., human rights, life, liberty, pursuit of happiness, democracy, freedom, and equality), and the scientific/rational stage was characterized by empirical science. Did Comte get this right?

If Comte had bet on the decline of religion, a "short" in stock market speak, he would have died broke. **Any** declines at all in religiosity were to take nearly 150 years, and even now, around 85 percent of the world are still religious in some respect.

However, Comte was right in a sense. Prior to the modern era, religion dominated science, art, and morals—the "Big Three": Truth, Beauty, and Goodness. Scientists were there to discover God's laws on earth. Art was concerned primarily with religious themes. Morals were dictated by church doctrine. With the advent of the modern era, church domination of the spheres of science, art, and morality was dissolved. Freeing of these areas from Church domination "unleashed tremendous creativity and allowed unprecedented advancement."[17]

This was a good and necessary thing, particularly for science. While the church could still burn scientists such as Giordano Bruno at the stake, threaten to torture Galileo until he recanted, and fight Copernicus' ideas on the solar system for a century, humanity wasn't going to make progress anytime soon. As a result of its emancipation, science exploded, making substantially more progress in a century than in the previous 2,000 years.

Figure I-2: The Creation of Adam, from the Sistine Chapel, by Michelangelo. Before the Early Modern Era, art was dominated by religious themes and imagery.

But the divorce between science and religion has been messy, with centuries of fighting over custody of the kids. Throughout the 20th century, and until today, the secular and religious worldviews

---

[17] See Ken Wilber, *Marriage of Sense and Soul*

clashed in schools, courts, legislative bodies, and workplaces. For some, science has negated the need for religion, and for others science and religion are Non-Overlapping Magisteria (NOMA),[18] each with different spheres of influence. Science takes care of the world of fact and explanation, and religion takes care of the world of morals and meaning.

While I disagree with NOMA, (e.g. in my opinion, science can and must inform moral decisions), it is a very pragmatic stance. This is something akin to the worldview of the Catholic Church and famous religious scientists such as Francis Collins, a legendary geneticist who is also deeply religious. In his view, **"one can be intellectually in a rigorous position and argue that science and faith are compatible."**[19]

Though pragmatic, NOMA is problematic. We must wonder whether religious ethics help us with 21st-century ethical issues at the frontiers of science, AI, cloning, climate change, and a surveillance culture. Religious texts are conflicted on moral issues and replete with exhortations to violence. If we select texts that we ethically approve of (such as the New Testament versus the Old,) what super-scriptural criteria are we using? Where did they come from? This implies that over time a higher moral order has evolved that allows us to discriminate and select which passages meet our ethical standards.

The problem with the divorce, from this book's point of view, is that whatever wisdom had been locked up in religious writings, to do with purpose, calling, and community, was cast out with the secularist bathwater. Even in the 21st century, we have yet to reconcile the different approaches to ethics that religious and secular worldviews might endorse and the "NOMA line" would seem to make that reconciliation harder.

---

[18] An idea proposed by Stephen J Gould, Harvard biologist and philosopher of science.
[19] "The Question of God", interview with Dr. Francis Collins on PBS, 2004

NIETZSCHE AND THE DEATH OF GOD

"God is dead."

– NIETZSCHE

"Nietzsche is dead." – God

CHRISTIAN T-SHIRT LOGO

In typical melodramatic prose, Nietzsche proclaims:

"God is dead... And we have killed him... What was holiest and mightiest of all that the world has yet owned has bled to death under our knives: who will wipe this blood off us?"

Nietzsche is much misunderstood, partly because of his fondness for dramatic metaphor. The philosopher was not talking literally about the murder of a deity, and he did **not** think the death of God was a grand triumph and unequivocally good. He rather thought that 19th-century materialism, secularization, and rationality had undermined our most sacred beliefs and traditions. He thought that the death of sacredness and tradition had undermined the **moral foundations of our world**, saying, "For some time now our whole European culture has been moving as toward a catastrophe."

Why? Because when Westerners gave up Christianity, they pulled the moral rug out from under their feet. Society, feared Nietzsche, would descend into nihilism. We would seek out dictators and autocrats to provide a false sense of moral certainty and meaning about the world that we had lost. The 20th and 21st centuries have certainly provided fuel for Nietzsche's argument.

Nietzsche thought that the responsibility for crafting our own lives and meaning without reference to higher authority (either religious authority or secular authority), was utterly terrifying. He was saying, "you do you," but in a much more revolutionary way, discard

FIGURE I – 3: "Crucifixion" by Andrea Mantegna, 1458: Does the decline in religion herald a second Fall of Man threatening our moral foundations?

all the strictures and comforts of modern society that shackle you and strike out your own. Be a renegade!

Both Nietzsche and some Enlightenment philosophers told a story of the decline of religion and the progress of humankind – a story of secularization. However, the "secularization hypothesis" is among the most argued topics in the sociology of religion—the picture is not black and white.

The fall of religion? The secularization hypothesis

Comte's speculation about human progress is what postmodernists (derisively) call a grand narrative, a comprehensive story that explains history, knowledge, and progress. Think: the Christian "fall of man," Freudian psychology, globalization, capitalism, and Marxist utopianism. **Secularization** is one such "grand narrative"—the world has **and will become** more secular—but does it hold? We've seen that religion's hold on Truth, Beauty, and Goodness was released, but also that until about 1950, the percentage of non-believers in the world was no greater than 1%. What has happened since?

Contemporary demographic data suggests that society has become more secularized. When asked whether "religion is 'very important to them,'" now only 53% of Americans respond positively, whereas the percentage was once over 90. Even in deeply religious America, the percentage of "no religion" has doubled in just this century to around 25%, but from a Comtean perspective, the US remains **a stronghold of continued religiosity.** Contrast this with Europe, where the percentage who say that religion is important to them is roughly in the low teens and in Scandinavia and Japan, it has crept into single digits.

When religious **behaviors** are measured, the decline is starker still. Many of those who say they believe no longer practice – they "believe without belonging." Many nonreligious parents baptize their children for social, familial, or cultural reasons (or perhaps as "insurance," in case they are wrong about the God thing.) Even so, in France, baptism numbers have fallen from about 75% to about 25% over the last few decades. In Ireland, by far the most religious Western nation in the mid-20th century, nearly 90% attended Mass in 1979. That has tumbled to 35% on average and is less than 20% in Dublin.

The secularization picture is much more complex than this demographic decline: **religious beliefs and behaviors** are but one facet of a complex topic. Behaviors are readily visible, but shifts in values, changes in influence on other spheres, and centrality of religion are much harder to measure. However, on a two-hundred-year view, secularization looks like an established trend. But for every trend, there is a backlash.

SECULARIZATION AND ITS DISCONTENTS

In the manner predicted by 19th-century German philosopher Georg Hegel, there is a counter-trend – a backlash against secularization.

Some forms of religion, such as prosperity theology (discussed later), are on the rise. In the developing world, there is evidence that religiosity is increasing. Birthrates among believers are much higher – which is a counterweight to the increased percentage of secular people. This means that the world as a whole will be **more religious** in 2050 if the trend continues (although in the West, much less religious.)

We have also seen a militant backlash against modernity and secularization in the form of **fundamentalism**. There are fundamentalist strains in (at least) Judaism, Hinduism, Christianity, and Islam. Rather than quietly ceding to secular culture, they take the fight to the secularists. In the still deeply religious US, evangelical voters have considerable political power, not just in policy making, but also in trying to remake the historical narrative of the US as a secular country into a Christian one. In the Islamic world (Turkey, Indonesia, and most of the Middle East), governments have become more theocratic. In Israel, once a multi-faith socialist democracy, religious fundamentalists have had a significant voice in right-of-center governments for a generation – the moderate Prime Minister and Nobel Peace Prize winner Yitzhak Rabin was murdered in 1995 by a fundamentalist and ultranationalist Yigal Amir, acting without regret under "orders of God," who believed the Oslo peace process with Palestinians was a threat to Israel and the occupied Palestinian territories.

The other backlash against secularization is spirituality. And while religion may be slowly in decline, spirituality is on the rise—some sociologists have gone so far to as to describe this as a **spiritual revolution**. Perhaps without religion, as Nietzsche predicted, people still crave meaning?

THE SPIRITUAL REVOLUTION

Attitudes toward spirituality had begun to shift away from exclusively "old-time religion" in the early 20th century, and that shift accelerated as that century ended. By the late 20th century, spirituality was the fastest-growing subject in nonfiction books. Pew Research's 2016 study on religion in America found that while **religiosity was falling**, as measured by daily prayer, church attendance, and belief in God, **spirituality was rising**.[20] More people today describe periodic "spiritual peace and well-being" experiences, and more people "wonder about the Universe" than a decade ago. This growth and diversification was found "...in Eastern religions, in evangelical and fundamentalist teachings, in mysticism and New Age movements, in Goddess worship and other ancient religious rituals, in the mainline churches and synagogues, in Twelve-Step recovery groups, in concern about the environment, in holistic health, and in personal and social transformation.[21]"

As the internet evolved in the 1990s, it accelerated the **diversification** and spread of spiritual ideas. Mainstream Eastern traditions, the Abrahamic religions, and state religions such as the Church of England began to lose their monopoly on spiritual information as anyone with a keyboard and sufficient zeal could publicly communicate their ideas across the globe.

The mathematical phenomenon called the **majority illusion** means that even fringe beliefs seem popular because **within** a network, they will seem commonplace. Whatever you believe today – in aliens, "Q," ayahuasca, the Illuminati, birtherism, a flat earth, or Soros' New World Order – **filter bubbles** and **algorithms** make it look like everybody in your network shares those beliefs. You feel the support and belonging of a big community while your whacky views are on the fringe.

This has been an essential driver of proliferation and diversification of spiritual beliefs; for example, you and your internet followers can compete frock-to-frock with the Vatican – persuade, share, build community online, and proselytize. In our century, militant groups

---

like the Islamic State have used social media to develop a well-funded, global network from ragtag groups in dozens of countries.

Sure spirituality has grown and diversified, but does that make a revolution? Perhaps that is hyperbole, but for the moment, those are established trends that do not seem to be slowing. In the next chapter, we try to define spirituality – an elusive and rapidly changing idea – more closely.

21st-century spirituality

Covered in this chapter:

The missionary's position (on spirituality)

History of a "personal God"

The spiritual revolution and the three types of spirituality

Where do the three types converge?

CHAPTER 2

21ST-CENTURY SPIRITUALITY

"Spirituality exists wherever we struggle with the issues of how our lives fit into the greater scheme of things... We encounter spiritual issues every time we wonder where the universe comes from, why we are here, or what happens when we die. We also become spiritual when we become moved by values such as beauty, love, or creativity that seem to reveal a meaning or power beyond our visible world. An idea or practice is 'spiritual' when it reveals our personal desire to establish a felt-relationship with the deepest meanings or powers governing life."

PROFESSOR ROBERT FULLER

Primatologist Frans de Waal recounts that in a conference at the American Academy of Religion, "One participant suggested that they start by defining religion, but another cautioned that the last time they tried to do that, half the audience stomped out of the room. And this in an academy named after the topic!"

Therefore, cautiously, we will take two approaches to defining today's spirituality. One tack we can take is to research what people mean when they use the word today. For example, survey thousands of people and study what terms, concepts, beliefs, and behaviors they associate with the term. (You could call this an ethnographic approach, or "bottom-up.")

We might also take a top-down approach and use a definition that scholars use – a "theoretical" one. There we meet the problem that a) the definition does not keep up with contemporary use, and b) even scholars have perspectives—their own paths, whether they are psychologists, sociologists, philosophers, or theologians. Scholars often criticize the bottom-up approach, claiming that when people describe spirituality in so many different ways, the term becomes meaningless. (And people who consider themselves spiritual tend not to care if scholars think they are, so the approaches conflict!)

We will do both to create a broad definition of spirituality which includes multiple theistic and non-theistic beliefs because otherwise the term fails to mirror the diversity of spiritual beliefs around us. For reasons that follow in the rest of this book, we will lean heavily on the following definition:

*Spirituality is **growing** and **striving** for **meaning**, **purpose**, **goodness**, and **connectedness**.*

This level of universality creates a broad tent which includes yogis, mystics, pagans, New Agers, Buddhists, the traditionally religious, Taoists, Emersonian environmentalists, Humanists, and many more. Those four elements (meaning, purpose, goodness, and connectedness) are proposed as the **common ground** shared between spiritual traditions; they, as we see later, affect personal and organizational outcomes such as well-being, motivation, and ethics.

Though abstract, the spiritual seeker can make them more concrete, "customize them" if you will forgive: for example, connection might be connected to God, or connected to community, or connected to Source; or, "goodness" might vary, pursuing justice, or service, or healing, or piety. Moreover, this customization is essential for spirituality to become the deeply personal thing that it must.

"Growing and striving" describe the **process of spirituality**. This addition is distinctive, although not unique. Many people, including scholars, ignore the idea that spirituality should be a dynamic aspect of our lives, not a static one. Chapter III is devoted to this idea.

Before further exploring the bottom-up definition of spirituality, what do scholars say about today's proliferation of different spiritual paths?

THE MISSIONARY'S POSITION (ON SPIRITUALITY)

"So, while we must avoid too much indefiniteness and abstraction on one hand, we must also avoid hard and fast definitions on the other hand. For no words in our human language are adequate or accurate when applied to spiritual realities..."

EVELYN UNDERHILL, THE SPIRITUAL LIFE

The tome, *World Spirituality: An Encyclopedic History of the Religious Quest* is 25 volumes long! Spirituality is a hard term to define, but not for want of effort! I suspect you know what your spirituality means to you, but only by understanding spirituality more broadly can we begin to bridge the divide and talk about spiritual concepts that matter to us all – that bring us together.

Today, people mean a great many things when they use the word "spiritual." However, philosopher and theologian Phillip Blond[22] laments this diversity saying that "God has been **pluralized** into a **general spirituality** and identified with virtually anything whatsoever thus creating a conceptual emptiness." Psychologists of religion Robert A. Emmons and Cheryl A. Crumpler wonder, "Can one speak of holiness or divinity without God? [From] wherein would these terms derive their meaning?"

These scholars want to reclaim the word "spiritual" to accord

---

[22] Blond, P., "The primacy of theology and the question of perception", In Heelas, P. (ed.) Religion, Modernity, and Postmodernity, Blackwell: Oxford (1998)

with the religious perspective—**an intellectual trap into which nearly every type of spirituality writer falls**. What does one, in their shoes, say to a Yogi, or Buddhist, or Humanist, or Chopra aco-lyte who fails their test of belief— "You aren't really spiritual; get with the program"?

A more ecumenical view, one that does not rely on a God-con-cept, was advanced by famed theologian Ninian Smart who defined spirituality as: "That body of beliefs, rituals, values, norms, and narratives that address the place of humankind in relation to the universe, and proffer a coherent worldview in which faith, devotion, a sense of the sacred, and adherence to ultimate values play an important role." Scholars differ, but each has a perspective.

Astute readers might well challenge me. "Do you, too, have a perspective?" Well, you got me, I do. While in arguing for a pluralistic, broad definition, I'm stating a **cultural fact**—people do, in fact, use the term "spirituality" broadly. With my scholar hat on (top-down), I'm also advancing the opinion that this is a valid philosophical and historical treatment. I don't see "secular spirituality" as at all oxymoronic. Why? **So human** is the search for meaning, purpose, goodness, and connectedness that it seems facile to restrict it to the traditionally religious. In this book, we are concerned with **work-place spirituality,** and I don't want my remarks restricted to the 5, 10, 20, or 50% of people who are traditionally religious (depending on where one lives).

How did spirituality become such a diverse phenomenon? The term's roots are deep within all the world's religions. However, it has come to mean much more than it once did, something personal and not necessarily connected to institutional religion.

HISTORY OF A "PERSONAL GOD"

Although spirituality means different things to different people today, that was not always the case. In the West, during the pre-modern[23] period, the spiritual journeys of ordinary men and women were mediated by priests and the institution of the church. Spirituality was part of religion. Scripture, which only priests could read, described the spiritual experiences of historical figures, mystics, prophets, and saints, but these spiritual experiences were **beyond the reach** of ordinary men and women. Spirituality, as offered to them, was second hand. "These monks, preachers and other 'artists of religious life' set standards of piety which clashed not just with sinful inclinations, but also with the very stuff of life, and thereby cast the prospects of 'eternal life' out of reach of all but these few saints. Salvation was the luxury of a chosen few, not a 'viable proposition for the ordinary people wishing to carry on the business of life as usual'."[24]

The Reformation, with its emphasis on the "priesthood of all believers," challenged the pre-modern relationship between humanity and religion, it became personal rather than mediated. It also loosened the power of the clergy and therefore paved the way for the scientific and democratic revolutions that transformed social and political power structures in the 1700s. One way of looking at today's eclectic and varied use of the term "spirituality" is that it was made possible by the Reformation. The monopoly that the pre-Reformation church had on spiritual experience and on spiritual journeys was broken up, paving the way **first** for today's **personal spirituality** and thus paving the way for a spiritual and mental life independent of clerical authority. (Although it is unlikely that Martin Luther would look upon today's spiritual eclecticism favorably!)

This personalization can mean that the path you choose accords with your personality. In Hinduism, six types of spiritual pursuit

---

[23] Pre-modern, early modern, and modern are terms philosophers and historians use to refer to periods roughly post-medieval to pre-17th century, the 17th and 18th centuries, and the 19th century, up until World War II. The modern era (aka modernity) is associated with reason, science, capitalism, urbanization, industrialization, globalization, and technological advancement.

[24] Heelas, P., "On differentiation and de-differentiation", *Religion, Modernity, and Post-modernity*, Blackwell: Oxford (1998)

give us a useful way to think about spiritual diversity: *hatha* (the body), *raja* (the being or mind), *bhakti* (the emotional and experiential), *jnana* (the intellectual or metaphysical), *kriya* (purification), and *karma* (selfless behaviors.) If you look around, you will find heart-centered people, people dedicated to service, people for whom spirituality is more intellectual, and people whose main path is through regular prayer. Many people make the mistake of thinking their orientation is **the** orientation, for example thinking that spiritual people must necessarily be heart-centered, or service-oriented, or of a certain faith, or meditators, or environmentally conscious.

Charles Glock, a sociologist of religion, identified **ideological, intellectual, ritualistic, experiential, and consequential aspects** of an individual's religion. (In simpler words, the books, beliefs, behaviors, experiences, and "results" of religion.) These matter to us because they tell us that within a faith or spiritual path, there will be vast differences in expression; you can love the beliefs without the books, or the books without the experience, or the ritual without the beliefs, and so on.

For example, many Catholics attend Mass for community and devotion but shy away from beliefs such as the Virgin Birth or its moral teachings around reproduction. I love Buddhist meditation and yoga but shy away from their metaphysical accompaniments. You may love the spiritual experience that accompanies Nature but remain ideologically committed to your birth religion.

Today's personalization also means people craft their path with practices or beliefs from other, seemingly opposing, traditions. Most Americans self-identify as Christians, but many of those, roughly six in ten, also hold a New Age belief – perhaps reincarnation, astrology, psychics, or the idea of "spiritual energy" in physical objects or people.[25]

Many of today's most eminent theologians endorse this cross-fertilization. Says Ninian Smart, "One of the effects of religions getting

---

[25] Gecewicz, C., New Age Beliefs common among both religious and nonreligious Americans, Pew Research Center, October 1st, 2018

together is that they borrow from one another. An example is the growing number of Catholics practicing Yoga and meditation techniques borrowed from Buddhism and Hinduism. These borrowings, I think, fertilize the religions."

Personal spirituality means we get the power to choose our own path, and you might say there are as many paths as there are people (around 7.5 billion of us.) But with power comes responsibility, and we need to craft it and work for it – our enlightenment cannot be outsourced.

This rest of this chapter tries to blend scholarship and ethnography (one of the reasons it has been called metamodern.)[26] We listen to what scholars have said about spirituality while listening also to what people say today when they call themselves spiritual. That leads us to a need to categorize those 7.5 billion spiritual paths in a way that we can understand them better and find some common ground between.

THE SPIRITUAL REVOLUTION AND THE THREE KINDS OF SPIRITUALITY

If the demography of world religions is complex and diverse, that of spirituality is many times more so. The view I present here is that **spirituality has turned the linguistic tables, and religion is now one of many possible spiritual paths,** rather than spirituality being (as it once was) a facet of religion. **The three types of spirituality are religious, secular, and mystical.** The following table (Figure II-2) describes these and some of their characteristics. Such a table does not begin to capture the hundreds of different possible categorizations of spirituality. The generalizations below are gross (in both the literal and slang meanings of the term.)

---

[26] For the philosophically curious, I define metamodern at the end of this chapter. For now, it is a response, or backlash against postmodernism that embraces some of its better ideas and discards some of its worst.

Gibbons' typology of spirituality

	Religious	Secular	Mystical
Example	Christianity, Hinduism	Humanism, Nature, Activism	Buddhism, Taoism, New Age
Theistic beliefs	Central	None	Diverse – "Universe", "Tao", "Goddess", "Nirvana"
Spiritual needs	Met through communion with Divine	Met through agency and activity	Met through spiritual practice and ritual
Unique values	Faith, piety, community	Reason, justice, human flourishing	Unity, harmony, oneness
Ethics	Simplistic – rule based	Complex, contextual, dilemmas, cosmopolitan	Personal, "right living," sometimes agnostic on global issues
Politics	Lean conservative	Lean left	Lean left, though sometimes politically disengaged
Typical practices	Worship, prayer	Nature walk, service, protest, community organizing	Attunement, meditation, yoga, movement, ritual
Nature of reality	Dual – divine and earthly	Singular	Transient, connected, illusory
Nature of humanity	Sinful – redemption through religion	Work in progress, institutions and systems matter	Varied, self-development matters
Personal change results from...	Grace, confession, cleansing, divine direction	Effort, agency, self-awareness	Practices and ritual
Attitude to systemic change...	Tread conservatively	Mandatory, urgent	Emergent

NB: These are broad, gross generalizations and there is variation even within a single doctrine, say within Catholicism, as well as between doctrines in a category (Islam and Hinduism), and the non-religious doctrines vary so much that any generalization must be held lightly.

© PAUL GIBBONS   PAULGIBBONS.NET

Figure II-1: A 1999 typology of spirituality that tries to make sense of the magnificent diversity of spirituality.

Every time you carve something complex into boxes, you create a little clarity but destroy a little precision. The table suggests that typical religious practices are worship and prayer. Yet, there is a significant mystical strand in all Abrahamic religions, such as a substantial literature on Christian meditation, or Sufism in Islam, or Kabbalah in Judaism. Hinduism could probably fit in either the mystical or religious spirituality categories. Buddhism is (perhaps wrongly) called a religion but belongs in the mystical category more than the religious. Secular spirituality tends to be non-theistic, but many nature-based spiritualities are pantheistic, or animistic, or even monotheistic (such as Goddess spirituality). Further, it is commonplace for people today to pick 'n mix, choosing aspects of the three types and crafting a highly individualized path.

Despite its imperfections, this typology is essential to our analysis because each type has a different attitude toward spiritual fulfillment and toward work, and each has different consequences and outcomes, as we see in coming chapters. The rest of this chapter explores how they differ, conflict, and converge.

Exploring the three types – religious spirituality

Religious spirituality needs perhaps the least explanation. While traditional religion has undergone occasional radical change (such as Vatican II in the 1960s and evangelicalism in the 20th-century United States), mainstream religion has remained essentially stable. This stability in a chaotic, changing, and sometimes troubled world is a feature, not a bug although one might worry about ethical precepts not keeping up.

The connection, across generations, to shared beliefs and traditions, is powerful. To say you are a Lutheran now means about what it meant 100 years ago. That connection to history is a very powerful part of traditional religion – feeling connected, to Peter, or Abraham, or Mohammed and the saints and sages of the millennia as well as to the culture and rituals of one's religion is hard to replicate in more modern spiritualities.

For the religiously spiritual, belief in God is the *sine qua non* of a spiritual belief system, and spirituality is connecting with a deity who, even today, may have many other names: Elohim, the Great

Spirit, Energy, Bríghde, Brahman, the Tao, Kami, Dharma, Bahá, the Universe, Teutatis, Yahweh, Jah, Pachamama, Ra, Higher Power, Ranginui, Source, Satnam, Jehovah, Odin, Higher Self, and Allah.[27] Add to that list pantheistic and polytheistic belief systems, and it becomes much longer. Then, to complicate matters further, consider that some of the terms above mean different things to different people. Even the term "God" conceals a myriad of meaning. So our list, despite its length, **conceals** some of the complexity and diversity of theistic beliefs.

Most holders of these beliefs consider their name for God to be the best name – some people will take offense that I mention Jah, God, and Source adjacently. But from a 10,000-meter-high view, all those beliefs require an element of faith in unseen beings. I'm interested in where common ground might lie between different spiritual paths, and this, the domain of metaphysical beliefs is the worst place to look – that is, the most emotionally charged and perhaps why people stormed out of de Waal's Academy of Religion conference.

Some writers on spirituality seek to distance themselves from religion. I have many times heard someone triumphantly (and with just a little superiority) claim, "I'm spiritual, not religious," as if you cannot be both and one is better than the other. **For many of these spiritual-but-not-religious folks, spirituality is an evolution of religion—a more advanced form, and categorically different.**

That worldview seems to me charged with egotism. Psychologist Kenneth Pargament agrees and even challenges the view that religion is distinct from spirituality. He laments, "Religion is associated [incorrectly] with the organizational, the ritual and the ideological, and spirituality with the personal, the affective, the experiential and the thoughtful." One of psychology's founders, William James,

---

[27] Some of these refer to a Supreme Being, while others refer to a divine place or path. There are people today devoted to each of these with the same fervor as a someone from an Abrahamic religion is devoted to their God. Rather than fading into history, many of these are resurgent.

might agree defining religion as "the feelings, acts, and experiences of individual men in their solitude" and not in terms of a deity or a church. As I won't allow religionists the view that non-theists are unspiritual, I'm neither going to allow the "spiritual but not religious" to grab the high ground (as some, not all, would like to.)

Religion though, compared to mysticism is a fairly scripted path, codified in ancient times and updated through writings of theologians, scholars, and spiritual leaders – for example, Papal Encyclicals. Mystical spirituality is harder to pin down.

Exploring the three types – mystical spirituality

"[religion should] ... comfort the afflicted
and afflict the comfortable."
FINLEY DUNNE

There is perhaps more diversity of thought, ideology, and practices within mysticism than any other of our three types. According to theologian Peter Moore, "the term mysticism is problematic but indispensable." Rather than a problematic formal definition, here is a list of traditions and associated mystical concepts: New Age, Shamanism, alternate states of consciousness, ecstasy, contemplative traditions, the Tao, Chi, Zen, occult, Buddhism, Reiki, Universe, Reality, Oneness, interconnectedness, Tantra, energy, Kabbalah, chakra, Divine, Sufism, Union, Atman, collective unconscious, Gnosticism, Theosophy, extra-sense perception, Quakerism, Cosmic Consciousness, and Spiritualism.

Mystics from different ages include Rumi, Ramakrishna, St. Francis of Assisi, Theresa of Avila, Lao Tzu, Confucius, Carl Jung, Jean d 'Arc, Baal Shem Tov, Hermann Hesse, Ghazzālī, Evelyn Underhill, Gautama Buddha, and Khalil Gibran. Writers associated with contemporary mysticism are Eckhart Tolle, Deepak Chopra, Ken Wilber, Barbara Marx Hubbard, Marianne Williamson, Ram Dass, Jon

Kabat-Zinn, Wayne Dyer, Alan Watts, Louise Hay, Neale Donald Walsh, Thomas Merton, Jean Houston, and the Dalai Lama. That is a long, eclectic list of names, stretching across human history. What does Deepak Chopra have to do with Theresa of Avila or Gautama Buddha?

What unites mystics is the view that we are all part of the Universe and connected to every other living being materially and spiritually. They are also united in their emphasis on spiritual experience, particularly **"numinous experience"** of another Reality. (In fact, some are dualists, believing there is a greater Reality which their practices apprehend, and some are monists, believing that there is one True Reality, but without their specific practice, one doesn't see it.) Some of those experiences are "extrovertive," looking out through the senses at "the One," some are introvertive, looking inward into the mind to achieve more pure states of consciousness. Then there are theistic, atheistic, and polytheistic strands of mysticism. The practices of mysticism often aim at personal transformation or realization of the "true Self" through spiritual practice.

Mysticism overlaps with religious spirituality, and many of the above religious mystics were faithful to their parent religion. Until the 20th century, when spirituality was still a subset of religion, the older mystics above were the spiritual groundbreakers. Spirituality was often the esoteric path within traditional religion.

It may seem that many of these mystics are on the fringe, a small group when compared to orthodox religion, but most of the sales boom in books on spirituality in the 1990s were in this category. Further, may people incorporate mystical ideas into more orthodox paths. Consider how many people you may know who have finished *The Prophet, The Power of Now, Be Here Now, A Course in Miracles, Eat-Pray-Love, Wherever You Go – There You Are, The Four Agreements, Conversations with God, The Celestine Prophecy, or The Alchemist.* If forced to guess, I would say that the number of people in the world who sample from the mystical traditions number in the billions.

Exploring the three types – secular spirituality

"Spirituality is the subtle awareness that transcends our petty self-interest. Thus, there is spirituality in nature, in art, in the bonds of love and fellow-feeling that hold a community together, in the reverence for life..."
PROFESSOR ROBERT FULLER

Secular spirituality has its roots in the early 20th century. It grew and diversified further during the 1960s' countercultural movement, and again in the 1990s with the rise of modern Humanism and Environmentalism. It is the fastest-growing area today, but many people in this category who are dedicated to learning and striving for meaning, purpose, goodness, and connectedness eschew the term spiritual. Their life is informed by deep ethical commitments, they may sample from mystical practices such as meditation and yoga and may be incredibly active trying to effect change in the world. Yet, people in this category avoid the idea of a deity or an Alternative Reality. Their "deity" might be Justice, Gaia, Humankind, Nature, Freedom, Science, Reason, Art, or Progress.

For a believer in a deity from orthodox religion, such transcendent conceptions may seem strange, or if not strange, un-spiritual: "Sure, I like nature (lowercase n) too, but it doesn't take the place of God." For the secularly spiritual, it might. Professor of Philosophy, Dan Dennett, one of the "Four Horsemen" new atheists, put it this way:

"Of course, I have spiritual moments. Sometimes I am transported by awe and joy and peace and wonder. People make the mistake of thinking spiritual experience such as that is associated with doctrine or belief. The world is a stunningly interesting and glorious place at every scale. The awe one can experience because one understands

65

*something about how the parts are put together is far
greater than the awe of incomprehension. The universe is
much more wonderful the more you know about it."*

Can earthly, secular, natural, and abstract "transcendent purposes" take the place of a deity or the mystic's "other Reality"? In
humans, with minds as powerful as we have, I believe so – and certainly there are people of my acquaintance every bit as passionate
and zealous about their secular transcendent purpose as the theist
is about their deity.

Let's explore two important strands to secular spirituality:
Humanistic spirituality and Nature-centered spirituality.

Humanistic spirituality

*"Humanism is a progressive philosophy of life that,
without theism or other supernatural beliefs, affirms our
ability and responsibility to lead ethical lives of personal
fulfillment that aspire to the greater good."*
AMERICAN HUMANIST ASSOCIATION

The fastest-growing species on the spiritual landscape is Humanistic spirituality – made more complicated to describe because
some Humanists see those terms as oxymoronic. However, Humanist
philosopher Anthony Grayling offers a reconciliation: "I believe
passionately in the value of all things spiritual, by which I mean the
things of the human spirit, with its capacity for love and enjoyment,
creativity and kindness, hope and courage."

Humanistic spirituality holds that human flourishing, guided
by human reason and action, matters most: "the sole things that
matter to humans are the things that humans may take care of." [28]

---

[28] Zygmunt Bauman, professor of Sociology, in "The Project of Humanity"

Our trouble is that the many people who think that way do not use the label "Humanist" because nowhere, unlike with religion, is there a place to learn its history and catechism.[29]

Most distinctively, Humanistic spirituality sees meaning, purpose, awe, goodness, and connectedness as **human** without need for external meaning (a deity or afterlife), or for an external moral reference point. Humanists hunger for meaning because the deep need to connect with something greater than ourselves and to consider how our life fits into the bigger picture is divinely human.

In common with religion and mysticism is the embrace of mystery. The connection to science and reason does not presuppose that we have all the answers, or that the answers we now have are all correct. There is a kind of faith attached to this view that nature will reveal her secrets if we constantly revise our own thinking. Maria Popova, a brilliant essayist, and curator of spiritual, artistic, and scientific content, put it this way:

> *"That gap between what we yearn to know and what we might never know is filled with the creative restlessness responsible for almost all human achievement — our art and our science and our philosophy, those myriad tentacles by which we reach for the unknown knowing full well it might be unknowable, but reaching nonetheless."*[30]

Einstein and Da Vinci, though non-believers, saw around them the most awe-inspiring, magical, sacred, wondrous world—it may be **scientific spirituality** that furnishes some Humanists with the sorts of **experiences** described by mystics throughout the ages. As

---

[29] Although rare, there is a strand of, congregational Humanism – that is, church-like services and ethically-based communities such as Ethical Culture, Unitarian Universalism, or a few varieties of Quakerism. Congregational Humanism recognizes that the traditionally religious are exceptional at building community, creating social capital, guiding their children in values development, and mobilizing *en masse* to do service.

[30] Maria Popova, curator of Brain Pickings, brainpickings.org, in an interview with physicist Lisa Randall on religion and science.

astrophysicist and Humanist Carl Sagan said, "The nitrogen in our DNA, the calcium in our teeth, the iron in our blood, the carbon in our apple pies were made in the interiors of collapsing stars. We are made of starstuff." According to this view, the spiritual experience of science may motivate human beings to moral action, by revealing our connectedness to others and to the world.

However, Humanists also seek the miraculous in the everyday, simple, and earthly. As psychologist David Elkins says, Humanistic spirituality is *"opening our hearts and cultivating our capacity to experience* awe, reverence, and gratitude *and the ability to see the sacred in the ordinary, to feel the poignancy of life, and to know the passion of existence and to give ourselves over to that which is greater than ourselves."*

Humanists find guides for living in ancient writings less likely to be spirituality bestsellers, perhaps those from the Greek and Enlightenment philosophers. Stoics emphasize **personal responsibility, reason, human flourishing, constant learning, and dispassionate judgment.** The Enlightenment philosophers ushered humanity out of the Dark Ages and brought us **science, reason, progress, liberty, democracy, and equality.**

Humanism emphasizes realization of their human potential – **you get to work on yourself.** This worldview midwifed the proliferation of **self-improvement** books, personal growth workshops, and therapies of all sorts that occupy at least two aisles in your local bookstore. Adjacent to this belief is one of **personal responsibility.** As Seneca said,

> *"Let your philosophy scrape off your own faults, rather than be a way to rail against the faults of others."*

Rather than self-improvement for its own sake, the self-improvement and realization of potential of Humanism are directed toward the betterment of the world.

Humanistic spirituality shares the search for **goodness** with other types, but the measures of goodness tend to be human – fairness, liberty, human rights, and flourishing. All spirituality has a vision of the divine, but for the Humanist, the sacred is right here – this world and the people in it. We must constantly strive to better ourselves and our institutions, to transcend the necessity and the inevitability of our lives and the world, and to use our free will responsibly. That leads to a set of Humanist virtues, not very different from those of religionists or the mystical: reason, education, excellence, compassion, beauty, kindness, knowledge, tolerance, forgiveness, perseverance, prudence, and love.

Though those virtues and values are shared with the religious, the attitude to moral failure is different than in some religions: "in their view [morality] is like taking aim at a target, and missing; it is a bad shot; what you must do is aim again, and do better. In other moral regimes, failure is a blemish, a stain that remains, culpable and in need of grace or forgiveness from an outside source."[31]

It is hard to say whether Humanistic spirituality as a coherent movement will ever take root, though it continues to grow quickly. It simply is not, perhaps yet, a label many people attach to their lives. It is likely, perhaps inevitable, that its signature ideas, e.g. free-will, personal responsibility, compassion, fairness, human rights, ethics, personal growth, self-actualization, and reason will continue to percolate through human culture and become "the only way to think about things" although unrecognized as spirituality by people who endorse those virtues. The second and final form of secular spirituality is Nature-centered spirituality. Although not growing as quickly as Humanistic spirituality, many of its nature-centered spirituality's forms are newer than other spiritualities and birthed in the 1960s.

---

[31] From AC Grayling's, *The God Argument*, Bloomsbury (2014)

Nature-centered spirituality

"Those who dwell among the beauties and mysteries of the earth are never alone or weary of life."
RACHEL CARSON

Nature-centered spirituality is complex and diverse. It (at least) includes animism, shamanism,[32] pantheism, Gaian religion, Eco-Christianity, Goddess religion, pagan religion, Transcendentalism, Environmentalism, and some indigenous religions (Native American spirituality for example.) I see three strands, one that is close to paganism and indigenous religion, one that is modern and scientific embracing ecology, and another that is activist embracing politics to effect environmental change.

How do these fulfill the definition of spirituality? Whatever I say here, I will not say as well as have said the poets, so I've peppered my cumbersome prose with more artful words:

"Knowing that Nature never did betray
The heart that loved her; 'tis her privilege,
Through all the years of this our life, to lead
From joy to joy... "
WORDSWORTH, "TINTERN ABBEY"

As with other kinds of spirituality, meaning and purpose are central. As Dostoyevsky said, *"Though I do not believe in the order of things, still the sticky little leaves that come out in the spring are dear to me, the blue sky is dear to me..."* Three-quarters of Americans agree that being in nature gives meaning and purpose to their lives, but that isn't the same as spirituality with nature at the center. Many Nature-centered spiritualities suggest that the divine permeates nature and that the sacred can be understood by

---

[32] Shamanism finds itself in both mystical and nature-centered spiritualities.

veneration of nature. What is particularly useful about this view is that this veneration can peacefully co-exist alongside religion and mysticism although some strands of religion view Nature through the philosophy of **dispensationalism** believing, "Jesus is returning and the earth is going to burn up anyway, so go ahead and use it up." [33] Occasionally there is political strife between some strands of Christianity and Environmentalism, "Evangelicals see environmentalists as godless pagans and socialists."[34] These latter views, though significant demographically, are fading and increasingly religious people view care for nature as part of their sacred responsibility, "care for the creations and not just the Creator."

Goodness in the newest strands of this spirituality is focused on nature – on endangered species, melting ice caps, biosphere degradation, preserving beauty, fighting pollution, rising sea levels, and a warming planet. Furthermore, nature has moral value of its own, not merely for its ability to nurture human life, but the right to exist and regenerate itself and the right not to be desecrated without remorse. We close as we opened, with a spiritual thought from Rachel Carson:

> *"The more clearly we can focus our attention on the wonders and realities of the universe about us, the less taste we shall have for destruction."*

Could it be a ridiculous taks to group those three types under the same umbrella – spirituality? Where might there be common ground?

---

[33] Robinson, Rev. Tri, Savings God's Green Earth, Ampelon Publishing, 2006
[34] "God and the Environment," Grist Magazine, grist.org/series/god-the-environment

WHERE DO THE THREE KINDS OF SPIRITUALITY CONVERGE?

"Spiritual individuals are disposed to a vision of excellence, loveliness, or preeminent goodness, and they order their conduct to realize that vision."

JORGE SANTAYANA, SPANISH PHILOSOPHER

The question asked throughout the ages and in this book is whether all wisdom traditions converge around certain values. What could possibly unite the secularly spiritual, for whom supernatural beliefs seem strange with the traditionally religious who might think that replacing God with a conception such as "Source" or "Nature" is misguided (or even blasphemous). What could moreover unite mystics, pagans, Buddhists, and environmentalists? Meta-physical beliefs are the worst places to look for convergence, but how about meaning, purpose, goodness, and connectedness?

Figure II-2: Where do these belief systems meet?[35]

Included in our definition of spirituality are four content elements: meaning, purpose, goodness, and connectedness. I suggest

---

[35] Clockwise from top-left: Reverend William Barber, Bishop Katharine Jefferts Schori, Marianne Williamson, Rachel Carson, Pema Chödrön, Imam Elahi, and Marcus Aurelius

that these offer common ground not only for individuals but also for how we understand spirituality meets workplace outcomes such as motivation, leadership, values, talent, and culture. The reason that common ground matters is so diverse groups can talk about spiritual matters with mutual understanding. To do that, you have to see yours humbly, in the context of an immense variety of different traditions, and see **others' journeys as parallel to your own.**

Let's briefly define the four elements more closely.

The four elements

Purpose: It seems universal that humans are **inspired by purpose**, more so by noble purpose, and purpose beyond the self. So important is purpose that all of Chapter VIII is devoted to exploring it through the lens of philosophy. Defining spirituality as we have makes purpose **an organizing principle for life**, where ethics, values, and vocation come together. In the words of noted theologian Paul Tillich, "The ultimate concern gives depth, direction, and unity to all other concerns."

To illustrate, Nelson Mandela was imprisoned for life in 1962 in a toilet-sized jail cell on a remote island prison. Despite these conditions, Mandela ran for forty-five minutes in place, then shadowboxed, and then did 100 fingertip push-ups, 200 sit-ups, and calisthenics. When a guard jeered at him for this, Mandela replied, "I must be fit so I can lead my people to freedom." It seems to me Mandela's sense of purpose animated and organized his life, in prison and out.

Infusing your life with purpose takes effort. If you are religious, it might mean being prayerful in all you do. If you lean New Age, your purpose could include "healing" that can touch all aspects of your life, personal and professional. If your professional purpose is helping people realize their potential, perhaps you extend that toward yourself and the people you love.

Meaning: Creating a more meaningful life seems not to be about getting an answer to "what is the meaning of life?" It is about asking the right questions of ourselves at the right times. If you think about the popularity of inspirational books, it precisely, I think, because they provide a leg-up toward making meaning.

There is something wonderfully human about the search for meaning that non-human animals seem not to have. It is what makes us us. Viktor Frankl overstated the case, but only by a little, when he said, "Life is never made unbearable by circumstances, but only by lack of meaning and purpose." Lack of meaning creates a "God-sized hole in the soul" as the religious would have it. This affects working lives. Work, opined Studs Terkel, "is about a search for daily meaning as well as daily bread..."

Frankl's experience of Auschwitz teaches us that life can be full of hellish circumstance leaving us adrift, but the meaning we make is our own – and ultimately the only true freedom that we have.

> *"We who lived in concentration camps can remember the men who walked through the huts comforting others, giving away their last piece of bread. They may have been few in number, but they offer sufficient proof that everything can be taken from a man but one thing: the last of human freedoms — to choose one's own attitude in any given set of circumstances — to choose one's own way."*

When Nietzsche talked about the death of God, he was metaphorically referring to the loss of meaning that 19th-century industrialization, secularization, culture change, and science had ushered in. (You might wonder what he'd think of the loss of meaning in the 21st century.) Recall, he didn't think "God's death" was straightforwardly a good thing – the loss of the foundational meaning underpinning European society was, he thought, catastrophic.

The loss of meaning "out there" means **humans have a lot of inside work to do** – to make their lives meaningful. The oft-told parable of the three stonecutters illustrates the importance of a meaning-making and a mindset shift. In this tale, a traveling monk approaches three different stonecutters and asks what they are doing. The first, miserable, says "I'm cutting this friggin' rock." The second, happier, says, "I'm building an immense wall." The third, joyful, says, "I'm creating a magnificent cathedral." This illustrates, again, that meaning isn't "out there" but is created; it's created in this case by **the narrative—the why of our work.**

We get to choose which stonecutter we will be.

Goodness: Most people **want to do good**, or at least do no harm. For workplaces, research shows (we visit all the evidence in Volume II) that people are much more engaged in businesses that make an effort to do good.

Humans disagree vehemently on a conception of the good, but there are some universals. The Dalai Lama offered such a list, "love and compassion, patience, tolerance, forgiveness, contentment, a sense of responsibility, a sense of harmony – which brings happiness to both self and others." This universalism is not to trivialize how difficult and conflict-ridden reconciling different notions of the good may be. Even if we do agree, say on human welfare as a good, the fight may remain over who is entitled, or who gets what share.

That is great triumph of political philosophy, creating institutions where differing conceptions of goodness can work and prosper together, in a community, a nation, and perhaps one day, in the world at large – in the old days, we just killed each other over whose "goodness" was better. (Which seems absurd when phrased that way.)

We are imperfect beasts, always falling short of the standards we set for ourselves, and we often allow our standards to slip in the face of circumstance. I used to say, "if you always live up to your own standards, they aren't high enough" – we need to stretch, to be a little kinder, do a bit more for others, and to lend ourselves to worthy causes. (Oh, and to burn fewer hydrocarbons and use less plastic!) We get to choose our conception of the good, but a reasonable standard is to try to leave the world a bit better by the end of the day than it was at the beginning. (From the point of view of the planet, not only do we not leave it better each day, we leave it considerably worse!)

Connectedness: One of my mentors, Richard Strozzi-Heckler, said, "... on the savannah, if you were cast out from the herd, you became lunch." Our ability to connect around shared purpose helped us survive and accelerated our cultural evolution – our primate cousins from that time do mostly as they did back then. Connectedness and collaboration allowed us to do more. Today, this ability to connect a million people in a company, twenty million people in a city, a billion in a country, and nearly eight billion around the world is a human superpower.

In the words of Christian mystic, Thomas Merton, "We do not exist for ourselves alone, and it is only when we are fully convinced of this fact that we begin to love ourselves properly and thus also love others." Connectedness, in spirituality, is not just social connectedness, but connectedness to self, tribe, and to the world. Even in million-person companies, we can feel alone and isolated. The responsibility for staying connected remains with us.

This is worth pondering in the 21st-century. Our physical and virtual connectedness are unlike ever before – however... Can we humans rise to the challenge of connecting spiritually and emotionally with our brethren, perhaps those half a planet away?

The fifth element – experience

The sixth chapter, on mindfulness, talks further about spiritual experience. While beliefs diverge into dozens of different transcendent conceptions, scholars think that spirituality converges in the domain of experience. In *The Varieties of Religious Experience*, William James saw spirituality as something experiential and common across all religious traditions, suggesting that experiences such as oneness, epiphany, altered consciousness, trance, deep mystical, and enlightenment shared a common ground. We may differ in our **abstract concepts of the divine** but perhaps share the experience of spirituality.

If one views spirituality in the ways described above, it is accessible to believers and non-believers of every kind. I hope that you can view your own spirituality in the context of others' and see their journey as parallel to your own even if they look different on the surface.

The next chapter takes us to the first half of our definition "**growing and striving**" and the idea **spirituality can be developed** and indeed **must be developed** if we are to fully flourish. Perhaps spirituality is not only part of our evolutionary heritage, fundamental to human nature, or a cultural phenomenon, but something that must rather be cultivated **as we develop, or if we are to develop.**

We all have the **capacity** to experience James' spiritual experiences: wonder, awe, reverence, and sacredness. But what does capacity matter if you don't make use of it? **Cultivation** of such attitudes is more important. Experiencing them is a habit of mind worth developing (again, whether you are clergy, scientist, artist, or businessperson). By investigating philosophical and psychological perspectives, we can better understand how spiritual cultivation can develop through one's lifetime.

EPILOGUE: METAMODERNITY – INTELLECTUAL CLAPTRAP OR A "MIDDLE-WAY"

Hegel, the 19th-century philosopher, thought history proceeded in cycles of change and then over-reaction to change. The modern era, up to about 1950, is associated with ideologies such as rationality, progress, capitalism, universalism, and individualism. Postmodernism, perhaps up until the turn of the millennium, argued that those narratives disregarded alternative stories about the past. The postmodern argument goes that our history, our institutions, our religions, our ideas about the world, and our science, were written by middle-aged white men. So while the ideas and institutions that we inherit from the past **masquerade as rational or inevitable**, they are not an essential feature of the world, but better viewed as reflections of the power structures that created them and people with power seizing more of it.

The postmodern view is, up to a point, trivially true. We cannot walk in the shoes of an African slave or a 19th-century native American, or a woman just about anywhere in the world; they didn't write our history books, and if they did, the stories would be different. They would not just be stories of prosperity, conquest, progress, and liberation – they would be far bleaker.

We see both forces at work today. There are many great books, such as Steven Pinker's brilliant *Enlightenment Now*, that wish to celebrate the progress that we have made and where we are (with facts!) But there are equally persuasive, equally factual, stories about how much prosperity, conquest, progress, and liberation are (respectively) unequal, colonial, environmentally destructive, and still oppressive. Partly which story you tell depends whether you live in Cambridge, or Compton. In a perverse way, it is amusing to watch "1%-ers" or elite academics beaming about how wonderful the world is from Georgetown (Mayfair for Brits), and the bottom third, (or women, or immigrants, or post-colonial countries, or people of color,) wondering wtf they are talking about. People in the middle with decent but not lavish lives, don't feel either group speaks for them and "check out."

Both modernism and postmodernism are failures. Modernity paved over the differences between people, and postmodernism became all about difference – about culture wars, and identities (in caricature) shouting at one another. "Nothing ever gets solved because the contending forces angrily oppose and caricature one another until (in fact) both are degraded and destroyed in number and in spirit."[36] Modernity was blindly optimistic, postmodernism deeply cynical. Modernity said, "forget all that historical stuff" – look at how bright the future is. Postmodernism said, "whoa buddy, that is easy for you to say – my history isn't so pretty and its legacy lives on and pre-determines my future."

The optimistic spirit of modernity was perhaps blindly so, the notion that we can improve the world with science and technology without worry. I'm inspired by that spirit, but new technologies made 20th-century warfare profoundly bloodier by enabling humanity to kill each other by the millions. Modernists were more alive to technology's potential and less with its consequences. In the rush to progress, they didn't really worry about what might be happening to little things like our habitat.

In our times, the viewpoints of modernism and postmodernism seem irreconcilable. In the US, where I now live, that means differences are resolved purely by use of political power. You get 51 votes you get your ideology through, and the other 49 votes... well, better

---

[36] Abrahamson, S., Ten Basic Principles of Metamodernism, Huffington Post, December 6th, 2017.

...uck next time. When the political tide turns, the other side's ideas of progress are forced out – resulting in a zigzagging of immoderate policies. We've lost the idea of dialogue and engagement to polemics and culture wars. Lost with those is the possibility of solutions that make use of the best thinking from both sides.

Metamodernism tries not to "average" these two conflicting movements, but to allow us to flexibly make use of both – to "oscillate" as they say. We should ask, before we try to hand wave away polarization of worldviews saying "just oscillate," whether this is a fantasy. I think not. There are, for sure, universal values but we need to be careful which values we claim are so – democracy, much as we would like to be universal, is not either in theory, nor historically, nor presently the only way to structure government. (I happen to be a fan, but that is beside the point.)

Metamodernism allows some universal values and truths while remaining committed to pluralism. We have done that here. We take a top-down and a bottom-up approach to spirituality - embracing pluralism but holding onto the idea that certain truths and values hold up better under scrutiny. We need the hopefulness and optimism of Enlightenment and the anxieties of postmodernity about concentration of power. We need reverence for truth and knowledge and understanding that some knowledge is contextual. This book, the critical reader will discern, hopes for a universalism of spiritual values that "sits above" beliefs about the Universe, or God.

Another standpoint of this book is the importance of reason and science. Appeals to reason, facts, and science – aren't always, as the postmodernist would have it, power grabs by elites who control the systems that generate them. They are functionally good for the world. We need them, but also to appreciate the limits of human reason and to remember when science was used to justify racial oppression and eugenics.

Another meta-narrative of this book is human progress, which is a dirty word in postmodernism. For the postmodernists, "progress" was code for the imposition of Western values. "Hey, make progress so you can become just like us," say the modernizers. "No thanks – we like our traditions, values, and ways of life, and we want modernity, if at all, on our terms."

Postmodernists reject the idea of progress because it has been defined in terms of Westernization, industrialization, and urbanization. While they make a good point, progress is a real thing. In 18th-century medicine, doctors killed people with leeches. Antibiotics work better. Metamodern ideas allow the idea of progress while being conscious of the fact that the term has been one of oppression.

We, I think, can progress capitalism, business, workplaces, and human experience of work by doing a little oscillation – to take just one example, viewing capitalism as a vital force for human progress while considering its deep structural inequalities, environmental harm, and corruption of democratic structures.

Spiritual growth and development

Covered in this chapter:

Revelation or search?

Ancient ideas on spiritual growth

CHAPTER 3

SPIRITUAL GROWTH AND DEVELOPMENT

Spirituality is growing and striving for meaning, purpose, goodness, and connectedness.

While meaning, purpose, goodness, and connectedness are the **content** of spirituality**, growing and striving** speaks to the **process** of spirituality. We wondered in chapter I whether spirituality was innate in some respect, but in this chapter, I suggest that it is a source of and an area for growth and change – rather than being innate or static. Wherever you are, or whichever tradition you inherit or choose, you can grow within it. By this, I'm implying that spirituality is **not a passive pursuit** and has to do with growth and striving to act in accordance with one's principles in daily life.

This of one the distinctive aspects of this book that it sets apart from just having specific beliefs and practices or espousing certain virtues or values. Historically, this idea is found in writings of St. Ignatius, 12-step programs, and in pockets of the Abrahamic religions, Hinduism, modern Stoicism, and Buddhism. Spiritual growth is also central to mystical and secular spirituality, although secularists may prefer the term personal growth.

This developmental perspective is empowering. You start from where you are, and if you lose your way, you restart from where you are. When people go through life changes, the source of meaning in their life changes. For instance, if work is an important source of meaning for you, that source of meaning will change when you retire. If parenting is an important source of meaning, that will change when your nest empties. "Restart from where you are" means you get to work on and redirect your meaning, purpose, goodness, and connectedness no matter your context or how it changes.

Revelation or search?

"Satisfaction lies in the effort, not in the attainment. Full effort is full victory."
GANDHI

In my late 20s, I was disillusioned by a life on Wall Street, miserably wondering when my life's purpose and vocation would appear on a tablet of stone for me to pursue. Was it medicine, science, economics, math, or something I had yet to discover? The angst of waiting for revelation was visceral.

Through the writings of M. Scott Peck,[37] whose books integrate Western psychotherapy with spiritual growth, I realized that **the thing I was waiting for was me**. (Possibly, the thing you are waiting for is you.) My growth process did not appear as a flash of insight, but Peck suggested it was a lifelong voyage of discovery. This growth perspective cured all my anxiety about what my purpose in life might be. I was relieved that I could chill out and focus on the questions rather than pine for answers. That also made for a more empowering narrative for my hedonistic Wall Street years. They, too, were part of the growth process – learning what I wasn't about – instead of wasted years I had to wish away.

Even though you hunger for meaning and purpose, those

---

[37] For example, Peck, M.S., *Further Along the Road Less Travelled: The Unending Journey Toward Spiritual Growth*, Touchstone: NY (1998)

won't necessarily appear to you in a flash of insight one day. Most treatments of spiritual growth that I have researched have two dimensions: a **revelatory** dimension and a **seeking** dimension. For a theist, the revelation might come from their God; for a Humanist, the revelation will perhaps likely come from knowledge – either self-knowledge or discovering more about the world. Both of those require a level of openness and humility – you cannot learn about yourself or the world, or receive insight if your views are already too rigid. As Emily Dickenson penned, "*The door to the soul should always stand ajar...*"

Just passively waiting for insight is not recommended by most faith traditions. As Christians put it, "God needs a partner in his plans for your life." There is an amusing parable from Judaism which has Mordechai complaining to God on his death bed about how hard he had prayed every day, to no avail, to win the lottery. God replied, "But, I did answer your prayers! I was waiting for you to buy a ticket." Whatever your worldview, **action and openness** seem to be important.

We share this common ground of actively searching for meaning and purpose– your search, your employees' search, and the search of people who are suffering. Although it seems sometimes that our ideas of meaning, purpose, and goodness might differ, **we can value the search in each other**. We will often encounter people at different stages of their search – it helps to understand where they might be and relate it to our own journey. While there may be as many jour-neys as there have been travelers, some scholars, theologians, and psychologists have tried to generalize about the growth process.

What do scholars think the spiritual growth process looks like? Peck suggests a framework of spiritual growth (based on the work of renowned developmental psychologists and theologians) that is summarized in the table below.[38] His model suggests that as part

---

[38] The big names are Jean Piaget, Erik Erikson, James Fowler, and Lawrence Kohlberg, three developmental psychologists and a theologian.

of individual spiritual development, there will be times of questioning, times of belief, times of disbelief, and times when these stages intersect. At the final stage, belief **and** doubt are embraced, scripture (religious or non-religious) is deeply personal, spirituality becomes a "get to" rather than a "have to." The integration of life and spirituality becomes active, not passive, and constant, not periodic.

Peck's stages of spiritual development

Chaotic	Pre-spiritual, unprincipled, amoral, anti-social/ sociopathic
Formal	Institutional spirituality, dependent, dogmatic, submissive
Sceptical	Individual, socially committed, idealists, agnostic/ atheist
Mystical	Embrace paradox and mystery, understand interconnectedness, engage in spiritual questioning, interpret scripture symbolically and individually, belief as a choice rather than obligation, maintenance of spiritual practice, acceptance of diversity

© PAUL GIBBONS   PAULGIBBONS.NET

Table III-1: Peck's stages of spiritual development

Try on Peck's model for size. How does it fit with your own journey? There are many developmental models in this book, particularly when we talk about leadership. I use them but "hold them lightly" simply because no author of a developmental model ever created one with themselves at the bottom – there is a level of subjectivity no matter how much the authors might suggest otherwise.

Ancient ideas on spiritual growth

"Such power as I possess for working in the political field is derived entirely from my experiments in the spiritual field."

GANDHI

Depending on your beliefs, revelation may play a role in spiritual development, but no theologian I've encountered says development requires anything but sustained effort, perhaps to fertilize the ground for revelation. How do we play our part? How do religion and philosophy say we can go about growing spiritually; how do we take on spiritual learning?

The seven elements below are common to most spiritual traditions' conceptions of spiritual development. There are hundreds of volumes, ancient and new, on this topic; this is an attempt to synthesize these commonalities in a nutshell.

- **Integration:** While some ancient monastic traditions were renunciate – that is, they saw leaving the world as essential to spiritual growth, today that is not a common view. Religious traditions talk about manifesting the divine in the world; mystical traditions talk about healing others; Humanistic and nature spirituality talk about systemic and institutional change. To grow authentically, practice has to happen in the temple of life – what the Greeks called *phronesis*, applied wisdom. (Phronesis is a good word: if you look at the name of this book's publisher, it is Phronesis Media, what I named my tiny publishing company.)

- **Spiritual study:**[39] To the credit of modern humans, spirituality was among the fastest-growing segments of the book market during some of the last 30 years. This explosion of interest happened even in the most secular countries in the world, i.e. European ones. Most strands of spirituality value spiritual study as part of spiritual growth, *lectio divina* in Christianity, *talmud Torah*[40] in the Jewish faith, Jnana yoga in Hinduism, and inspirational and self-help reading from the New Age traditions. Wherever you look, studying spiritual ideas and reading about the spiritual journeys of others is part of the spiritual growth process. Perhaps Renaissance theologian Erasmus said it best, "study as if you were to live forever."

---

[39] Nobody reads these days, so study includes of course, audiobooks, podcasts, YouTube, online learning, discussion groups, and other flavors of knowledge acquisition.

[40] From Latin, divine reading; from the ancient Hebrew, sacred learning.

Figure III – 2: Whatever your path, spiritual study is part of it.

- **Reflection:** Judaism has a concept called *teshuvah*, which means "returning" – a course correction – when one has strayed. The Ignatian spiritual tradition has the *Examen,* a spiritual exercise with roots in Stoicism's daily reflection practice, and which became, in the 20th century, the inspiration for the Twelve-Step programs. The objective is to awaken sensitivity and self-awareness, motives, and desires and discover where you are called upon to grow. This practice is essential in every performance domain, from competitive sports to leadership.

- **Service:** From the Christian Bible to socialist thought, service to others is virtuous. Luke 12: 48 says, "From those to whom much is given, much is expected." Karl Marx, with deep concern for community, suggests that "those who are most able must help those most in need." In my view, service makes the whole of humankind rise to greater than the sum of its human parts. The elegant paradox of service is that it helps the server and not just the served. This is a pillar of 12-step recovery programs where addicts struggle with post-addiction emotional issues – rather than a pint of Häagen-Dazs or another earthly "fix," the counsel is: "If you want to feel better about your life, help someone else feel better about theirs."

- **Spiritual practices:** Some practices stimulate experiences described as spiritual such as peace, harmony, oneness, and connectedness. These practices may include a walk in nature, a run, a hug, prayer, meditation, yoga, music, art, or dozens more. Only you know what creates such experiences for you, and if you don't know, you have an exciting journey ahead of you.

- **Stoicism:** While Modern Stoicism is becoming a spiritual path, the stoicism referred to here is more general: "the endurance of pain or hardship without complaint, and with regulated emotions." Psychologists often claim that intimate relationships are the greatest test of our spiritual condition and the most fertile ground for spiritual growth because true intimacy may cause the most pain. The second greatest test might be work, where we spend a great deal of time, and when we bump into other humans who may trigger us, and where our frustrations and anxieties may come to the fore. The essential message, in both contexts, is to embrace the hard stuff in life because **that is where your growth will come from**: "If you love those who love you, what credit is that to you? Even sinners love those who love them." (Luke 6:33) Twelve-Step programs call this, in more salacious terms, an AFGO: ("another fucking growth opportunity"). Can we love the jerks, the haters, the trolls, the bigots, the malign, and the miscreants? Can we embrace our own pain, be it loneliness or loss? The practice of stoicism allows us to take the negative feelings we experience and alchemically allow them to heal and transform.

- **Discipline:** Fortitude and discipline are common to all ideas on spiritual growth. Aristotle said that we become what we repeatedly do, and that the Greek virtues of wisdom, prudence, justice, fortitude, courage, liberality, magnificence, magnanimity, and temperance were easier to say than to live. Similarly, Hindus see loving devotion (bhakti yoga) as a discipline to be practiced, not a feeling. The Dalai Lama talks most about the discipline it takes to live Buddhist principles of loving-kindness, peace, and compassion.

The elements of growth above are called **generative practices** that improve **all of life** by way of **virtuous circles**. If you nurture relationships, you are nurtured by them. If you generate community and develop others, feedback loops accelerate your personal development and the expansion of your community. If you exercise, you strengthen your mental and physical capacities. By "paying it forward," you create a more compassionate world. If you develop your mind, you grow your capacity to learn and develop it further. You grow spiritually by practicing growing and helping others grow.

Developmental models such as these invite us to devote ourselves to personal growth with passion, energy, and imagination. Integrated with models of human development, they suggest that part of the developmental process of maturation, growth, and self-actualization is partly spiritual. They become important as we talk about leadership development in chapter IX, because any conception of spiritual leadership must hold the spiritual growth and development of followers as a priority.

However, there are spiritual growth traps. One into which I've fallen is being so absorbed in one's own growth and development that it becomes another ego trip and a further example of self-centeredness. The expression: "more evolved than thou" or "more enlightened than thou" pokes fun at ourselves and others for whom spiritual growth became a chance to be uppity. In my view, inner growth that does not produce outer results – in the world, in relationships, as a parent, or at work is a kind of spiritual self-indulgence. There is also a parallel trap, elaborated later, which involves trying to effect change without being willing to take on the hard work of inner transformation.

Even though our own conception of the divine may be
precious to us, can we come to treasure the search
in our brethren and thus find a common humanity?
Can we value this in our work colleagues?

21ST-CENTURY SPIRITUALITY

This chapter concludes our look at contemporary spiritualty, where it came from in historical and evolutionary terms, and samples insights from across traditions which, in my view, humans share. Table III – 3 summarizes the discussion from the last two chapters.

A metamodern framework for understanding 21st - century spirituality

Types	Content	Growing and striving
• Religious	• Purpose	• Integration
• Secular	• Meaning	• Stoicism
• Mystical	• Goodness	• Spiritual practices
	• Connectedness	• Service
		• Discipline
		• Reflection
		• Spiritual study

© PAUL GIBBONS PAULGIBBONS.NET

Figure III-3: 21st-century metamodern spirituality

While I've drawn from multiple academic and spiritual traditions in preparing this framework, there are varieties of spirituality with which I'm less acquainted and about which less is written (those captured in purely oral traditions). For example, while I've done my share of sweat lodges and smudging, I'm less familiar with Native spirituality, shamanism, and pagan traditions. As you read on, I ask is that you "try on" the definition, growing and striving for meaning, purpose, goodness, and connectedness like a cloak, applying it to your path and those of other paths in your circles. By the end of the book, if you "feel warmer," I will be delighted.

In the next chapter, we talk about the relationship between spirituality and work, where our notions of joyful work come from, and whether, maybe, workers have been sold a bill of goods. Is there a darker side of work: "workification" and workaholism?

CHAPTER

The history and gospel of work

Covered in this chapter:

The case against work

Spirituality and de-motivation

Separation of church and work

CHAPTER 4

THE HISTORY AND GOSPEL OF WORK

*"I slept and dreamt that life was joy. I awoke and saw that
life was duty. I worked — and behold, duty was joy."*

RABINDRANATH TAGORE

However obvious joyful work sounds as an ideal to people of our time, historically, this has not been the case. Accounts of work from religious texts are mostly harsh; they suggest we inherit the punishment meted out to Adam and Eve upon their expulsion from the Garden of Eden.[41]

*"Through painful toil you will eat of it all the days of your life…It
will produce thorns and thistles for you … By the sweat of your
brow you will eat your food until you return to the ground"*

GENESIS 3:17–19

But despite all that hardship, remember to work hard, miserable though it may be:

*"Whatever you do, work at it with all of your
hearts, as working for the Lord…"*

COLOSSIANS 3:23

---

[41] There are other Biblical accounts of work. Certainly ministry, healing, and teaching are ennobled by the Bible. Paul believed in the value of manual labor so that he could carry out his apostolic mission without charge.

Likewise in other cultures. To the ancient Hebrews, work was a product of original sin. To the ancient Greeks, workers were beneath the heroic warrior class, artisans, and *aristos*. In the Indian caste system, laborers (*shudras*) were the lowest, below priests, warriors, and traders.

After this historical start, how did hard work become a virtue rather than a penance? How did work come to be revered? How did Rosie the Riveter become a World War II icon? When and from where did we get the notion that work **should** be joyful? How did businesspeople (both in terms of esteem and income) rise to the top of social hierarchies?[42]

Figure IV –1: "Rosie the Riveter" inspired a social movement that helped increase the number of working American women and became, for many, a feminist icon.

---

[42] Amusingly, to me anyhow, when I moved from medicine to finance, more than one of my scientist mentors snootily looked down upon this as "going into trade" – not a fitting occupation for bright young men. How times change!

At the end of the Middle Ages, Europe saw the emergence of the merchant class and merchant guilds. Before this, you were born into the nobility, with dough, or a peasant, without it. The idea of **accumulating wealth** in one's lifetime was new for the not-high-born. Furthermore, buying something for one price, and selling it for a higher price was frowned upon by the church – business was not morally praiseworthy! This emerging class of businesspeople began to flex their economic and political muscles and in doing so reversed church thinking. Within the Christian religion, getting rich, over the next century, became worthy – piety and wealth were linked, no longer opposites.

When ideas about wealth changed, so did ideas about work. Andrew Taggart, a contemporary philosopher, offers a historical summary of work's meaning. "In ancient times, physical labor was contemptible. With the rise of the medieval times, work began to be seen as valuable, but its value was **instrumental** in nature – that is, valuable for what it produced. Later came a transformational shift in perspective from the protestant work ethic: work came to be seen as having **intrinsic value**, value in its own right. Finally, Victorian philosopher Thomas Carlyle introduced the 'gospel of work.' For Carlyle, work had "**supreme value**" – as important as all other virtues including goodness, honesty, kindness, service, and courage.

That is, I believe, where we land in the 21st century: working hard is supremely virtuous.

We see evidence of "the gospel" in our culture. Our work, what we do and how much, defines us to a very great extent. Today, people answer questions that were once theological and philosophical in a vocational way. What do you want from life? What gives you meaning? What is the good life? What is most important? Now, such questions are often viewed and answered through the lens of work, career, and one's occupation.

Contrast this with other cultures and other times. For the early Greeks, the "good life" was the **virtuous life**. For the Stoics, it was **equanimity and peace of mind**, for the Epicureans, **pleasure**. For the Roman Empire, it was **valor and courage**. In religious societies, **piety and devotion** were of supreme importance. Today, we raise kids to achieve and to work hard. To work hard and become rich is virtuous and highly regarded in its own right, almost irrespective of how you do that (inside the generous boundaries of the law.) Work and wealth are perhaps even more culturally noble than a life of service or (say) developing a cure for a life-threatening disease, and certainly more than the pastoral professions, carers, and teachers.

It is difficult to visualize the culture you live in but take a step back and think about ours. Consider today's list of most admired people (not mine necessarily, from surveys)— the list is increasingly **dominated by business leaders** such as Bill Gates, Warren Buffett, Jeff Bezos, Jack Ma, Oprah Winfrey, Jack Welch, Bob Iger, Karoline Nystrøm, Jamie Dimon, Lars Sorensen, Lakshmi Mittal, Sheryl Sandberg, Ginni Rometty, and Indra Nooyi[43]. Where are the artists and scientists? Where are the educators? Where are the spiritual leaders? (There aren't any is the answer, apart from Pope Francis.) Consider the same list (US centric) from 100 years ago. It had Charles Lindbergh (explorer), F. Scott Fitzgerald (writer), Babe Ruth (athlete), Duke Ellington (musician), Eleanor Roosevelt (activist), Shirley Temple (actress, diplomat), Amelia Earhart (aviatrix, explorer), Albert Einstein (scientist), Marie Curie (scientist), Sigmund Freud (doctor), and Jonas Salk (scientist.) There were few businesspeople on those lists, mostly luminous characters such as Henry Ford, John D. Rockefeller, J.P. Morgan, and Randolph Hearst. The kind of people our culture venerated 100 years ago seem less weighted toward wealthy businesspeople.

---

[43] It is quite possible that the Europeans will not recognize the Americans and vice-versa. Further this list substantially underrepresents Asia which makes me suspicious of the methodology they use for "most admired people in the world." Some business leaders are also philanthropists. And there are hundreds of such lists. Perhaps take them with a grain of salt.

The case against working

"...You never told me being rich was so lonely
Nobody know me,
Oh well, hard to complain from this five-star hotel..."
MAC MILLER, RAPPER (1992-2018)

Joy, meaning, purpose, and community at work is an idealization or an aspiration. We conference speakers, business authors, and "gurus" gush about such matters endlessly. Consider the list of top-10 business speakers and how many of them have messages such as those at the core. Assess for yourself whether this is a megatrend by considering how many business books on passion, community, connection, meaning, and purpose are published today compared to a decade ago.

However, aspirations are only valuable insofar as we don't pretend they correspond in any way to how things are today – **then they become delusions**. Gurus discuss these noble aspirations as if already a secular workplace trend. Not a chance! The percentage of disengaged workers in the United States seems to hover around 65%, and over half say their work is meaningless. We are miles from our ideal, and if HR practitioners and business leaders are in any way serious about meaning, joy, and purpose, there is substantial work to do.

The work required to transform workplaces will be
fundamental and systemic and not just paying a guru
$50k to give workers a sugar high at a conference.

Figure IV – 2: Les Casseurs de Pierres (The Stonebreakers, Gustave Courbet, 1849) was in the style of social realism depicting the backbreaking hardships of manual labor.

The dark side of "the gospel"

Motivational noises are no substitute for real change in the way we think about work and workplaces. In fact, the gospel of work was criticized by thinkers from the get-go. Let us go back and consider the context in which the **gospel of work** was written – the 1800s. Recall to mind images from Victorian factories and coal mines and consider "Les Casseurs" above. What about that work was sacred? According to Bertrand Russell[44], "... the gospel of work was the morality of the Slave State, ... the kinds of murderous toil that developed under its rule—actual chattel slavery, fifteen-hour workdays in abominable conditions, child labor—has been disastrous." Carlyle's gospel was the uplifting motivational speech of the 19th century and Russell pointed out the 19th-century reality. How much have things changed?

Even in the mid-20th century, Studs Terkel's book *Working* recorded stories of over a hundred workers in as many different

[44] A legendary polymathic thinker, and according to Wikipedia, "a British philosopher, logician, mathematician, historian, writer, essayist, social critic, political activist, and Nobel laureate." (Not bad for one dude.)

occupations. The stories reveal hostile attitudes to work. He concludes, "to survive the day is triumph enough for the walking wounded among many of us" and describes "the ambiguity of attitudes towards the job as something more than Orwellian acceptance, something less than Luddite sabotage."[45]

The Terkelian story is a reality for many. David Graeber, a professor of anthropology at the London School of Economics, says companies pay people to carry out an endless array of tasks that make no meaningful contribution to society. Economist John Maynard Keynes predicted that technology might make workers more productive, leading to a 15-hour workweek. Instead, Graeber (author of *Bullshit Jobs*) argues that technology has been used to make people work **more** in pointless jobs they hate.

We saw that the protestant work ethic held **all** work as worthy—what you did was less important; work was man's way of serving and glorifying God. As part of this ethic, Scottish Calvinists and American Puritans even disdained leisure and fun. Work wasn't just a good thing; after worshipping God, it was the G.O.A.T![46]

The institution of business, more than any other carries the torch for hard work. Ask yourself why – who benefits? In the words of Bertrand Russell, "The idleness of landowners is only rendered possible by the industry of others. Indeed, their desire for comfortable idleness is historically the source of the whole gospel of work. The last thing they have ever wished is that others should follow their example."

Let's again take a step back and consider whose idea "the gospel" was, why they might have said it, and what were the consequences of that view. The protestant work ethic comes to us chiefly from 16th-century theologian and reformer John Calvin. Calvin's ideas included the notion of an "elect and holy" who were **predestined**

---

[45] Of course, there are other views of work today. The "postindustrial" view, the 4th industrial revolution, holds that technology will liberate workers from mundane and repetitive work and allow the pursuit of more creative and intellectual work.

[46] The Greatest of All Time, perhaps coined by hip hop trio De La Soul in 1993.

to obtain a greater share of material wealth. Whom did Calvin want to work harder? Not the clergy, royalty, or landowners!

Nope, his exhortations were toward poor suckers like the rest of us; bluntly, for you peasants, **hard work is good, but it won't do you much good,** because, you know, "elect and holy predestination" and all that. If you look deeply, you can see echoes of this cultural remnant today—people on the margins (say the bottom third) of society are expected to work hard, yet even in rich countries, **they cannot expect any comfort let alone luxury or joy**, nor is that likely to change in my generation or the next so structurally hardwired is this inequality and lack of social mobility. Nearly 1/3 of Americans (100 million people) and 20% of Britons fall into a category called "working poor" – who, even though employed, face a level of economic insecurity, periodic inability to pay rent and monthly bills, or at risk of being financially crippled by a medical or other emergency.[47] Is the idea of workplace spirituality a dubious luxury of the elite – who exhort the people that they employ for skimpy wages to derive greater meaning, connection, and joy from their work? Above all, in believing that work should be a spiritual pursuit, we should not fall into the trap of restricting the finding of work we love to the genteel classes.

We may also wonder about the notion of calling which, as we saw above, can be a powerful motivator in life – through connecting with one's deeper purpose. Although I'm passionate about the idea, and over my years as a coach helped many people to find and pursue theirs, I've worried whether "calling" was for the very few, the elite. Sociologist Ken Roberts[48] criticizes the notion of calling, suggesting that because social class differences and opportunity structures are the critical determinants of career choice, most people's choices are constrained.

While idealistic types, such as me, believe work should be a

---

[47] See "An Overview of America's Working Poor" from www.policylink.org

[48] Roberts, K., "The sociology of work entry and occupation choice", In Watts, Super, and Kidd (Eds.) *Career Development in Britain*, Hobson's Press Cambridge (1981)

spiritual pursuit, we should remain grounded and wonder whether workplaces and society are set up to nurture this. There are reasons for skepticism. The "gospel of work" may not just be a curse for workers at the bottom; even people who are "making it," at the tippy top of the economic ladder, may find themselves cursed because their lives have become too focused on work to the detriment of all else.

SPIRITUALITY AND DE-MOTIVATION

Most workplace spirituality writing tells us that there is a link between spirituality and the motivation to work. Is this true? No. As a generalization, it is false.

Let's first consider whether people who are religiously spiritual work harder? Scholar Stephen Blackwood's empirical research concluded, "there is little religious basis for the work ethic and a corresponding insignificant role for religion in effecting change in commitment to the work ethic over time." He goes further, saying, "religious type (Protestant, Catholic, Jewish) does not appear to affect motivation to work when socio-economic factors are controlled for." [49] In short, work motivation appears unrelated to religion. As for other types of spirituality, we simply do not know whether the mystically spiritual, Buddhists, New Agers, environmentalists, or Humanists are motivated to work harder or more engaged.

The opposite might even be true! Some spiritual and religious traditions value **balance** more than hard-driving achievement. Integrating your sense of spirituality with your work might have the opposite effect—a **negative one**—on your motivation to work (at least to excess.) A spiritual outlook will mandate a reflective and broader outlook on life's goals. Some of those goals will be directed toward friends, family, leisure, and health, all of which "spread out" your motivation.

Up until 2012 or so, I did a ton of C-level coaching and team development. During those decades, I grew close to hundreds of executives and still yet to encounter someone who thinks they ought to work more and a great many who think they ought to work less.

I belabor this point, that workplace spirituality may **decrease work centrism** and work motivation rather than increase it because almost everything I have read on workplace spirituality asserts the opposite. The idea that spiritually "awake" employees will be more motivated to work and produce results for the company is generally false—we can never say **all** spirituality will motivate **all** work[49].

We are going over to the dark side of work, but we will come to two Jedi ideas shortly – "**ideal work**" and "**spiritual fit**" that are motivational.

The dark side of work culture – workification, workaholism, and burnout

"One of the symptoms of an approaching nervous breakdown is the belief that one's work is terribly important."
BERTRAND RUSSELL

Returning to philosopher Andrew Taggart's thinking, life is becoming more "workified." Americans work an **average** of 54 hours per week, and many work much more. It is not uncommon to work two jobs or have a "side hustle" to make ends meet. Technology has not delivered a reduction in working hours since the 1970s, but an increase! This workification trend is not **just** longer hours. It is not **just** that people's identities are closely tied to their work.

---

[49] For the non-academic reader, motivation is one of the most studied topics in industrial and organizational psychology, spawning thousands of books and hundreds of thousands of articles. For the academic reader, my review of the "spirituality literature" concluded roughly that observed correlations were weak, spirituality measures were flawed, spirituality measures overlapped with criterion variables, and research methods were always observational.

(Ask yourself what the second or third question you might ask the person sitting next to you on an airplane might be!)

Taggart goes farther, saying that other aspects of our lives have become more work-like. We "work out" at the gym; we "work on" relationships; we do spiritual "work"; we "work on" issues with a therapist. If you are a contemporary parent, you are at least partly your child's scheduler, taxi driver, manager of activities and logistics, and co-ordinator of playdates, soccer, academic enhancements, and summer camps. Parenting is more work-like now than thirty years ago.

If Taggart is correct about this, there is a systemic problem – sewn into our culture, our incentives, our norms, and our employment and vacation policies.

Workification of life may lead to workaholism and burnout. Workaholism is particularly pernicious because **working hard is admired culturally**, as are the economic benefits (to the business and the individual) of doing so.

> *Workaholism is worse, in that respect, than alcoholism because being constantly drunk isn't admired, and the alcoholic can "just" stop drinking, but overwork is admired and nobody can just stop working.*

Overwork has systemic, reinforcing effects. My coaching practice had businesspeople earning more than $1 million a year who worked, in their view, too much. This cost them health, friendships, marriages, and family lives, and more. The more you work, the less you nurture these other areas and the more they suck – like a garden, the less you tend it, the less pleasant it is to spend time there, the more onerous that task of upkeep beccomes and so on. The less fit you are, the less enticing going to the gym sounds. The more you fight with your spouse, the less spending time at home sounds appealing. You then, naturally and humanly, avoid the areas that suck and work more – a vicious cycle that can lead to burnout.

Burnout, according to the medical journal The Lancet is "... a work-related syndrome involving emotional exhaustion, depersonalization, and a sense of reduced personal accomplishment." The Mayo Clinic identifies six causes: lack of control, unclear job expectations, dysfunctional work relationships, extremes of activity, lack of social support, and work-life imbalance. I know few people that don't have at least one of those all of the time.

Many of us, in the modern world, have teetered on the edge of workaholism and burnout at various stages in our lives.

SEPARATION OF CHURCH AND WORK

"He who has a why to live can endure almost any how."
FRIEDRICH NIETZSCHE

Psychologists of Religion cite a disconnect between the values people use in different spheres of their lives, called "the separation thesis." In caricature, people may be spiritual at home and in church, but in the workplace, not so much. Even among self-avowed "spiritual people," work tends to be seen as a **separate secular enterprise**. They compartmentalize their lives and justify "non-spiritual" attitudes and actions.[50]

If we, as leaders, want to help people bring their deepest selves, beliefs, and values to work, we need to create workplaces with the right environment, culture, job design, reward systems, recruitment and talent management, and leadership culture for people to express their passions and live their highest values.

However, individuals can never completely duck **personal responsibility** – it is we who have to end the separation of "soul

---

[50] Spilka, B., Hood, R., Gorsuch, R., *The Psychology of Religion: An Empirical Approach,* Prentice Hall: NJ (1985)

and work." If your workplace makes this hard or impossible, as many do, you either need to double-down on spiritual development, or "get out of Dodge[51]."

Integrating your spiritual path with work may be tough, and it cuts both ways. You need to choose your work (vocation) so it is aligned with your values, and you need to practice the principles you espouse at work, with your colleagues. To decompartmentalize, individuals must be willing and committed to treating their spiritual lives and work in an integrated fashion. This means not only viewing work as central to the fulfillment of their spiritual path, but also viewing their spiritual paths as the route to achievement and satisfaction at work. In practical and Buddhist **eight-fold path** terms, this means:

- Choosing the right path ("right livelihood," "right understanding.")
- Walking that path well ("mindfulness," "concentration," "right effort.")
- Treating others in a principled way ("right speech," "right intention.")
- Behaving in accordance with one's ethics ("right action".)

The implication of this worldview is clear—if you want spirituality at work, then **be spiritual at work**. In other words, find a spiritual path that is consonant with your worldview, and start putting its principles into practice in your work life. If you want meaning and purpose at work, seek it also in the mundane and prosaic aspects of working life. Your experience at work will be a complex interplay of what you do (the content), where you do it (the work environment or context), and the attitudes and values you bring. Insofar as your spiritual life brings you joy, connection, meaning, purpose, and connection, then your work life will begin to do so also.

---

[51] An Americanism: leave some place in a great hurry, originally Dodge City, Kansas during the gunslinger days.

Remember also that such integration may initially bring discomfort. It was said that religion **comforts the afflicted and afflicts the comfortable**. If your vocation is unaligned with your principles, upon reflection that might require courage and fortitude to change. If your employer's business purpose conflicts with your own, or their manner of doing business does not pass the moral tests of your tradition, you may again have to change. Or, you may have to change yourself, your outlook, and your attitude. Or you may need to remove some old habits and adopt some new ones. None of these changes is supposed to be easy, but they are supposed to be worth it.

It is also worth, nay essential, to make your own list of what ideal work would look like, and where you might consciously make sacrifices for the sake of practicalities, and which other ideals you've unconsciously abandoned.

IDEAL WORK – A BALANCE OF GETTING AND GIVING, INTRINSIC AND EXTRINSIC VALUE, SPIRITUAL AND SECULAR REWARDS

"The role of work in human dignity and the esteem accorded to traditional work has become fragile and uncertain."
HARVARD PHILOSOPHER, MICHAEL SANDEL

Even though ideal work may be a seldom realized goal, we should in this book, and you should, create a template of that ideal. Why do we work? What values and things of value get us out of bed?

Psychologists divide motivation into intrinsic and extrinsic—that is, doing something for its own sake or doing it for external goodies (such as pay). It is an axiom of motivational psychology that the more you focus on extrinsic motivation, the more you kill off intrinsic motivation. In business, the more you focus on "hard" rewards, the more you kill off the joy of doing the thing.

That isn't the whole picture: the **narrative** (the story we tell ourselves) about our work—whatever that work may be—can determine our experience of it. **It may not be that some work is more spiritual than other work, but rather that some narratives are more spiritual than other narratives**. For example, when my firm won its biggest contract to date, approximately ten times bigger than our previous biggest, it was a leadership development program for an investment bank. I wondered whether helping an investment bank earn another 0.1% Return on Assets was how I wanted to spend my life. Did the world need richer bankers? I had to change my narrative and focus on the fact that I was supporting people to become better leaders and helping them and their teams realize their potential to bring the maximum of my passion and skills to the job.

There are eleven dimensions of **ideal work** (we could call this the "Art of the Ideal") taken from a mix of spiritual traditions but chiefly the Buddhist concept of "right work."

- **Intrinsic worth:** Sometimes the work itself will have **intrinsic worth** – i.e., work that has value in its own right. (If you had Warren Buffett's moolah, you'd do it for free.) In contrast, there is busy work, meaningless tasks disconnected from big picture, and disconnected from your passions. If it weren't for the paycheck or the bennies, you'd be outta there pronto.

- **Spiritual growth:** The work contributes to your spiritual growth– that is (using this book's definition) your striving for meaning, purpose, goodness, and connectedness." Crappy work stifles or impedes your spiritual growth – and you be required to do all the spiritual "heavy lifting" to make meaningless work meaningful, or you feel disconnected from yourself.

- **Secular growth:** Helps you grow in self-actualizing ways as a person and as a professional. If you find it hard to imagine how you will have grown professionally or personally in ten years, then "bounce" (as the kids say.)

- **Balance of giving and getting:** Sometimes work will be about **what we get**, and sometimes it will be about **what we contribute to others.** "Right work" is a mix of giving to and getting from others – you contribute value to others you work with and they contribute to you. When giving and getting are out of balance, it is either give, give, give until the tank is empty, or always all about you (in which case you are probably miserable.)

- **Purpose and meaning:** There is a later chapter on purpose, but here the most important thing is that the corporate purpose and/ or the work you do is aligned with your purpose – that your role meets the tests of human flourishing at work that we explore in Chapter VII.

- **Provides valuable value:** "Right work" provides value to others (valuable value I would add – just selling people stuff, say junk food or cigarettes or drugs, isn't valuable value.) Not-so-right work does harm or is exploitative (like selling ARM mortgages, or worthless supplements.)

- **Ethical alignment:** As with purpose, we want our employer's ethics to live up to our own and their values to be aligned with ours.

- **Nurturing culture and climate:** You work in an environment which contributes to your flourishing, including culture and climate at work. Workplace climate is "how the weather feels at work" and includes **emotional safety**, camaraderie and *esprit de corps.* Workplace culture sets norms of behavior including those norms around hot button issues such as diversity and work-family.

- **Safe and secure:** Work is safe physically – or the danger at work is danger you signed up for – which may be the case in fire departments, the police, and the military. It isn't the case when a worker being exposed to asbestos or coal dust or toxic chemicals isn't. Work must also be secure – the risk of sudden or unjust termination is appropriately low.

- **Secular rewards:** It goes with saying that compensation, if not immediate then prospective, must be commensurate with your role. However, younger generations repeatedly say that they would give up some material rewards for other non-material benefits such as those described here.
- **Spiritual rewards:** Spiritual rewards can be seen as the opportunity to give or pay-it-forward. Some jobs, carers, teachers, health workers, and ministers are obviously about giving. In other jobs, it may depend on the narrative you create – if you are an artist, businessperson, or scientist, do you view your work through the lens of contribution to the world?

This list is far from the last word on what makes ideal work, but it may be worth taking your current job and running through the list as a checklist which you can find in Figure IV -3 below.

We would like these things to go together and there is evidence that socially responsible companies are great to work for in other respects – if they do some things well, they do all things well. However, on occasion, I've consulted to non-profits that have very noble external missions which have very toxic cultures – it isn't the case that virtuous purpose makes for a virtuous organization. Yoga teachers can be very purpose-driven, yoga for them is how they make money, but also their spiritual path, how they serve the world – yet there is more than one example of an industrial scale yoga business where the culture was rife with harassment and abuse. The same applies on occasion to churches, noble in purpose by design, but where fraud and sexual misconduct are rife.

And there is no law that says that a cigarette manufacturer must have a toxic internal culture. This is an important point. We cannot assume that if we get one aspect of ideal work right that the rest will fall into line. For example, if we create a nurturing culture, that we ethics follow, or if we get rewards right, that people will self-actualize.

Dimensions of Ideal Work

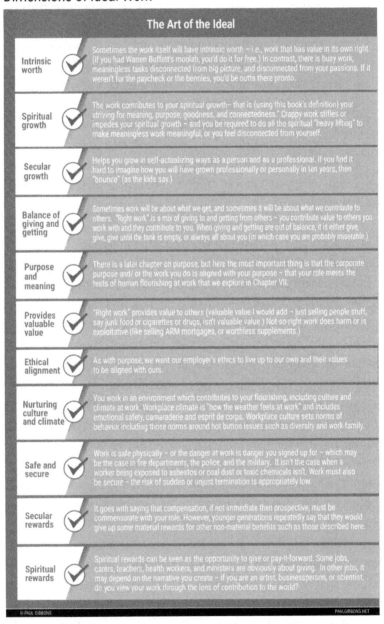

Figure IV-3: An ideal work checklist (The Art of the Ideal)

Some responsibility for creating ideal work comes from workplaces, what role might business play?

THE WORKPLACE AND HR AGENDA

"How can we ensure that Americans who do not inhabit the privileged ranks of the professional classes find dignified work that enables them to support a family, contribute to their community and win social esteem?"
PHILOSOPHY PROFESSOR, MICHAEL SANDEL

Embracing these ideas sets a challenging agenda for workplaces that want to approach the conditions for ideal work. (Partly the point of this book.) Are they suitably organized, with the right **culture and climate**, and with the right **people policies** and **development and learning curricula** so that these aims can be achieved? Who is responsible for culture and does it, as it must, appear on the CEO agenda?

The importance of culture, climate, meaning, and purpose, demands a shift in mindset toward designing work that is fit and meaningful for humans rather than paying them a lot to do work that has little meaning.

If we managed to do that, we might have fewer people suffering through the week and "working for the weekend"—perhaps more happiness and less misery in the working world if such aspects of work were more deeply considered.

HR departments have historically spent most of their effort on extrinsic, secular rewards such as pay and promotion and less on culture and climate. That is changing. HR departments have come to worry more about purpose, meaning, and self-actualization, but such efforts are hard to build into business processes and structures. For example, HR departments often offer workers a chance to do philanthropic work on the company's dime. Some of this time can be spent on development, building schools, upgrading neighborhoods, or giving back in other ways adding, if you will, a little spirituality to the secular benefits of working for their organization. HR departments often "own" culture and climate but in practice, they are much harder to manage than meat and potatoes HR. (There is a much longer analysis of service in our chapter on corporate social responsibility and philanthropy in Volume II.)

In addition to opportunities to give back, businesses may want to offer wellness programs and things such as yoga and meditation. (Both are **empirically** exceptionally good things for mental, physical, and spiritual health as explored in a later chapter.) However, yoga and meditation are seen by some Christians as religious practices and thus heretical. (It is somewhat ironic because spiritually oriented yogis deprecate Western-style yoga because of its distance from the spiritual roots of yoga – they see "gym yoga" as too secular!) Workplaces wish to offer Muslims a place to pray, but what if that conflicts with Christians, Yogis, and Buddhists? (What you **call the place** can even be controversial.)

If workplaces wish to nurture "soul" at work, business must put some boundaries around its expression.[52] Sometimes well-intentioned policies, such as meat-free Friday or WeWork's meat-free expenses policy can be seen as a heavy-handed imposition of values – that is, paternalism. There can also be problems with proselytization. Should we permit lunchtime prayer meetings, or a religious poster, or invitations to church services, or a Quran on a desk? What about teaching meditation during management development? What about sponsoring team environmental service projects (such as a forest cleanup) for people who may be ambivalent toward the environment?

---

[52] The August 1999 Harvard Business Review has a case study that presents this dilemma.

We also must ask ourselves, as business leaders, whether this is worth the trouble. As we see in Volume II, when we talk about conflict, the number of spirituality – and religion-related lawsuits has soared in recent decades. While we want to offer workers a path to finding personal meaning and purpose that is aligned with their career goals **and our corporate purpose**, is that too tall an order? Do we open a Pandora's box and force ourselves to adjudicate on issues we would rather not?

The answer to whether it might be worth it will depend on the arguments and evidence in the second section of this book, **Loving Your Work and Leading Others**. First, let's look at how people choose work and the notions of calling and spiritual fit.

Vocation and "spiritual fit"

CHAPTER 5

VOCATION AND SPIRITUAL FIT

"Most people's jobs are too small for their spirits."
STUDS TERKEL, FROM WORKING

People spend nearly half their waking lives at work, perhaps 100,000 hours in a lifetime. In the previous chapter, we argued that the time one spends working should be **joyfully and purposefully** spent, contributions should be a source of **meaning and fulfillment**, and social interactions should be a significant source of **community and connectedness**.

In this chapter, we start with questions about vocation and mindset: Which matters more: what you do, or how you do it? Can you bring a spiritual mindset, say of gratitude or service, to **any** job? How much responsibility for the worker's experience lies with the worker, and how much with the employer?

CHOOSING WORK – BALANCING SECULAR AND SPIRITUAL

"Discovering vocation does not mean scrambling toward some prize just beyond my reach but accepting the treasure of true self I already possess."
FATHER THOMAS MERTON

One workplace spirituality "killer-app" is vocation choice, sometimes called fulfilling your purpose in life, finding your calling, or "following your bliss." This subject has birthed hundreds of books. A few, such as *Connections between Spirit and Work in Career Development*, are academic in approach. Others are more inspirational and practical, such as *True Work, The Purpose Driven Life, The Leaders Way, The Work We Were Born To Do*, and *The Art of Work*.

The above books rightly say that the feeling of being called may be immensely powerful. For the called, it may provide motivation to make drastic life changes. Calling provides a narrative for work that can help you soar in the good times and transcend the bad times. It helps leaders lead with greater passion and charisma—indeed, many leadership development programs help leaders create a powerful **career narrative** about their highs and lows and the learning from those that has shaped who they are. In my programs, leaders used to explore this by creating a timeline of life and leadership experiences that had shaped their vision and values and that shape what is unique about them and what they stand for as a leader.

There is a question of whether calling comes from "out there," the Universe, a Higher Power, God, or whether (as existentialists would have it) there is no purpose "out there," but **we are liberated to choose for ourselves**. Different strokes.

For the existentialists or people without a deity, this freedom of choice, of accepting responsibility for those choices, and of doing the work of creating meaning can be hard. In the words of Jean-Paul Sartre, "Man is **condemned** to be free; because once thrown into the world, he is responsible for everything he does. It is up to you to give [life] a meaning."

When reflecting upon your calling, using one of the many guides available, you want first to focus on the spiritual, the meaning derived from work, and on intrinsic satisfaction rather than on skills, interests, job opportunities, financial rewards, and traditional views of success. Secular concerns press upon us all the time, so we give priority to the less urgent but more important. There are various tools career coaches use to help with this: narratives, dreams, symbols, poetry, visualization, and insights from the past.

Once you've used these "spiritual tools," you balance spiritual with secular concerns.

One simple tool, *the Ikigai* ("reason to live" in Japanese), helps readers think through the tension between the secular and spiritual worlds[53].

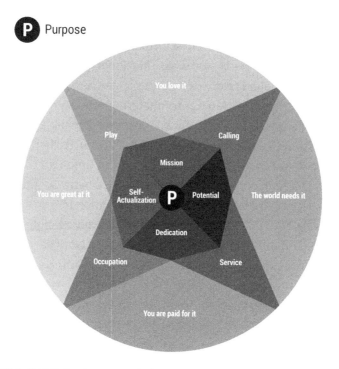

Diagram V-1: The Ikigai career purpose tool

To use this tool, spend about an hour thinking about each of the petals and the tensions between them. Ask yourself which petal is most or least fulfilling in your current role. (I have formalized this process with a questionnaire and in workshops, but the do-it-yourself approach works well if you dedicate the time to it.)

---

[53] You can find the *ikigai* and dozens of tools on purpose and calling in *Reboot Your Career,* a workbook that I co-authored with career coaching specialist Tim Ragan in 2016.

Where some books on calling are wrong

"If you're having work problems, I feel bad for you son. I got 99 problems but meaning ain't one."
99 PROBLEMS, JAY-Z, PARAPHRASE

Coaches and self-help gurus sometimes draw a distinction between societal and parental influences, the tangible pressures of living (paying rent), and what the "inner-self" or "real you" or "true self" is called to do.

This distinction is false and unhelpful because there is no "you" bereft of any historical or cultural influences – your likes and dislikes, talents and shortfalls, personality, and values were shaped from an early age by dozens of influences. You can't untangle the threads and find a "pure you" in there. Humans have many scripts running – you just get to choose which you pay attention to. You also get to choose to set some influences aside and give more weight to others.

We gain information about the world of work as we mature. Sometimes I advise young people that early jobs are as much about finding out what you dislike as what you like. Choosing a career is always a balancing act of dozens of factors including some fairly prosaic geographical ones such as where you prefer to live, where your spouse prefers to live, where the schools are good, where parents, friends, and relatives live, as well as all the different factors covered by the *Ikigai*.

Another faulty assumption of many spiritually oriented career counselors and coaches is that the practical matters of earning a living, developing skills, and finding a job will "unfold" once finding a calling unlocks the passion and commitment that lie within you. I don't think this is helpful or true. There is a certain kind of spirituality, usually New Age, that holds that once you find your calling and put your career intentions "out there," the Universe will provide a living. Well, as they say in the Middle East, "...trust Allah but tether your camel." Even though the Universe is on your team, put the hard work in. Circumstances, opportunity, luck, the economic environment, and your job-hunting skills will play a part in the realization of your calling. Adults need to balance **passion and practicalities** in the world of work – and (again) need to balance secular and spiritual concerns. (There is a 12-Step expression: "God does the steerin', I do the rowin.'" For Humanists, it might be, "the purpose I've created does the steerin', and I do the rowin.'")

Another faulty assumption of **some** spiritual approaches to calling is that finding your calling and doing it is necessarily a source of great joy. Maybe. Life stories of great saints suggest that not everyone who is "called" finds it easy. It sometimes demands great change and sacrifice. You might be called to earn a quarter of what you do now. Or are you ready to uproot your family? Are you ready to go back to school? Do you want to be called to sacrifice? Do organizations want their workers to be called? Typically, in the 21st century, we want the "goodies" from calling or vocation without the sacrifice.

Coaching people out the door

"They attain perfection when they find joy in their work."
THE BHAGAVAD GITA

Finally, coaches focus on worker self-actualization for (or so they should even if they are performance coaching), but many times when I've coached a mid-career executive on career matters (paid for by the company), they decide to go self-actualize somewhere else. When my firm ran a leadership development program for a few dozen senior investment bankers (partners in a big firm), we talked about choice, self-expression, joy, balance, work-family, and goal setting. Five of our initial group of 12 were gone within a year (retired, began independent consulting, or moved to another firm).

In the long run, empowering self-actualization that leads to someone quitting may benefit the business, creating an opening for someone whose passions may be more aligned. (After all, you should prefer employees who are passionate about being there.) The employee's departure increases the amount of big-picture happiness in the world—you've done a good thing. In the short run, though, it looks like financial folly—investing in executive coaching to watch your employees leave and then incurring the cost of losing and rehiring a worker.

The challenge for businesses is how to improve their recruiting and interviewing processes to better identify those who are truly called to work for them. How can organizations best hone and express their mission so prospective employees can discern whether they should be working there?

There is a bigger challenge we get to later which is how businesses can they make sure their insides live up to the glossy outsides of recruitment pitches.

THE SPIRITUAL FIT

"...you are someone who has a particular passion or a particular personal philosophy, and you're able to turn work into an instrument of realizing the deeper meaning in pursuing your personal philosophy or passion."

SATYA NADELLA, MICROSOFT CEO

Satya is talking about what I call the **"spiritual fit"** how well one's purpose and values fit with the specific mission of our employer. However, a courtship might produce a fit and result in two people deciding to marry but working on the fit does not stop there. Even if you find a job in the Ikigai sweet spot – that is:

- Work that the **world needs,**
- Work we are **passionate** about,
- Work that **tests us** and uses our skills,
- Work that **remunerates** us well,

126

... the "marriage" demands work on both sides. For firms, the fit isn't just about hiring workers who fit, it is about helping new workers onboard.

Back in the day, even at my blue-chip former employers, the boss "onboarded" new hires, thus: "there is your desk, the bathroom is down the hall, and the coffee machine a bit further." That is it. There was no effort to help new hires fit – to help them make sense of the values of their new firm, and how their skills might contribute to their passion and purpose. Our connection to purpose, if it happened, was left to chance.

In the 1990s, PwC offered new employees a whole day onboarding! That whole day was then seen as indulgent by some but would seem ridiculously short to today's HR professionals – and today PwC's process is six months long. Leading firms take onboarding very seriously: Google also devotes six months to it, kicking off with an intensive two-week immersion into "being Googly" (the culture) but also the structure and strategy of the business and the architecture of the platform.

Hiring and onboarding help with internal fit. One could recommend companies look more deeply into values and purpose at the recruitment stage, but as values questions become more personal, they may veer into off-limits territory or may be potentially discriminatory. Fits won't be perfect or permanent – some employees don't know what job they want until they see it – and at 25, you ain't seen much. Some jobs look juicy from the outside but don't feel right once you are in them. (And sometimes you don't know what you got 'til it's gone.)

Choosing the right profession and the right company to work for can be a long journey. You have to constantly reassess your priorities, values, fit with your employer, and whether the path you are on is one you value and admire. Steven Covey said cleverly, "there is no use racing up the ladder of success if it is leaning against the wrong wall."

However, I recommend **strongly against** daily or even monthly questioning of values and fit and purpose in life. I think that is a recipe for misery. Rumination, experts say, is among the unhealthiest psychological habits. The question "Is this the right job or profession for me" is one to be taken seriously, but only periodically – semi-annually, or annually. Once you commit, you stop asking the question for another six or twelve months – when it pops into your head, you set it aside.

Having said that, you should put your values, fit, and purpose to work in daily life – questioning yourself hard on whether you are living up to them. That is the spiritual challenge – not to get too comfortable with yourself, but also having a depth of self-compassion for your stumbles. Few of us can walk in and say "take this job and shove it" without consequences. Daily, you recommit to where you are and to the sorts of attitudes that make you happier and make you a nicer person to work with.

This, clearly, speaks to the necessity of making time for annual (or so) reflection upon your purpose and values – again not ruminating daily, but when the time that you set aside comes, engaging in purposeful life-design (or re-design.) Once, you commit to change, it will still take a long while to enact your new vision or profession. When I coached mid- or late-career people who desired or were approaching a major career transition, I used to advise that such transitions take a year to envision, plan, and execute. If you are retiring from a 40-year career, I suggest (unless your only goal is the hammock) that it takes five years to build up a portfolio of stimulating, enriching service and commercial opportunities.

A final source of misery is people who suffer at work, decide to change, and who fail to take action. They wake up each day with "I need to change jobs" for months or years without acting – getting a little unhappier and a weakening sense of their own power and agency. Usually, they need support in planning and being held accountable for taking the baby steps to realize the change.

This discussion has mostly been about fitting the job to yourself, that is finding work that aligns with your purpose and calling. However, there is another spiritual job alluded to above, fitting yourself to the job with the right mindset.

IT AIN'T WHAT YOU DO, IT'S THE WAY THAT YOU DO IT[54]

"For works do not sanctify us, but we should sanctify the works."

MEISTER ECKHART

While vocation choice concerns itself with "doing the work you love," the alternative is "loving the work you do." In other words, how do you "get your head right"? Which work attitudes and beliefs affect your experience of work? For example, if work is approached as a place of **service** or giving, rather than a place of being served or getting, would one enjoy it more? Was St. Francis right in saying, "It is better to understand than to be understood, to comfort than to be comforted, to love than to be loved, better to give than to receive"? Is the secret of happiness not doing what one likes, but liking what one does? At one spiritual retreat I spent time with a Benedictine Abbott and even though 25 years ago, I remember his questions: How is life treating you, Paul? More to the point though, **how are you treating life?**

---

[54] From poppy one-hit wonder group Bananarama and Fun Boy Three in the 1980s. Try to get that earworm out of your head now.

Meaning making

"Do not indulge in dreams of having what you have not, but reckon up the chief of the blessings you do possess, and then thankfully remember how you would crave for them if they were not yours."

MARCUS AURELIUS

Ancient spiritual texts and modern writers on humanism suggest that taking personal responsibility for meaning "**creates the work reality**." Viktor Frankl was able to find meaning in a concentration camp. In the yogic spiritual tradition, the concept of Karma Yoga suggests that working with love and enthusiasm can turn a chore into a spiritually enriching experience. The Buddhist spiritual path (*bodhisattva*) recommends going forth for the welfare and benefit of the world to prevent suffering. In Hinduism, the concept of right livelihood affects one's *karma,* one's inheritance in the next life. Christian monks maintained *"laborare est orare"* (to work is to pray). These views suggest that enjoyment of work is "an inside job"—if you can bring the right attitude and actions to work, you can transform your experience of it.

Recall the parable of the stonecutters. The third stonecutter's narrative was: "I'm creating a magnificent cathedral." We get to decide which cathedrals we are building by creating our own narratives. This illustrates, again, that meaning isn't "out there" but is created; it's created in this case by—**the why of our work.**

Sadly, the prevalent and contrary view in society is that what happens determines what we feel and do: "He made me furious" or, "Work is killing me." If one's mood is determined by context, then it will ebb and flow with the fortunes of life. If the actions of others determine one's response, then there is no freedom, only reaction. Many spiritual orientations make you more responsible for your feelings and actions:

- "Very little is needed to make a happy life; it is all within yourself, in your way of thinking." (Marcus Aurelius)
- "In the long run, we shape our lives, and we shape ourselves. The process never ends until we die. And the choices we make are ultimately our own responsibility." (Eleanor Roosevelt)
- "Look at the word 'responsibility' – "response-ability" – the ability to choose your response." (Steven Covey)
- "Man should not ask what the meaning of his life is, but rather must recognize that it is he who is asked." (Viktor Frankl)
- "Do not let the behavior of others destroy your inner peace." (HH the Dalai Lama)

Their essential message is that our perception of the world, and our reaction to it, are a matter of choice. And right attitudes and right actions manifest themselves not only in an **improved internal experience**, but also in **relationships with others**, including our **relationship to the world**. This deeper connection to self, others, and world was part of our definition of spirituality, the practical face of the spiritual journey.

What do "real people" say gives their working life meaning. In a survey from US consulting firm BetterUp[55] conducted in 2018, today's workers report that they find most meaning:

- "... where I'm trying to make other people's lives better..."
- "...when I'm working to help others grow and see their potential..."
- "...when I am able to push my abilities to the utmost is the most fulfilling..."
- "...when my work revolves around helping others especially the disadvantaged and needy..."

This leads to a paradoxical situation. On one hand, meaning happens between our ears—and ultimately, **only we can be responsible**

---

[55] www.betterup.com

for the meaning we create. On the other hand, the employer, culture, work environment, job, and leadership can make it hard or easy to find meaning in a given job. Does the idea of personal responsibility for meaning-making give employers a free pass? Is it all "on you?" Of course not.

Here we find one of the most incisive criticisms of the whole idea of spirituality and business – the idea that finding meaning and purpose at work can be found if the individual works hard enough at it.

We saw that meaning and purpose can be found in the humblest of jobs: humans can reshape their narratives to a great extent. But, leaving all the spiritual heavy lifting to workers isn't right—for them to enjoy a shitty job, they would have to become spiritual giants, master meaning-makers. There is also something deeply cynical about expecting someone who earns ten times less than you to get with the program and find the right attitude to make "loading 16 tons"[56] meaningful.

The attitude of gratitude

"Cultivate the habit of being grateful for every good thing that comes to you, and to give thanks continuously. And because all things have contributed to your advancement, you should include all things in your gratitude."
RALPH WALDO EMERSON

One attitude, though not by any means a uniquely spiritual one,

---

[56] "You load 16 tons, and whaddya get? Another day older and deeper in debt. St. Peter don't you call me, 'cos I can't go. I owe my soul to the company store." (Folk song from 1947.)

is gratitude.[57] Gratitude means being thankful, not just for specifics, as when a colleague does you a kindness, but generally, toward life, toward the people in it, and for circumstances (even those that seem harsh). As the saying goes, "Happiness isn't getting what you want; it is wanting what you got."

But like most valuable things in life, the attitude of gratitude takes practice and cultivation. That general "attitude of gratitude" creates an other- rather than self-orientation—an appreciation for what one has, rather than entitlement and grasping for what one lacks. As British author G.K. Chesterton said, "I would maintain that thanks are the highest form of thought and that gratitude is happiness doubled by wonder."

Another way that the gratitude mindset is expressed is a **"get to" rather than "have to" orientation**. "Have to" people see a world with little choice, one whether they comply (grudgingly) with demands put upon them. "Get to" people may be doing the same thing, but with a different narrative—I "get to" do what I'm doing. This simple shift in narrative can be transformative.

Nietzsche, of course, had an even deeper take on gratitude. He suggested that true gratitude was being willing to live your life, just as it has happened, over and over again in **eternal recurrence**. (One of his signature ideas.) Only then, said he, when you accept all that has been, and are willing to live as such over and over, will peace and gratitude be found. *"And then you will find every pain and every pleasure, every friend and every enemy, every hope and every error, every blade of grass and every ray of sunshine once more, and the whole fabric of things which make up your life."*[58]

One of the biggest obstacles to having attitudes at work (and

---

[57] Sometimes spiritual writers use the terms spirituality as if "all that good stuff" – humility, integrity, gratitude, passion, and conscience were uniquely spiritual. You can arrive at those attitudes through Humanistic psychology or many other ways. (No psychologist would take exception to the mentioned goodies.) We should not pretend that only spirituality, or only our own version of it is the only path to desirable human qualities – although our position is that the word "umbrellas" inner and outer work and includes those virtues and an ethical stance on life..

[58] From *The Gay Science*, published in 1882.

in life) that create a better experience is the intrusion of negative thoughts. Everybody "knows" they should be grateful, everybody "knows" that they are the author of their own experience – but that "knowledge" can be of little use when the sniveling shipwreck of a human being in the next cubicle tries to take credit for your work, or you have to work past 9PM for the third time this week.

Everybody has thoughts that are not in the interest of the thinker. Everybody has impulses to do the wrong thing. Most of us ruminate a downward spiral of worry, fantasy, and resentment at least sometimes. How do we overcome negative thoughts, sometimes called the "itty bitty shitty committee" in your head? Let's look at mindfulness.

The science of mindfulness and flow

CHAPTER 6

THE SCIENCE OF MINDFULNESS AND FLOW[59]

This is more evidence for the positive effects of mindfulness than there is for any other self-improvement technique you will find in the self-help section of your local bookstore.

MINDFULNESS IN BUSINESS

"In the end, just three things matter: How well we have lived. How well we have loved. How well we have learned to let go."

JACK KORNFIELD

Even those of us writing on spirituality and work in 2000 could not have predicted which ideas and practices would be taken up by 2020. In those days, outside our community of hippie scholars and workplace spirituality evangelicals, the ideas were seen as fruity by orthodox business and HR departments. One topic that broke through was mindfulness, partly because research during the intervening decades from neuroscience, cognitive psychology, and

---

[59] This chapter is a much-updated version of a tiny section of a chapter called The Science of Changing Hearts and Minds in my 2015 book, *The Science of Organizational Change*. (2nd edition, 2019).

medicine began to categorically show its benefits. The breakthrough was also due to the take-up by big-name, much-admired (in some respects) Silicon Valley companies such as Google.

What did researchers discover during the last few decades about a spiritual tradition that traces its history back to 1500 BCE?

DEFINING MINDFULNESS

"If you just sit and observe, you will see how restless your mind is. If you try to calm it, it only makes it worse, but over time it does calm, and when it does, there's room to hear more subtle things—that's when your intuition starts to blossom, and you start to see things more clearly..."
STEVE JOBS

As someone fascinated by peak human mental performance,[60] I have often wondered whether minds can be trained like muscles. Athletes who desire optimal muscular, physical performance work on endurance, stamina, strength, agility, and flexibility, as well as the specific skills of their discipline. This was not always the case. Tiger Woods, it is said, was the first golfer to practice yoga and weightlifting to develop those **foundational** physical faculties alongside his (ample) skills with the clubs. Even in the physical domain, building foundational physical abilities is a relatively new thing— there were few gyms in the 1960s either for athletes or for common folk.

Is it possible that in the 21st century, we will learn better how to train our **foundational mental skills** the way athletes develop their endurance, stamina, strength, agility, and flexibility? Foundational mental skills include attentional control, situational awareness,

---

[60] I'm a mindsports geek and compete internationally at chess, bridge, poker, backgammon, and strategy games.

cognitive flexibility, emotion regulation, processing speed, working memory, purposeful control of reasoning, and impulse inhibition.[61]

Are there push-ups for the mind that develop those mental "muscles?"

There are. Mindfulness practices improve not just thinking, but creativity, emotional life, and social skills. In 21st-century workforces, as data science and AI make work more technological, increasing our human capabilities and capacities has become even more important than before. Could mindfulness help with this? Do pushups for the mind increase all human capabilities? And, what do we mean by mindfulness practices?

HOW TO DO MINDFUL

"Meditation is essentially training our attention
so that we can be more aware—not only of
our own inner workings but also of what is
happening around us in the here and now."
SHARON SALZBERG

According to two researchers, mindfulness practices are "a family of self-regulation practices that aim to bring mental processes under voluntary control through focusing attention and awareness."[62] Mindfulness practices develop and habituate **metacognitive** processes that control mental life so that those metacognitive processes are readily available.[63]

Despite its roots in mystical traditions, we use the term

---

[61] Adapted from Jurado, M. B., & Rosselli, M. (2007). "The elusive nature of executive functions: A review of our current understanding." Neuropsychological Review, 17(3), pp. 213–233.

[62] Walsh, R. & Shapiro, S. (2006). "The meeting of meditative disciplines and western psychology: A mutually enriching dialogue." American Psychologist, 61(3), pp. 227–239.

[63] Our discussion will be purely of its benefits on thinking and the control of emotion, and not on metaphysical or ethical components.

"mindfulness" in completely secular ways. Moreover, to repeat myself, there is more **empirical evidence** for the effectiveness of mindfulness practice than there is for any other method of personal change found in the psychology section of your local bookstore or on commercial brain-training sites.[64]

The most common mindfulness practice in the West is meditation:[65] paying attention, intentionally and nonjudgmentally, in the present moment. The most common form of meditation is just to sit quietly and observe the breath, an automatic, subtle process that requires intense concentration to follow for any length of time. When attention wanders, as it more or less instantly and constantly does in the unpracticed, the objective is to notice the wandering and to return your attention to the breath. This deepens and widens our awareness so that we are more profoundly and broadly aware of our internal states and the workings of our mind.

The astonishing thing, in my experience, is what happens when you try to do this in any sustained way. First, it is incredibly difficult. My attempts to focus on the breath unleash a stream of thoughts like sitting trackside at the Monaco Grand Prix. Second, things come up. In my case, boredom, restlessness, irritation, rumination, and dreaming are all part of my default (hidden) cognitive makeup, and meditation brings them front and center in all their ugliness. (And, even mindfully writing that sentence reveals the self-critical inner voice that is injurious to my well-being! During meditation, and sometimes during writing, one **"sees oneself seeing"** and gets to observe harmful patterns in thought that are deeply ingrained.)

Although meditation is a practice **within** various religions including Christianity, Buddhism, and many forms of mysticism, **it can be a completely secular practice**. That is—it works fine, if detached from

---

[64] The evidence for "brain-training websites" is skimpy. (Don't waste money on those, meditate instead.) Although performance on the onsite exercises improves, few of those enhanced skills transfer to real-life situations. See Owen, A., et al. (2010). "Putting brain training to the test." Nature, 465(7299), pp. 755–778.

[65] In China, the practices are Tai-Chi, or Qigong; in India, it is Yoga, which when not taught as a "stretch class" ("acroyoga" or "health club yoga") has mindfulness benefits.

doctrine of any kind. Meditation attempts to release the practitioner from ceaseless chatter of beliefs. (You can hold onto your beliefs, but they stop holding onto you.) In the words of Peter Matthiessen:[66]

> *"The central feature of the practice of meditation and hard work known as Zen is that, as it has no patience with mysticism, far less the occult. Nor does it have any time with moralism, the prescriptions or distortions we would impose on the world, obscuring it from our view. It asks, it insists rather, that we take this moment for what it is, undistracted, and not cloud it with needless worries of what might have been or fantasies of what might come to be."*

The plethora of benefits to be gained from practicing meditation follows from seeing those thoughts more clearly and from practicing setting them aside. Over time, rare glimpses of what it is like to have a "mind like a still pond" become longer and more frequent. The promise of mindfulness practices is that the "still pond" state can be trained so that it becomes habitual.

ANECDOTAL BENEFITS OF MINDFULNESS PRACTICES

Before delving into the empirical evidence for mindfulness, let us review the anecdotal, descriptive evidence that gives a flavor on how that simple exercise produces such immense psychological benefit.

Mindfulness practices strengthen control of **attention and concentration** (deficits made worse by 21st-century technology and culture). In paying full attention to the present during meditation, and by returning to the object of concentration repeatedly, the

---

[66] From *The Snow Leopard*, Peter Matthiessen Penguin, 1978

practice of fully paying attention to just one thing develops as does a muscle during training. With time, the wanderings become shorter because the practitioner develops a **meta-attentional** faculty that quickly notes distraction.

Although the practice of meditation is 4,000 years old (and designed a little before TikTok, the 24-hour news cycle, and Twitter), it seems an elegant solution to our world full of distractions and competing demands. In the world of work (or school), being able to concentrate hard and at length on just one thing is an asset. In relationships, being able to fully attend to what someone is saying without a wandering mind is gold dust.

This thinking about thinking, the metacognitive faculty, "sits above" thinking and feeling processes and monitors and regulates them. This permits the practitioner to "step outside her thinking," to interrogate assumptions, and to gain perspective. Meditation teacher Jon Kabat-Zinn said, "When you pay attention to boredom, it gets unbelievably interesting." For example, are the thoughts ruminating about the past, incessantly planning the future, engaging in fantasy, or simmering about life's injustices? Those mental predilections offer clues to default mental processes. Or one might also observe a mental life preoccupied with abstract thought (like mine.). None of those is bad, but neither are they always contextually appropriate. **Ergo, mindfulness is about having more choice about what we do with our minds.**

This thinking about thinking, in turn, leads to more cognitive flexibility and more choice. This third-person perspective creates more choice in how people react to stimuli, which creates the possibility of different, perhaps more creative, choices. David Rock, the neuroscience author, calls this faculty "the director" and our mental lives "a stage." The director makes sure that the right actors are on stage (in working memory) and that they are performing their correct parts.

Some of what enters the stage are emotional responses and habitual impulses. Having a strong "director" makes the practitioner a more accurate observer of her emotional life and impulses, which enhances the ability to regulate emotions (sometimes called emotional intelligence) and inhibit impulses. Those contribute to balance, maturity, wisdom, acceptance, and equanimity by widening what Viktor Frankl called "the gap between stimulus and response."

Mindfulness practices, finally, develop a **special kind of self-awareness**. Many people have completed psychological profiling of some kind in their career, revealing baseline psychological "resting states." However, self-awareness must include in-the-moment awareness or what McKinsey authors Boaz and Fox call **"state awareness."**[67] This state awareness is much more important than "profile awareness" (such as Myers-Briggs) because it informs the leader of their disposition right now, in the moment. Psychometrics, by comparison, are Self-Awareness 101. (My other, business-oriented writing debunks many psychometrics which, astonishingly, are a billion-dollar industry even though most scholars pooh-pooh their validity.)

Mindfulness practices develop kindness and compassion. Beginning meditators often slap themselves back to attention angrily and self-critically. "There I freaking go again." They might notice that they are not very kind to themselves, and noticing this harsh inner voice is the beginning of self-compassion. Buddhists suggest that practicing this **self-compassion** is the ground of a much deeper compassion (which they call "loving-kindness"): **kinder to oneself means kinder to others.** This creates a suite of social and societal benefits such as empathy, connection, and perspective-taking.

Finally, mindfulness practice cultivates an ability to "be with" or accept what happens in the moment. Philosopher Ken Wilber describes how meditation aides the process of "interiorization" where "the organism achieves increased independence from its environment, ... and is no longer buffeted by immediate fluctuations."

---

[67] Boaz, N., & Fox, E. A. (2004, Mar.). Change leader, change thyself. McKinsey Quarterly. Retrieved from http://www.mckinsey.com/insights/leading_in_the_21st_century/change_leader_change_thyself.

Wilber argues that this leads to greater detachment and decreasing egocentrism. Insofar as spirituality involves an emphasis on **personal responsibility** for feelings and actions, meditation is claimed to be one practical method of achieving the **detachment** and responsibility called for by the spiritual worldview.

When you sit back and reminisce about your life, it is almost a given that the most enjoyable and memorable moments are the ones in which you were **completely present**. Being "present" is associated with peak performance and peak psychological states, as described by author Mihaly Csikszentmihalyi in his seminal book *Flow: The Psychology of Optimal Experience*. Acceptance of what "comes up" is, according to Eastern traditions, the root of happiness. In the words of mindfulness teacher Pema Chödrön,

> *"In meditation, we discover our inherent restlessness. Sometimes we get up and leave. Sometimes we sit there but our bodies wiggle and squirm and our minds go far away. This can be so uncomfortable that we feel it is impossible to stay. Yet this feeling can teach us not just about ourselves but what it is to be human...we really do not want to stay with the nakedness of our present experience. It goes against the grain to stay present. These are the times when only gentleness and a sense of humor can give us the strength to settle down... so whenever we wander off, we gently encourage ourselves to "stay" and settle down. Are we experiencing restlessness? Stay! Are fear and loathing out of control? Stay! Aching knees and throbbing back? Stay! What is for lunch? Stay! I cannot stand this another minute! Stay!"*[68]

One final feature of mindfulness practices is that they are **generative practices** as we visited in the section on spiritual growth. This

---

[68] Chödrön, P. (2007). *The places that scare you: A guide to fearlessness in difficult times*. Boston: Shamabala.

means that they, and the associated benefits, **support the mastery of other skills** in the same way that strength, stamina, endurance, agility, and flexibility make learning and mastering specific skills (throwing, catching, hitting, swinging a golf club) easier.

Enhanced mental awareness and control help make all other mental exertions easier. In business, for example, effectively countering cognitive biases requires a level of self-monitoring and cognitive flexibility; behavioral and habit change requires catching an old habit to replace it with a new one; influencing requires nonjudgment and empathy for facts to have a chance; negotiation and conflict resolution require the ability to "be centered."

The table below summarizes this astonishing catalog of benefits.

Anecdotal benefits of mindfulness practices

• Control of attention and concentration	• Increased (state) self-awareness
• Increased situational awareness	• Happiness
• Cognitive flexibility, choice	• Emotion and impulse regulation
• Metacognitive faculties	

© PAUL GIBBONS — PAULGIBBONS.NET

Diagram VI-1: Anecdotal benefits of mindfulness practices

I leave it to the reader to assess whether, if accurate, those would be an enhancement to their business/leadership life.

The healthy skeptic in all of us must wonder which are proven and which are overhyped. We turn now to see what science suggests about the truth of these descriptive/anecdotal benefits.

SCIENCE OF MINDFULNESS PRACTICES

Initial interest in mindfulness (and the practices which surround it such as meditation, yoga, and Tai-Chi) arose in alternative communities beginning at the start of the twentieth century and accelerated with 1960's counterculture. Saffron robes and long gray beards kept "serious" researchers away for decades.

The few early studies found positive results for **cardiovascular outcomes** (blood pressure and heart rate) and stress reduction. The beneficial effects of meditation on physiological stress (e.g., high blood pressure), anxiety, neurosis, phobias, and drug and alcohol abuse were documented in the 1980s. Research then accelerated, and researchers began to study **mental health** outcomes finding that mindfulness produces numerous mental health benefits. These include prevention of depression relapse, addiction relief, control of ADHD behaviors, alleviation of stress-related medical conditions, pain management, and help with anxiety disorders.[69] These clinical effects attest to the general power of mindfulness practices to shift conditions that can be resistant to drug treatments and psychotherapies.

By inference, if sitting quietly and observing the breath improves the well-being of the distressed, we should wonder whether it might develop peak mental performance in the completely untroubled (in whichever galaxy they are to be found. As Freud said, "Each of us is a little neurotic in our own way.") Very recent research suggests we can do more than just infer.

In the 1980s, research on non-clinical populations found meditation linked to **positive outcomes** such as confidence, self-control, empathy, and self-actualization. Only at the beginning of this century did hundreds of researchers worldwide start to **study high performance in the healthy** and application of mindfulness in a business setting.

---

[69] Hussain, D., & Bhushan, B. (2010). "Psychology of meditation and health: Present status and future directions." International Journal of Psychology and Psychological Therapy, 10(3), pp. 439–451.

Figure VI-2: Eastern mysticism meets Western neuroscience. Professor Richard Davidson from the University of Wisconsin uses MRI, PET, and EEG[70] to study meditators' brains.

In a recent review, Professor Jeffrey Greeson of Johns Hopkins University reviewed 52 of the most recent mindfulness research papers. His findings are summarized (along with selected others) in the following table:

Benefits of mindfulness practices with strong empirical support

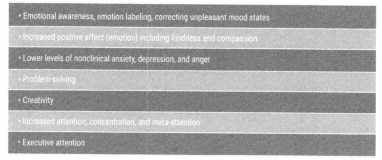

- Emotional awareness, emotion labeling, correcting unpleasant mood states
- Increased positive affect (emotion) including kindness and compassion
- Lower levels of nonclinical anxiety, depression, and anger
- Problem-solving
- Creativity
- Increased attention, concentration, and meta-attention
- Executive attention

Diagram VI - 3: Research-based benefits of mindfulness practices.

---

[70] Magnetic Resonance Imaging, Positron Emission Tomography, and Electroencephalogram respectively.

Diagram IV – 3: Research-based benefits of mindfulness practices.

Still, high-quality research is hard to come by. Comparing meditators and nonmeditators, for example, will not yield useful results because the effect of meditation cannot be isolated from other lifestyle choices. (Are the meditators all vegan, cyclist craftspeople with no stress?)

Good (controlled) studies need to teach people to meditate and contrast their results with randomly assigned control groups (who maybe practice yoga, relaxation, or nothing.) But in long-term studies, people drop out, and short-term studies have their work cut out for them to generate the benefits. As with all new research areas, categorical answers are a work in progress.

This summary of research findings correlates reasonably well with the anecdotal/descriptive benefits outlined above. We now turn in greater detail to how mindfulness practices work and, finally, how to use them in a corporate setting.

WHERE CAN I BUY ME SOME?

"When the mind becomes clean and tranquil, then there is no need to practice meditation; we will automatically be meditating always."
SWAMI SATCHIDANANDA

Were any family of pharmaceuticals able to produce such a wide spectrum of interesting clinical and cognitive benefits as mindfulness, a dozen drug companies would each invest billions in bringing the first product to market. If all this came in a pill, I would take it daily; wouldn't you?

Peculiarly, most people have some sense of what the mindful state feels like: present, in the moment, in the zone, or in the flow. Mindfulness practices are about achieving that state on demand or getting back to it when far away.

The chief obstacle, say many businesspeople, is time. The Dalai Lama, über meditator, meditates for two 90-minute sessions per day. As an example to potential meditators who would give it a try, he sets a scary standard. I know that if I set myself a lofty target of 30 minutes twice per day, I will likely fail (because I have). I do not deal well with failure (part of the reason I should meditate in the first place), but rather than deal with my perfectionism, the fear of failure, I allow my practice to lapse for many months at a time. Suggestions that I start again with one, two, or five minutes a day always seem wimpy even though research on habits suggest that is **exactly** how you should begin (or re-begin.) The message is: how you approach meditation reveals aspects of the self such as your attitudes to self-care, discipline, learning, and more. That, too, is part of the learner's journey – why do I find it easy to make time for Twitter, but not five minutes doing something I know is beneficial? It is **all an invitation to greater self-awareness** of our conditioning and habits, some of which gets in our way.

Research has good news for people who think as I do. It seems that you do not have to have been meditating for 30 years to get the benefits. Y.Y. Tang, Professor at Texas Tech University, investigated **new meditators in a corporate setting** and found that after just one week of daily 20-minute sessions, the new meditators scored higher on tests of attention and mood and had **lower levels of the stress hormone, cortisol**. This is truly fascinating, for here is a 4,000-year-old spiritual practice producing, it seems, biochemical changes in the body.

Even more good news is that short periods of meditation produce bursts of the mindfulness experience, and some practitioners even advertise the one-minute meditation and the one-second meditation. Can you switch from autopilot to being fully present just for a second? Some businesspeople use this mini practice just before starting a key meeting, wanting to bring their fullest awareness and attention to the proceedings. One senior VP reported that he had trained himself to do this every time he touched a doorknob.

There is a certain false economy in passing up the chance to establish a personal practice. Each of us has our daily distraction demons, and part of my irrationality is the ability to spend five minutes re-reading the news online ten times a day, rather than five minutes mindfully giving myself a break (with all the attendant long-term benefits). There is an important cognitive bias called **hyperbolic discounting**, which means future benefits are heavily discounted compared to present "demands" (assuming Instagram ranks as such.) The piece of cake or the salacious news story provides a dopamine rush, and the metacognitive faculties that integrate cortical control of impulses have to work hard to weigh weight-control or long-term productivity against the power of instant gratification. So, too, with mindfulness. Long-term abstract benefits, as described, are in conflict with today's habits.

Another obstacle newcomers stumble upon is the internal dialogue: "My mind is too frantic to meditate." That may be true, but if one believes the potential benefits, that is like saying "I am too unfit to go to the gym," or "too inflexible to stretch." Nobody hops off the couch and runs a 5k, nor do first-timers walk into a gym and bench-press 100 kilos. Setting ridiculously high initial standards and being unwilling to be a novice are the enemies of personal progress and change. (Again, how you approach mindfulness practices reveals a lot about the self.)

Looked at through the lens of economics, ten minutes per day would only have to make the rest of the other ten hours (550 minutes) two percent more pleasurable, productive, or less stressful to be worth the investment. Who can claim 98 percent productive efficiency over an entire day?

In building the habit, we can try to implement some of the new research on habit formation. "Minihabits" are a way to develop constructive habits with the emphasis on repetition rather than length. That means one minute done consecutively for seven days is much more valuable than one session of ten minutes on the weekend because for beginners, a habit's formation matters more than the duration of its failed attempts.

There is also a powerful concept called "action triggers," that is, linking a new behavior to an old one. These "when-then" action triggers look like, "When I take off my shoes, then I will meditate for five minutes." In a rather beautiful virtuous circle, the minihabit of meditation may bring the benefit of more conscious control of impulses, which can lead to greater power over more important habits. Could starting with one minute a day, and building gradually, unleash a sea of positive personal change?

DEVELOPING MINDFULNESS IN BUSINESS

When I was an executive coach, those executives with more presence, clarity of thought, focus, and productive relationships prospered. Many of them had a natural reflective, mindful outlook on life. Others less so, and we often worked to help them build a mindfulness practice.

Since 2005, all the (many dozens) of leadership programs I have designed have had a mindfulness component. We called it, secularly, "attention training" to slide it under the radar of skeptical senior leaders. One program that ran for several years was for 300 partners at KPMG. Following our ten- or twenty-minute practice, they would report a sense of calm, a quieter mind, clarity of thought, disappearance of stressful thoughts, and that they were more present. They were intellectually and experientially sold on the benefits. Terrific! Practice at home or the office, we implored them, for ten minutes a day for the duration of the program, and the habit of this state of mind will become more permanent! Our encouragements that they might take this up were met with a sincere interest and solemn commitment, yet few gave it a serious sustained try in their lives and even less so after the program had ended.

Likewise, in a nine-day leadership program for HSBC Bank, we introduced a mindfulness practice and used it daily during the program. Again, the enthusiasm and perceived value of the practice during the program were great, but there was very little take-up once people returned to their busy work lives.

Naturally, enjoying very close relationships with the program participants, we asked, "Why?" One reason stood head and shoulders above the rest. Habit. They knew it was good for them, and they had felt its benefits, but after 25 years of throwing on a suit, dashing for the 6:43, and keeping their foot on the gas until their evening collapse, the practice of stopping for even one, two, five, or 20 minutes was too hard to initiate and sustain.

Fast-forward from London 2005 to Silicon Valley 2020, and Google's Search Inside Yourself program has benefited from 21st-century research and gets better take-up of the mindfulness practices. Much can be learned from Google's experience. In our programs, mindfulness was presented as an adjunct to other leadership material; in Google's, mindfulness is the focus. The company brought in world-famous psychologists and teachers and linked the practice to neuroscience (much loved by the engineers).

The culture at Google, though a long-hours culture, encourages novelty and individuality. In our early 21st -century development programs, we missed the social and cultural dimensions of behavioral change that Google seems to have captured. With a program this popular at a much-admired, high-growth, 21st-century business and a well-selling book called Search Inside Yourself, perhaps mindfulness in business is an idea whose time has finally come. A few decades ago, people used to sneak off for five-minute smoke breaks a dozen times per day, and that was permitted by corporate cultures of the time. Perhaps it will soon become legitimate to take five-minute "sit breaks." Today there are mindfulness programs at other admired companies such as Apple, Facebook, Twitter, eBay, Intel, Nike, LinkedIn, McKinsey, IBM, Cisco, and General Mills.

I'm always fascinated by little changes that produce outsized results. As a consultant, I've often witnessed massive investments producing few results! Meditation is the former – a doctrine-free, incredibly simple, high-leverage activity that can be transformational in effect on the mind.

There are writers and thinkers who get prissy about corporate meditation, sometimes calling it McMindfulness. There are those who get snotty about corporate yoga without the accompanying *dharma* (which includes renouncing violence and becoming a vegetarian) – they call this "gym yoga" or "stretch class." I have no time for this critique. People must start where they are – not from where the above spiritual killjoys would like them to. One reason mindfulness meditation has existed for as long as it has and is growing in uptake today is because of its adaptability to different cultures and contexts. It is adapting to ours – and while I criticize our culture and context plenty, people living more mindful and choiceful lives, however, they get there seems unambiguously a good thing.

FROM MINDFULNESS TO FLOW AND SPIRITUAL EXPERIENCE AT WORK

"Art and religion are, then, two roads from which men escape from circumstance to ecstasy."

CLIVE BELL

Psychiatrist Gerald May[71] categorized types of spiritual experiences and described the "unitive" spiritual experience as "swept up by life, caught in a suspended moment where time seems to stand still and awareness peaks in both of its directions." Aesthetic experience, he continued, is "unself-consciousness ...an act of mind whereby a person comes to know in a richer or deeper way some aspect or essence of experienced life ...a play of impulses at the fringe of

---

[71] May, G., *Will and Spirit*, HarperCollins: San Francisco (1982)

awareness." We have seen that even though spiritual beliefs diverge, people share a common ground of spiritual experience. What we also see is that spiritual, aesthetic, artistic, scientific, and nature experiences converge with spiritual experience.

Psychologists, starting in the 1990s, began to call such experiences "flow." In a now-famous book, Mihaly Czikszentmihalyi[72] describes "flow" as "a unified flowing from one moment to the next, in which we feel in control of our actions, and in which there is little distinction between self and environment; between stimulus and response; between past, present and future."

It is likely you have felt something like this, either provoked by spirituality, work, art, science, or nature. High performers call this in being "in the zone." These similar mental events all seem to involve an experience of absorption, loss of rumination, self-transcendence, pleasurable sensation, and a distorted sense of time.

Flow states and the pre-disposition to have them have been related to changes in prefrontal cortex activity and with dopamine receptor availability.[73] Although there does not appear to be a God spot in the brain, it does appear as if those peak experiences are "real" in the neurobiological sense. (I'm sure people reading this who have such experiences are saying "duh" – but for the skeptics, this grounding in biology of these experiences and meditative states might be reassuring.)

Can these peak experiences be reproduced in the workplace? Surprisingly, Czikszentmihalyi found that many of these types of experiences occurred **more at work**. But these experiences, in the untrained mind, tend to be fleeting and **hard to produce at will**. The question, as with mindfulness, is "where can I buy me some flow?"

Without wishing to appear glib, as if such singular experiences could be switched on and off without much effort as we do with

---

[72] Mee-hai Cheek-sent-mee-hai. Cziszentmihalyi, M., *Flow: The psychology of happiness*, Rider: London (1992)

[73] "The Emerging Neuroscience of Intrinsic Motivation: A New Frontier in Self-Determination Research, " S I. Di Domenico,* & R M. Ryan Frontiers in Human Neuroscience. 2017; 11: 145.

our handheld devices, certain aspects of work and the environment make the experiences more likely. This sets a high bar for the **design of work and workplaces.** The six most important elements appear to be:

Distraction: May warns us, "as soon as the experience is noticed and grasped, the unitive experience of oneness dissolves and the self re-emerges." The modern world and workplaces are set up to maximize distraction and minimize flow. Everyone "knows" they should switch off notifications, but the dopamine hit from the latest salacious tweet or "please drop everything" email from the boss is hard to resist.

Good work: Positive psychologists have associated flow with motivation, reward, and kind of work. Meaningful work, it is no surprise, is central, as is a high degree of intrinsic motivation. As Czikszentmihalyi says, "...make the experience so enjoyable that people will continue to do it even at great cost, for the sheer sake of doing it."

Autonomy: Work you choose yourself, directed toward goals you set yourself, is related to the frequency of flow experience. Csikszentmihalyi calls such individuals **"autotelic"** from the Greek for "self" and "goals.")

Challenge/ skills: Csikszentmihalyi studied chess players and rock climbers and found that a combination of level of challenge and level of skills utilization was optimal. There was a Goldilocks zone, where you are **maximally challenged**, but not overly so, bringing the best you can manage to the task. You will see in the human flourishing mode in the next chapter that engagement (optimal challenge) is one of the five dimensions.

Deliberate practice: A recent advance in learning theory involves deliberative practice, practice that is purposeful and systematic and directed at a specific area. If you think about a virtuoso pianist, they know the piece so well that there is automaticity with the basics that allows the virtuosity of expression they produce.

Meditation: As we saw, the goal of meditation is to bring that mindfulness, focus, interiorization, and detachment to everyday activities: research suggests that mindfulness training can increase these "flow" or "in-the-zone" states.

Flow is fascinating because it links the psychology of work with spirituality, the design of workplaces, flourishing, and neuroscience. We have found a sweet spot of purposeful work, with intrinsic value, in well-designed workplaces, helping generate flow (spiritual-like) experiences.

Happiness and flow at work are important and vast topics. What we should take away is the similarity of "in the zone" experiences to spiritual experiences – that work under the right conditions might provide experiences similar to those described by sages. The big-gest lesson from mindfulness and flow at work is that turning up at church or the ashram won't cut it. You have to get in the game—that is, be effortful along your spiritual path and double-check your motivations to make sure that the spiritual journey is not to gratify, but to pacify your ego. To restate how we began:

There is more evidence for the effects of mindfulness on an incredibly long list of critical psychological variables than there is for almost anything else (including drugs, most therapy, most of what you read in the spirituality literature, and everything you might read in the self-help section of your bookstore.)

In the next chapter, we look at two further ideas where spiritu-ality may provide insights: happiness and human flourishing.

The science of happiness and flourishing

Covered in this chapter:

CHAPTER 7

THE SCIENCE OF HAPPINESS AND FLOURISHING

"The secret of happiness: Find something more important than you are and dedicate your life to it."

PROFESSOR DANIEL DENNETT, PHILOSOPHER

This chapter is the story of an evolution in thought. Throughout history, philosophers, psychologists, and spiritual leaders have framed happiness as the ultimate goal in life. It is the ultimate goal, said Aristotle, because the question "why do you want to be happy" does not demand an answer – desiring happiness is sufficient unto itself. Moreover, happiness is often supplied as a **sufficient answer** to other deep fundamental questions such as "why do you like Game of Thrones?" or "why do you like fishing?" "Because it makes me happy" is enough – nobody follows up with "yeah, but why do you want to be happy?"

The evolution in thought starts with the worry about whether happiness is oversold as the ultimate goal in life and then debunks myths about happiness that make people miserable. But what is more important than happiness? Depth psychology, from the mid-20th century, offered us some answers such as Maslow's hierarchy of needs. But we argue that depth psychology is not deep enough – that there are better ideas on what matters to human beings – those ideas are contained within the idea of **human flourishing**. Then though, after evolving beyond Maslow and human flourishing, we wonder whether even those go far enough – or whether there are human concerns even deeper and higher than those.

THE HAPPINESS DISEASE

In the future, I may release a book called "The Happiness Disease" because I think happiness is misunderstood, misrepresented, hyped, packaged, and sold in a way that makes people miserable. Just as we are invited to compare our physiques with the Aphrodite and Adonis wannabes on magazine covers (see Figure VII – 1), we are invited to compare our inner lives with the smiles of gurus beaming from the covers of their books. In other words, to compare their **outsides** with our **insides** – i.e., how we feel. If you feel sad, down, afraid, or lonely, as we all sometimes do, that comparison can make you feel worse, as if there were something wrong with you, that some secret ingredient is missing. Therein lies the first truth about happiness—**comparison is not your friend.**

Figure VII – 1: This is what health and happiness looks like? Get real.

Feeling low then becomes something to fix. Rather than love and accept sadness, we grasp at happiness and try to make our insides feel like Tony Robbins looks on the outside. So, we buy the latest self-help book, indulge in retail therapy, or escape by having an affair. But sadness, when embraced, can be a good thing reminding us of something we care about that is lost, and as such sadness is a **source of meaning** and transformation. Loneliness may remind us that we need warmth more than we care to admit. "Fixing" feelings to make them go away, with avoidance behaviors, makes the emptiness deeper. "Feeling all the feels," say psychologists, builds self-understanding and self-compassion, the roots of long-term change. As Confucius said 2,500 years ago, "we should feel all our sorrows, but not sink under their oppression." If you are unhappy, psychologists say, "you have to feel it to heal it."

Acknowledging that we feel less than happy can be taboo in some cultures. Workplaces frequently have a tacit insistence that you report happiness all the time. "Among men,[74] "how are you?" must be met with a list of acceptable responses: "Awesome, man" or "living the dream, baby!" "Pretty good" is as low as you can acceptably go. Some of this back-slappy, high-five conversation is normal and fun, but when it prevents authentic self-expression, it disconnects what you say from how you feel and isn't useful.

There are three additional truths about happiness that the Greek and Roman Stoics understood that we have forgotten. Stoic truth one—thinking about how happy you are, or how happy you are not, is the best way to be **unhappy**. Stoic truth two—happiness is the byproduct of the good life, not the goal of the good life. The good life (depending on which Stoic you had cornered) was virtue, valor, justice, courage, prudence, honesty, generosity, dignity, friendship, or developing one's mind. For Epicurus, *"the virtues are inseparable from a happy life, and living happily is inseparable from the virtues."*

---

[74] I assume women have their own norms, greetings, and responses about expressing feelings at work. I don't know to what extent their interactions mirror what men do.

The "virtues horse" needs to come before the "happiness cart." We simply no longer think that way today. Can you imagine a book on being virtuous topping the New York Times bestseller list?

Figure VII - 2: Does all the ink spilled on happiness make us unhappy?

Stoic truth three—the happiest people take pleasure in small, sensual things of the day-to-day: walking their dog, cooking a meal, hugging their spouse, watching their children running in the yard, the first sip of coffee, the cool breeze, the first day of spring, the smell of cut grass and clean laundry, the excitement of the spine cracking on a new book, the feel of late afternoon sun, and the sound Netflix makes before the show starts.

Consider the Stoic truths from a modern perspective – do they still seem apt, or has our culture overtaken them? What have we learned in recent years about happiness? Rather than being over-turned, these more ancient truths have been reinforced by evidence from biology and economics – on genes and money.

Happiness, genes, and money

"It's like the more money we come across the more problems we see."

"MO' MONEY, MO' PROBLEMS, NOTORIOUS B.I.G.

"Twin studies" have shown that twins raised separately, in vastly different environments (poor, rich, urban, suburban, rural) have highly correlated levels of happiness. That means that genetically, some of us are melancholier, some more bubbly; and some people swing between those, while some are even-keeled. It is my theory,[75] that the worst states of mind are "unhappy about being unhappy" or "depressed about being depressed" or "anxious about being anxious" – in other words, there will be times when we feel each of those things, and we need to accept that the emotional tapestry of our lives will sometimes have darker tones. When those darker hues appear, lack of self-acceptance can spiral into shame or self-hatred. Freud famously talked about "ordinary unhappiness" as a healthy state of mind – one we should embrace. This, again, is one of the ways meditation is said to work, by enabling us to observe **how we feel** dispassionately and without judgment, arresting the" down about feeling down" spiral.

The twin studies tell us that again that comparing how happy we are with how happy others look is a trap. We are wired differently and self-acceptance, in a sense of your neurochemical makeup, is an essential psychological faculty.

Although we've argued that happiness is too shallow a goal, there is the age-old question of whether "money buys happiness" – what does research say? Wallis Simpson, The Duchess of Windsor, wife of King Edward VIII who abdicated to become her third husband, once said, "You can never be too rich or too thin." Maybe she was

---

[75] I have discussed this with very prominent experts on mental illness and addiction, however it is NOT to be construed as medical advice, nor a suggestion to start or discontinue any form of support.

right; I would not know, being neither. But **grasping** at being richer or thinner can be a source of misery.

Some psychologists have gone so far as to suggest that wealth without meaning is a source of unhappiness. For example, Abraham Maslow said, "Affluence itself throws into the clearest coldest light the spiritual, ethical and philosophical hunger of mankind." This suggests that money is not only not sufficient for happiness and also that it is possible to be rich and still have a "hole in the soul." It might even be worse, and was in my case a long time ago on Wall Street – "why with all this money am I unhappy – what is wrong with me?"

As US president Franklin Roosevelt said, "Happiness is not in the mere possession of money; it lies in the joy of achievement, in the thrill of creative effort." Economists, too, have worried about the link between money and happiness. In the 1970's American economist Richard Easterlin showed that US GNP per capita had risen by a factor of three since 1960, while measures of average happiness have remained virtually unchanged over the half-century. We had three times the moolah and were no happier for it. In fact, there is some evidence that happiness begins to **decline** at the highest levels of wealth. This is known as the Easterlin Paradox shown in figure V – 3.

Not surprisingly, the poorest people report substantially increased life satisfaction as their meager incomes increase. However, beyond a modest level, a household's increased income counts only in a limited way toward life satisfaction. Other things, according to economist Richard Layard, matter more: "community trust, mental and physical health, and the quality of governance and rule of law. Raising incomes can raise happiness, especially in poor societies, but fostering cooperation and community can do even more, especially in rich societies..."[76]

---

[76] From the World Happiness Report, 2012, edited by John Helliwell, Richard Layard, and Jeffrey Sachs

Wealth and Well-being: The Easterlin paradox

Figure VII - 3: Mo' money, mo' problems. Beyond a certain level, wealth only makes you a little happier, and beyond that perhaps less happy.

If our predisposition to happiness is inherited and it is largely unrelated to wealth, is there a better way to understand life that isn't just "hedonic?"

BEYOND HAPPINESS – TO DEPTH PSYCHOLOGY

"And although it might be best [to] have both happiness and depth, [it seems] we would give up some happiness in order to gain the depth."

PROFESSOR ROBERT NOZICK

Twentieth-century Harvard philosopher Robert Nozick gave us a tantalizing thought experiment that allows us to think through meaning in life. Imagine that scientists develop a pleasure machine that would stimulate your brain with pleasurable experiences indistinguishable from the real world. Would you prefer that to real life?

Before I advance some of Nozick's suggestions, consider Cypher, the baddie from The Matrix. Cypher betrays his real-world friends so he can go back into the Matrix, to live in a perfect, yet simulated world. "You know, I know this steak doesn't exist. I know that when I put it in my mouth, the Matrix is telling my brain that it is juicy and delicious. After nine years, you know what I realize? Ignorance is bliss." Would you follow Cypher back into the Matrix? People invariably say no to the pleasure machine and tell Cypher to take a hike, but the interesting question is "why?"

Figure VII-4: Does it matter that the steak isn't real?

Nozick thinks that part of what gives life meaning is **agency**— we like to achieve things and not just feel them. We want to think of ourselves as purposeful human beings and create identities for ourselves. We also do not want our experiences limited to those which a machine may create – we appreciate the diversity of life's experiences. In the Matrix, Agent Smith tells Morpheus that when the Matrix created a too-perfect world, humans rejected it – we, it seems, want **depth**, and perhaps even the suffering that gives pleasure meaning.

Maslow and depth psychology

"Pleasure in itself cannot give our existence meaning; thus the lack of pleasure cannot take away meaning from life, which now seems obvious to us."

VIKTOR FRANKL

Maslow, the mid-20th-century pioneer of depth psychology, believed that depth in life mattered as much as survival and happiness and proposed his framework of human needs in 1943 (see the following, familiar diagram). Maslow begins with fulfillment of basic needs, through needs for community and self-regard, and finally our need to self-actualize (realize our potential).

Diagram VII-5: The OG motivation model. What lies beyond self-actualization and Maslow's hierarchy?

Do Maslow's ideas exhaust the human hunger for depth and meaning? Happiness can be transitory, is there something more stable and substantial? It is a testament to Maslow that 80 years hence, we still refer to his thinking, but Maslow's hierarchy and needs theories from the last century needed an update. Research had failed to find evidence to support the idea of a hierarchy and our intuition should guide us toward the idea that even people living in extreme privation may find esteem, belongingness, love, and self-actualization. Indeed, later in life, Maslow updated his ideas to include transcendence and spirituality, but this diagram looms largest as his legacy.

We had to wait until the 1990s to get a better model—and the one we got includes ideas from spirituality, ancient Greek philosophy, and 21st-century philosophy.

BEYOND DEPTH PSYCHOLOGY TO HUMAN FLOURISHING

"I now think that the gold standard for measuring well-being is flourishing and that the goal of positive psychology is to increase flourishing."
PROFESSOR MARTIN SELIGMAN, A FOUNDER OF POSITIVE PSYCHOLOGY

Consider whom we admire and why. Is a soldier doing her duty happy? Does caring for a sick friend or child make you happy? Does summiting Everest make you happy? Does working 18 hours a day on a mission-driven startup make you happy? Are artists and scientists happy, or do they seek deeper fulfillment? Our intuitions should guide us toward "maybe – but being happy isn't what motivates those actions." We admire the **duty and service** of the solider, the **selfless love** of the carer, the energy and **pursuit of excellence** of the startup, and the **search for knowledge and beauty** of scientists and artists.

This should guide us toward the notion that there is more to the good life than happiness. The "answer" (not 42 as in the movie) may be human flourishing.

Human flourishing is an ancient Greek concept (*eudæmonia*) further developed by 21st-century **positive psychologists**. I find it fascinating because it is a scientifically tested idea wherein psychology, philosophy, and spirituality appear to converge.[77] The model, of human flourishing at work, is slightly modified from the Greek version, informed by positive psychology research, but specific to work. It includes the dimensions of:

- **Spiritual fulfillment**: leading a meaningful life.
- **Engagement**: being fully absorbed by work, in the zone, and experiencing flow.
- **Relationships**: having a healthy community and nurturing relationships at work.
- **Excellence**: building new skills; setting and achieving goals that are valuable and meaningful to you.
- **Affect**: feeling happy and optimistic about work.

You can see that happiness makes it onto the list, but this model answers our questions about carers, scientists, entrepreneurs, and mountain climbers – what motivates them and what we admire about them.

The following "pop quiz" will help you think more broadly about your flourishing at work thus saving you a trip to BuzzFeed. There is no benchmark except for your own standards – only you know what a 5/5 looks like for you.

---

[77] There are other scales of human flourishing, some with ten dimensions, others with eight. "Tested" in this context means that certain tests of validity are met – the so-called "convergent validity." That is often **not** the case with popular organizational psychology instruments such as MBTI and DiSC, despite the fact that those are part of a hundred-million-dollar industry.

Human Flourishing at Work

Score (1-5)

I feel, that through my work, I am contributing to something worthwhile	
I lead a purposeful and meaningful life	
My career is aligned with my values and mission	
Spiritual fulfillment	
I am fully engaged and interested in my daily activities	
I am constantly learning and continually challenged	
I sometimes lose track of time doing work I enjoy	
Engagement	
My work relationships are supportive, rich, and rewarding	
I actively contribute to the happiness and well-being of others	
I feel respected and valued at work	
Relationships	
I continually achieve success	
I accomplish important goals I set for myself	
I am competent and capable in the activities that matter to me	
Excellence	
I am optimistic about my future	
I look forward to Mondays (more generally, to working)	
I am happy at work most of the time	
Positive affect	
TOTAL	

Figure VII-6: Are you flourishing at work?

Having completed the quiz, you might have identified gaps. Perhaps it shed light upon some blind spots you may have been ignoring. If you find a gap, ask yourself what is missing and what might close it.

Human flourishing also sets an agenda for workplaces. If positive psychologists and the Greeks are right that this is a robust model of human meaning and motivation, are businesses set up to support human flourishing at work (as part of their quest to humanize?) Not yet – even if this Humanizing Business series is a step in that direction, it is a baby step.

But both Maslow and flourishing are, on a closer look, "all about me." So while they invite us to be the best we can be and to self-actualize, they are somewhat silent on what might be best for those around us and the world at large. That is, flourishing has nothing to steer us toward the virtuous life.

Just as 1950s ideas were updated by human flourishing, in this century thinkers began to wonder whether the self should be at the apex or whether there are higher satisfactions that we might aspire to at work than just personal ones.

BEYOND FLOURISHING TO PURPOSE

"When it's over, I want to say all my life
I was a bride married to amazement.
I was the bridegroom, taking the world into my arms."
MARY OLIVER, A CONTEMPORARY POET

The ancient Greeks pointed to a paradox millennia ago, the more you strive for happiness, it will elude you. Point your strivings elsewhere. Viktor Frankl, half a century ago, said likewise: "The more one forgets himself — **by giving himself to a cause to serve or another person to love** — the more human he is and the more he actualizes himself. What is called self-actualization is not an attainable aim at all, for the simple reason that the more one would strive for it, the more he would miss it. In other words, **self-actualization is possible only as a side-effect of self-transcendence."**

One possible solution to that paradox is found in the field of

171

transpersonal psychology – a field that adds transcendent experiences to human experiences, and that tries to combine spirituality and psychology for a more holistic understanding of humankind. However, transpersonal psychology requires that there are some experiences humans have that are not human experiences, a big metaphysical pill to swallow, even if spiritual experiences are quantitatively different from the day-to-day.

A more humanistic idea is that there is no other place we can get to, nor should want to get to other than right here. The world is magnificent enough; the world and the humans on it are more worthy of our attentions than are other realms. Our suggestion in the next chapter is that human purpose supplies the transcendent dimension we need while keeping our feet on the ground.

EPILOGUE: UNDERSTANDING RESEARCH ON SPIRITUALITY AND WELL-BEING

"Happiness and freedom being with a clear understanding of one principle. Some things are within your control, and some things are not."

EPICTETUS

In the chapter we argued that happiness was too shallow a goal. However, a great deal of research is nevertheless focused on whether spirituality affects happiness. This epilogue summarizes some of the findings. But first, How does it affect mental health?

Spirituality and mental health

Mental health is a significant issue for business. *Forbes* claims that 300 million people suffer from depression globally and that depression and anxiety cost global business $1 trillion annually, not to mention the harder-to-measure and more important human costs.

Spirituality helps people make sense of difficulties, puts troubles into perspective, creates resilience, encourages self-reflection, leads to greater connection with others, and creates a sense of belonging, say prominent psychoanalysts such as Erich Fromm, Gerald May, and M. Scott Peck. These psychotherapists insist that to treat an individual with a **psychological condition**, we need to attend to not only **cognitive and emotional** aspects of the psyche but also **spiritual beliefs**. In other words, beliefs about the nature of the universe (hostile or safe), the existence of an afterlife, and the nature of sin and forgiveness and so forth affect internal psychological states and mental health. Finally, current health sciences literature (e.g., medicine, counseling psychology, nursing, and psychotherapy) contains a wealth of research relating spirituality to both positive psychological and physical health outcomes.

We should be careful though. Before accepting sweeping assertions, we should look at the evidence. That evidence is largely positive. A study by the Fetzer Institute links religiosity to "lower levels of depression and psychological distress and reduced morbidity and mortality[78]." Others have found a **"u-shaped" relationship**: psychologists Masters & Bergin report that "stronger spiritual beliefs were related to lower levels of psychological distress ... but people with no spiritual beliefs [also] had low levels of distress."[79] We see this u-shaped pattern throughout psychology of religion research, in mental health, and also in ethics and well-being. (Could spirituality be as Mr. Miyagi[80] suggested, something you do wholeheartedly or not at all? "Walk left side road, safe. Walk right side, safe. Walk middle? Sooner or later...get squish like grape.")

Mental health is critical, but we can set the bar higher. Perhaps spirituality, on balance, eases discomfort – but does it make you feel better about life? Does spirituality improve **wellness**, health, and happiness in those without mental health concerns?

Spirituality and well-being

To read some authors, you might think spirituality is inevitably related to happiness. This is simply not always the case. Whether one

[78] Fetzer Institute, "Multidimensional Measurement of Religiousness/ Spirituality for Use in Health Research", Jan. 1999

[79] Masters, K. & Bergin, A., in Schumaker (ed.) *Religion and Mental Health*, Oxford University Press: Oxford (1992)

[80] The wise Asian sensei in The Karate Kid (1984)

looks at the mystical tradition, the religious tradition, or the secular tradition, spiritual beliefs can be discomforting. Deep reflection on one's life may not always be pleasant, and that is why many people avoid it. Mystical experiences can be associated with bliss, but also with painful feelings linked to the dissociation of the ego.[81] Rose tinted views ignore the fact that having a moral compass **makes life decisions much more painful sometimes**. Vulgarly, it is easier not to give a fig about ethics or meaning: business is business, dog eat dog, greed is good, the devil takes the hindmost.

Instead of measuring happiness, researchers prefer the broader Subjective Well-Being (SWB) that can be defined as "a person's cognitive and affective evaluations of his or her life including physical health, happiness, mental health, life satisfaction, and a sense of meaning and purpose.

Several studies have found a link between spirituality and SWB using definitions like ours. One such study defined spirituality as Purpose, Innerness, Interconnection, and Transcendence, and found a link to both the cognitive and emotional aspects of SWB.[82][83]

Despite most research on religion and spirituality pointing toward feeling good about life, there are many more things we do not know. For example, we do not know how mysticism may be related to well-being and life satisfaction. Neither do we understand the effect of secular spirituality on well-being. We know that **being in nature** is related to human well-being, reducing rumination, "a maladaptive pattern of self-referential thought that is associated with heightened risk for depression and other mental illnesses".[84]

[81] May, G., *Will and Spirit*, HarperCollins: San Francisco (1982)

[82] Daniela Villani, Angela Sorgente, Paola Iannello and Alessandro Antonietti "The Role of Spirituality and Religiosity in Subjective Well-Being of Individuals With Different Religious Status" Frontiers Psychology 09 July 2019

[83] While encouraging, research such as this point toward an unsolved problem in spirituality research – measures of SWB often have a spiritual component and measures of spirituality often have a happiness component. Sometimes correlations result from asking the same question a different way.

[84] Gregory N. Bratman, J. Paul Hamilton, Kevin S. Hahn, Gretchen C. Daily, and James J. Gross, PNAS July 14, 2015 112 (28) 8567-8572; first published June 29, 2015

However, the neuroscience of nature experience tells us nothing about whether a nature-centered spirituality or environmentalism improves well-being? Neither do we know much about Humanism and well-being. We know that Humanists have a deep commitment to human flourishing, but do they themselves have higher levels of well-being? Both Humanists and environmentalists have concerns that place other people, or the environment, first in their concerns. Are they better off, in terms of well-being, because of these commitments? We don't know. As newer kinds of spirituality emerge, we are left with more questions than answers as to which might, when compared with the traditionally religious, create higher or lower levels of subjective well-being.

Why you believe matters more than what you believe

> *"After all it is those who have a deep and*
> *real inner life who are best able to deal with*
> *the irritating details of outer life."*
>
> EVELYN UNDERHILL

Beliefs are not the only thing that matter. If we think about the **purpose of workplace spirituality research**, it is not to help people pick and choose between different beliefs. That is not useful: no believer is going to read research that says non-believers are happier and decide to jump ship (or vice versa.) Baptists won't start visiting shamans, and Humanists are unlikely to start going to Mass. That isn't the way beliefs work.

The astonishing **common thread** that people of all traditions may share, is not in the **content** of beliefs, whether you believe in Allah or Source or God, but rather **how earnestly** your beliefs and practices are pursued and **why you participate** in your spiritua

Spiritual 'mode," borrowing a term from the psychology of religion, is the **reason** you are spiritual. It can be intrinsic or extrinsic either you practice it for its own sake (intrinsic) or use your tradition as a means of avoiding guilt or obtaining status, security, self-justification, and sociability (extrinsic.) From a psychological point of view, the extrinsically spiritual fare poorly. According to Keith Pargament, those who attend church frequently, but are less intrinsically religious, show the **worst psychological profiles** on such dimensions as coping skills, self-attitudes, and world attitudes. He concludes, "A little religion seems just enough to bug people but not enough to bless them."[85] **This again reveals a u-shaped curve,** with the most and the least religious the happiest. If your spiritual quest is for the wrong reasons—material gain, security, or appearances—it may be detrimental to your well-being.

How earnestly you practice your tradition, the **salience**, matters also. Simply put, the harder you work at it, the better off you are psychologically. Just setting spiritual goals (whatever tradition you may follow) is beneficial. One researcher, psychologist Robert Emmons found that "**spiritual strivings** accounted for significant variance in well-being outcomes above and beyond the religious variables of attendance, the importance of religion, and prayer frequency."

This accords with our ideas on spiritual growth, that whichever tradition you practice, you should grow within it. That is, more important than what you believe, more important than how often you attend or practice, is that you try to develop spiritually. It is better to view spirituality as a development process. We will see later that many of the best leadership models are developmental and that self-awareness and personal growth are central to developing yourself as a leader.

Now we find a common thread between spirituality and religion in workplaces—**help people practice whatever they do more**

[85] Pargament, K., "The Psychology of Religion and Spirituality? Yes and No." The International Journal for the Psychology of Religion, 9 (1), pp. 3 - 16 (1999).

earnestly and more easily, and in an integrated fashion, and you quite possibly will enhance their well-being.

We can aspire to more for ourselves and our workplaces. There are desirable outcomes beyond well-being, just feeling good about life that spirituality may support.

CHAPTER

The philosophy of purpose

Covered in this chapter:

CHAPTER 8

THE PHILOSOPHY OF PURPOSE

"The secret of happiness: Find something more important than you are and dedicate your life to it."

PROFESSOR DANIEL DENNETT, PHILOSOPHER

DOES HUMANITY HAVE A PURPOSE?

Everything has a purpose, even a screwdriver. What do we mean when we talk about human purpose? What makes human purpose unique?

Perhaps little motivates and inspires humans more than the idea that we are living the greater purpose for which we were intended. Mark Twain once offered, "the two most important days of your life are the day you were born and the day you find out why." Does it matter if the "why" – why we were put here – comes from the Universe, or if it is more powerful to create or choose the narrative of why we are here and what we are supposed to do? French theologian and physician Albert Schweitzer recommended, "Life isn't about finding yourself; life is about creating yourself." However, either of those options may be a powerful guide.

Two tools from earlier in this book will set purpose searchers off on the right path: the *Ikigai* career purpose tool (Chapter V) and the human flourishing at work model (Chapter VII) blessed by the positive psychology movement. The latter is the most tested of theories you may find on purpose and meaning. This chapter provides a view of purpose from a philosophical as opposed to a psychological perspective.

Unlike a screwdriver, humans get to choose and create purpose for themselves – a freedom that a screwdriver does not possess. While Kant thought that freedom to choose was our greatest source of our humanity (our meaning and purpose), Nietzsche compared that freedom to a small boat on the open seas – both exhilarating and terrifying. Terrifying because we have all (I think) felt the emptiness and lack of fulfillment that comes from a life that feels purposeless. Exhilarating because once you do find or create your own purpose, and because the world of work and occupation choices is vast and varied, it can feel like your soul is on fire (as the Jesuits say.) The right dedication to search will find a you-sized ecological niche in which you flourish.

I recall one particularly acute feeling of purposelessness when my life was full of amazing accomplishments like splotches of bright paint on a canvas, but when I stepped back to look at the canvas, I didn't feel that the individual splotches collectively created a beautiful painting. That realization reminded me of a song you might remember: "And you may find yourself in a beautiful house / With a beautiful wife / And you may ask yourself, well / How did I get here?"[86] Thankfully, through a process of deep reflection and creation, I eventually did create a purpose for what my whole life was to be about, and that gave greater meaning to the bright splotch I was so busily painting. For me, eventually, the exhilaration replaced angst when I consciously created my own purpose – the narrative behind the splotches.

Human purpose should be grounded in what is unique about humans – our **superpowers**. What do I mean by "human superpowers"? We have seen some of them earlier: we are **adaptable** and

---

[86] Once in a Lifetime, The Talking Heads (1980)

able to prosper in deserts, jungles, and cities. We are **creative** and relentlessly create new tools for the betterment of humankind. We are **rational**, able to transcend animal instincts, and to envision and plan. We are also **social and collaborative** – human groups and teams are much greater than the sum of their parts.

This chapter talks about other human superpowers we haven't yet visited, grounded in philosophy, developmental psychology, and evolutionary biology: our pursuit of excellence, transcendental values, and philosophical ideas about the good life.

THE PURPOSE OF PURPOSE – THE "WHY"

"This is the true joy in life, being used for a purpose recognized by yourself as a mighty one. Being a force of nature instead of a feverish, selfish little clod of ailments and grievances, complaining that the world will not devote itself to making you happy."
GEORGE BERNARD SHAW, IRISH PLAYWRIGHT AND SOCIAL CRITIC

Why does purpose matter so much? what is the purpose of purpose? What makes work purposeful? Is purpose such a subjective, cultural, and personal concept that any generalizations are apt to be suspect? We can say a few general things.

We certainly do not want to restrict purposeful work to mission-driven startups, social enterprises, and *Médecins Sans Frontières*. Nor do we want to restrict it to innovation and creativity – although that spark seems to power purposeful work for many. Nor finally, do we want to restrict purposeful work to business and leadership (although that is what many of the popular books underscore), nor just to the professions.

Purpose has, in my model, four important jobs:

1. It offers **direction**, and if we use spiritual principles when choosing purpose, it offers **sound**, **valuable guidance**.

2. It offers **"height"** – we can create more **fulfilling lives** by using our creativity and vision.
3. It offers **depth**, inspiring us towards **self-transcendence** – operating beyond the self. That self-transcendence helps us find **nobler meaning** for our existence.
4. It offers a **timeless perspective** on our lives, how our lives will remain a contribution.

Your purpose should be grounded in your superpowers, what is unique about you. My own superpowers were my love of books and my desire to leave a legacy through my writing. This is grounded it in the *Ikigai* model: what I love doing, what I am good at, what the world needs, and what is remunerative (well, three out of four ain't bad.) You do you. Use intentional reflection to find that sweet spot for yourself.

Recall Nietzsche said that having the freedom to create meaning can be terrifying. Reflection may take courage. It is all too easy to push aside life's bigger questions such as "who am I?", "what guides me?", and "what do I want to give to life?" In the words of Viktor Frankl, you need to "let life question you." I would add, "periodically" because constant existential rumination, without serious reflection and action, is a recipe for misery.

This chapter takes two different slants on purpose. The first is Mastery – that is, the "how" of purpose. The second slant is the Transcendentals that offer a lens through which to understand the "what." Even though purpose should be grounded in our superpower talents, we should not rely on that inheritance alone. What is more inspiring and powerful is to take those talents and **pursue mastery**.

MASTERY AND THE LOVE OF EXCELLENCE

To me, mastery is that ability to lead a more
purposeful life, and then take all of life and turn
it into a platform, because that's all we have.
SATYA NADELLA, MICROSOFT CEO

I propose, unlike many alternative theories of high-performance motivation, such as Maslow's, that mastery matters – perhaps more than wealth or fame or security. Think along with me about **mastery and motivation** while considering the following:

- What motivates high performers? Serena Williams (tennis), Magnus Carlsen (chess), Kobe Bryant (basketball), Mikhail Baryshnikov (ballet), Serena Williams (tennis), and Cristiano Ronaldo (football)?

- What motivates artists and architects? Pablo Picasso (visual art), Adrian Smith (Burj Khalifa), Damien Hirst (visual), Zaha Hadid (Beijing airport), or Yo-Yo Ma (cellist)?

- What motivates scientists and thinkers? Jennifer Doudna (CRISPR-Cas9), Peter Higgs (Higgs Boson), Craig Venter (Human Genome), James Thomson (stem cells), or Tim Berners-Lee (World Wide Web)?

- What motivates engineers and inventors? Steve Wozniak (Apple)? James Dyson (appliances)? Robert Noyce (the microchip)? Elon Musk (re-usable rockets and much more)?

- What motivates journalists and historians? Katherine Graham (Washington Post publisher), Bob Woodward (Watergate), Barbara Ehrenreich (worker rights), Niall Ferguson (historian), Anderson Cooper (journalist), or Mary Beard (historian)?

- What motivates philanthropists and activists? Malala Yousafzai (education), Mèdecins sans Frontiers (health), Bishop Desmond Tutu (anti-apartheid), President Jimmy Carter (human rights), or Bill and Melinda Gates (third world poverty and health)?

Figure VIII-1 : The spirit of mastery: pushing the boundaries of human achievement.

Perhaps you share with me admiration for those who take their chosen craft to the highest level? Although I don't know which end of a kitchen knife to hold, watching Gordon Ramsay is like magic. Although not a sports fan, I find watching LeBron James awe-inspiring. We may not agree politically with scholars such as Niall Ferguson (conservative) or Barbara Ehrenreich (progressive), but we can admire their scholarship and attempts to advance our understanding of ourselves.

The spirit of mastery can be inspirational in every domain, from cooking and gardening to particle physics. The four-minute mile was an impossible feat when Roger Bannister broke it in 1954; now 1600 people have run sub-four miles including many high-school students. Bannister didn't just break the record for Roger, he broke it for us – when a human being sets a new standard of excellence it lifts standards and hopes around the world. Excellence, thought about correctly, reminds us all of what we are capable– not just as an endowment of the supremely talented.

The spirit of mastery is one of the marvels of our species. Over our long history and pre-history, the striving to better ourselves and to master a craft, from the stonemason and carpenter of the Middle Ages to the additive manufacturing expert of today, pushed the limits of human achievement and inspired others to do likewise.

So it is with business. The great enterprises of today remind us what business is capable of. When businesses excel, they both inspire us and remind us that excellence is something humans are capable of. And so also of leadership. By embodying mastery and excellence, a leader inspires and sets standards for followers. Rather than view such leaders as "unicorn" exceptions, let us view them as human. Let us not wait for the next one to be born but use the realization that **what one is capable of, more are capable of**, and start forging greatness out of the talent pool we now have.

Mastery can appear self-oriented. However just "being number one" for ego-centric reasons is not what powers people to the extraordinary heights of performance. To achieve such heights, you need to love the game for the game's sake. For the most part, that love reveals itself before age 10, long before neurotic impulses such as competing for fame and money take root. That is why sometimes in career coaching, the coach may inquire 'what did you love to do when you were a child?' or 'if money was never a concern, what then would you dedicate your life toward?'

Some famous authors who write about purpose invoke the phrase, "not the best **in** the world, but the best **for** the world." That clever-sounding phrase strikes me as a false choice – we are not forced to choose. Moreover, **the best in the world**, coupled with noble purpose, **will be the best for the world.** I have had the good fortune to know many candidates on those lists and though never "ego-free" (as if that were possible), never have they been fueled by self-love and have always been fueled by love of the craft and the pursuit of mastery.

Mastery has to be part of how we design purpose for our lives – but mastery of what? What purposes, have thinkers suggested, are worth mastering? What purposes should we embrace in our own work to feel truly fulfilled? These answers may lie in the Transcendentals, taken from Greek philosophy, that point us toward some of the most noble and worthwhile purposes available to humans.

TRANSCENDENTALS - TRUTH, BEAUTY, GOODNESS

"Three passions, simple but overwhelmingly strong have governed my life: the longing for love, the search for knowledge, and unbearable pity for the suffering of mankind."

BERTRAND RUSSELL

For the ancient Greeks, human purpose was to pursue the Transcendentals (the "Big Three"): Truth, Beauty, and Goodness.[87] The "Big Three" superseded (in the philosopher's mind) secular wants such as wealth, conquest, and happiness. While Greek values also included justice, prudence, courage, fortitude, and temperance, the Big Three superseded those also - they fall under Goodness.

Before plowing on, ask yourself whether our society a) aims at Truth, Beauty, and Goodness, b) whether it should, and c) whether business ought to play a role in that aspiration. Or, are we pointed in different directions? Do we stumble upon Truth, Beauty, and Goodness accidentally? Does business have different, purely materialistic objectives? Should it? Don't take for granted the importance of what I say about Truth, Beauty, and Goodness – think hard about whether and how we can intentionally orient ourselves and our endeavors toward them and whether doing so would bring us closer to noble outcomes.

Truth - "standing on the shoulders of giants[88]"

Truth, or **knowledge**, for the Greeks, was paramount. The quest for Truth is motivated by the hunger to know, discover, and learn. Today

---

[87] There are many more ideas than just this, self-knowledge, virtue, happiness, friendship, and pleasure all make appearances in Greek wisdom literature but these are the biggies.

[88] "If I have seen farther, it is by standing on the shoulders of Giants." (Isaac Newton to Robert Hooke, 1675)

people play chess, do crosswords, play Fantasy Football, and read difficult non-fiction books. Why? Because our species likes to think. Thinking is one of the things we do that is most specially human.[89] It is also the primary source of joy at work for many people. (Although some politicians seem to get on just fine without too much thinking.)

Thinking and the hunger for Truth were called "the Cognitive Revolution" by Yuval Harari in his gripping account of pre-history. Seventy thousand years ago, that hunger gave us the superpowers of **language and abstraction**. Language enabled humans to communicate with more sophistication and, crucially, provided the ability to **describe the unseen** through stories. This creation of narratives describing fictional or hypothetical entities birthed our **imagination** that allowed us to share a vision of what the future **might** hold.

> *A great deal of leaders' power comes from "selling their imagination," through **creative stories** they tell and those that are told about them.*

Language and storytelling helped us scale Truth, becoming our tool for organizing ourselves socially to achieve those visions by working toward shared and communicated goals – cities, trade, technology, temples, art, and science. With those developments to human evolution, we began to stand on the shoulders of earlier generations. Abstractions and predictions – unseen concepts – allowed humans to talk about potential tigers, or tiger habits, or future tigers, or predatory cats like tigers, as opposed to talking only about literal tigers, as in: "look out dude, here comes a tiger!"

Abstraction helped us abstractly. As humans traveled, new environments demanded we quickly abstract earlier knowledge about how to live and adapt to new environments. We take abstraction for granted, so adept are we today as conceptual, abstract thinkers,

---

[89] Yes, problem solving and some higher-level thinking takes place in higher mammals, particularly primates. Each year it seems we discover they think more than we thought.

but our ability to communicate about abstract concepts is a prized evolutionary trait our species developed over time.

Truth motivates us all to some degree, driving the curiosity and scientific impulse readily seen in most children (but sadly less often in adults). Developmental psychologist Jean Piaget described abstract thinking as thinking about things in a way that is removed from the hard facts of the "here and now" and from specific examples of things in real life. Abstract thinkers are able to reflect on events, ideas, attributes, and relationships separate from the objects that have those attributes or share those relationships. Abstraction develops slowly in children, but sometime around age 12, kids learn to turn concrete experience into abstract thinking. When we think concretely, we experience **this song**, but abstractions help us think about its melody, lyrics, and genre. Abstract thinking can further mentally transport us back to that high-school dance where we first heard the song. A concrete thinker can recognize that Jack fancies Jill, but a more abstract thinker can reflect on emotions such as affection and the nature of relationships. Concrete thinking witnesses a natural disaster, but abstract thinking helps us plan and problem solve for future, hypothetical natural disasters.

All this abstraction comes with a curse – leaving the world of the here and now, the visceral, and "reality." Romantic thinkers like Rousseau and those long before him bemoaned this, as do my New Age friends. When we think abstractly about the past, we are prone to regret and resentment. When we think about imagined futures, we are prone to anxiety (as well as flights of inspiration.) Spirituality, for example in New Age circles, is about the heart in the here and now, while abstraction "puts you in your head." There is some truth to this, but practicing mindfulness meditation trains us to be aware and flexibly switch between "modes" and to acknowledge let go of our abstract thoughts as they arise, returning present focus to our breath and feelings should that be appropriate. To be sure, we need to be connected to the here and now, but to privilege the immediate and the emotional to the exclusion of reason is to divorce ourselves from one of our superpowers.

Abstract thinking is also a source of moral reasoning. While my feelings may make me want to kill the truck driver who nearly shoves me off the road, the fact that I possess a frontal cortex means the abstraction "thou shalt not kill" overrides my emotional impulses, so the truck driver survives to swerve another day.

In the world of business and 21st-century work, no conception about what matters and motivates is complete without the hunger for Truth. There are professions dedicated to the advancement of knowledge—science and journalism, not solely, but most obviously. What would business look like if Truth were pursued as a central purpose? If they did, they would passionately avoid misrepresentation and fraud. (And we would see less "snake oil" on the shelves of pharmacies.) Internally, evidence, honesty, and integrity would be part of their culture. Their cultures would also value learning and knowledge more greatly.

I have suggested to many CEOs that learning is the most important faculty for the sustainability of their business and that that learning starts at the very top – the CEO should be the Chief Truth Officer (even though that sounds like an Orwellian statement) or the Chief Learning Officer. Both business' **ends and means** could and should favor Truth more than they now do.

Perhaps this meditation on Truth provides you some insight into your own purpose. Hopefully, but perhaps not. The pursuit of answers, Truth, is a human superpower, but perhaps the other two Transcendentals will speak more to you. As you read further on the Transcendentals, consider which of the three belongs in your purpose sweet spot.

Beauty – physical and spiritual inspiration

Beauty is not something often sought or found at work, but creating beauty gives work meaning for many people. The artistic impulse is as old as our species, from cave paintings at Lascaux, to early Egyptian jewelry, to Greek sculpture. Beauty can be technological – the elegance of a German luxury car or the sleek aesthetic of Apple AirPods. Beauty can be found in visual art, photography, cinematography, and today's "Sistine Chapels." We can find beauty in music, literature, or perhaps even in a beautifully crafted television ad (although that might be going too far.) This value, capable of profoundly inspiring us, seems missing from talk about business or how it may meet spiritualty – as if business' relationship with the beautiful ended at furnishing the lobby.

Beauty also inspires feelings of awe and wonderment similar to spiritual experience. For Einstein, the meeting of beauty, goodness, and knowledge evoked spiritual experience. In my view, it is too important to be left to artists and art. Today we neither design all cities, workplaces, shopfronts, products, nor even all houses with aesthetics in mind. For some of these creations, even "not ugly" can be an achievement. Figure VIII-2 contrasts the high-tech office with the call center, the revolting strip mall with a more elegant alternative, and social housing – the beautiful and the ugly.

But we can design beautiful offices, shops, and neighborhoods if we care enough to try. Though we can decorate cubicles with posters and photos and we can decorate urban blight with street art, or... (I can't think how to improve a strip mall), we can start from a better place. Strip malls are useful, but who finds them attractive? And why should inspiring beautiful workplaces exist only for investment bankers and tech bros? Would Amazon fulfillment center workers be more engaged, less stressed, and happier if not forced to work in a utilitarian nightmare?

Take social housing. When people grow up or work in the worst of such places, it is hard to convey the message "we care about your experience and your future." And who could wake up in eviscerated Gary, Indiana, or bombed-out Wolverhampton, UK and push themselves to be their most inspired and productive? By designing these places without concern for beauty, we send the message that

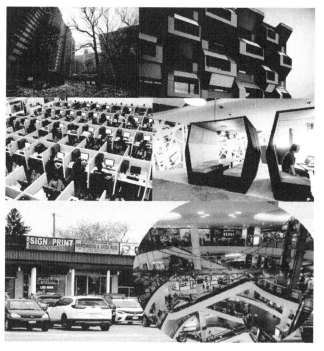

Figure VIII-2: Welcome to your new office/ home/ shopping experience.
Don't forget to be inspired and motivated today! (We can do better.)

we don't care about the people who live there, so we should not be surprised if kids raised there grow up not to care about a world that appears not to care about them. Moreover, experts such as Stacy Stewart from Fannie Mae (government housing finance in the US) say, "...poor design . . . can play a critical role in the way that people perceive and accept their surroundings and in how neighbors see them. . . . people feel isolated from the rest of the community. They feel stigmatized."

Likewise, if we are sincerely interested in worker experience, not just in customer experience or executive experience, we have to design beauty into workplaces, not just the lobby, the CEO's office, and the website.

Designing beauty into business is not just designing for our eyes – ears also matter. Julian Treasure, one of my first ever interviews when I was researching "the spiritual CEO," has made it his mission in life to transform the sound of business. Sound affects us physiologically, psychologically, cognitively, and behaviorally, yet we are besieged by "commercial" unwanted sound, "hold music," background noise, beeps, and musak.

Businesses do not spend a fraction of the money on customers' auditory experience that they spend on the visual: our soundscapes are much more harmful. After being on hold and putting up with distorted music and a cold voice saying, "We care about your experience, you are number ninety-four in line," what customer could be in a good mood? We put up with auditory ugliness because we have become used to it, but its toll on our stress and emotions persists. So Julian pursued his purpose, writing books, founding The Sound Agency, and giving two of the most-watched TED talks of all time on how we can create acoustical environments that nurture us rather than assault us.

Beauty need not just be sensual. Scientists find beauty in the structure of the universe and mathematicians in the elegance and symmetry of its rules. Architecture combines engineering and aesthetic beauty. There is also a kind of moral human beauty – warmth, sincerity, purity, integrity, authenticity, or passion. Culture and community can be beautiful – the way people treat each other and the types of things they do and share can be beautiful.

The third Transcendental, Goodness, is closer to many hearts than the first two. Perhaps justly so – but the transcendentals aren't exclusive. There is a reasonable line of thought that they converge, that Truth is Beautiful and Good, that Goodness requires Truth and Beauty, and the Beautiful contains a certain Truth and Goodness.

What motivates the nameless billions of people whose job is principally to care for or provide for others (and often without pay)? One theory is that we are drawn to do good for others and Goodness if the final purpose Transcendental.

Goodness, altruism, and human nature

"There are evidently some principles in human nature, which interest him in the fortune of others, and render their happiness necessary to him, though he derives nothing from it, except the pleasure of seeing it."
ADAM SMITH, THE THEORY OF MORAL SENTIMENTS

There are dozens of faces of goodness: justice, freedom, fairness, honesty, compassion, friendship, courage, honor, service, kindness, order, love, and many more. But goodness has been a lost concept when it comes to much contemporary work and business, the central paradigm, birthed in the history of business, that "goodness is not what business about." Nevertheless, our moral intuitions should guide us toward goodness, even (and especially) in business, because of the deep admiration we feel for those people in the world driven to selfless service and who put ethics, righteousness, and people before material comforts and profit. We admire goodness, but we give business a pass – allowing it a purely secular existence Business has the power to **scale goodness** – it can inspire on a bigger scale.

In experimental economics, people who are given money and free choice share it with strangers even when they have no self-interested rationale (within conventional economic models) for doing so. Why would Navy SEAL Michael Monsoor jump on a grenade to save others' lives? Why did Katniss sacrifice herself to save Prim, or Anna to save Elsa? One could argue, and nihilists do, that humans are altruistic purely out of self-interest and therefore that altruism does not exist. In this logic, the feelings we get from doing good for others provide us with pleasure, and ultimately that is why people do virtuous things – they want to feel good or look good. That argument misses a critical point, as we must wonder: how did helping others thus feeling good become linked in humans' emotional wiring? We could have been wired very differently!

Consider how a team of "ball-hogs" would fare against a team that collaborates. In pre-history, humans' propensity to help and work with others promoted cohesion and stability in small groups and become part of our cultural wiring. Over millennia, the **"cultural software"** that taught us to collaborate was codified in oral history and then in wisdom writings ("love thy neighbor as thyself") and in social norms such as kindness and service that conferred cultural advantage for those groups.

There is a robust debate in academic circles about how our capacity for altruism, **helping others at a cost to oneself,** arose and how our propensity toward helping others contributed to our flourishing as a species. Was it nature or nurture - genes or culture? Altruism seems partly genetically "hardwired," as there is a gene, AVPR1, that appears correlated with altruistic behaviors. We find that twins raised apart show similar empathy and sharing behaviors. Self-sacrifice is also genetically "wired" in a not-so-obvious way: if an individual dies defending their group, their offspring and genetically related others in the herd still may survive as a result of the sacrifice. Genetic hardwiring seems part of the explanation for altruism, but not the only one.

We are driven emotionally to altruism through compassion. The word's Latin roots mean to feel empathy together (*pati*, suffer; *com*, together). Insofar as we are a species that prospers through community and social bonding, feeling another's suffering is the vital ingredient that facilitates human altruism. Margaret Mead, the über-cultural anthropologist of the 20th century, was asked what evidence constituted the first sign of civilization – was it clay pots, jewelry, or tools? She explained that she had found a skeleton with a broken-then-healed femur. That marked civilization's birth for her. Why? Because a broken leg ought to have meant death – you couldn't have run, hunted, or defended yourself. No animal survives with a broken leg for very long. Yet, a healed femur meant someone had cared for and carried such a person to safety until they were healed – that evidence of helping others was, for Mead, how civilization started.

Still, it is harder to see how big group altruism, the tendency to help people half a planet away, might have evolved. Why do we send aid to victims of natural disasters? How did genes and culture (hardware and software) produce this strange behavior? Perhaps that small group altruism, "cultural software," became a habit of mind we applied to larger and larger groups. However, I prefer to think that it came about through a **revolution in philosophy,** the world of ideas – that our higher faculties, our ability to work from abstract noble principles, won the day over our baser, self-serving instincts. The development of our frontal cortex, bigger and more connected than in other mammals, can tame impulses from the limbic system.

The idea of "common humanity" was alien before the Enlightenment – we were divided by birth into rulers and the ruled, by skin color into races, by geography into competing nations, by religious belief into righteous and infidels. The Enlightenment project, birthed 300 years ago, meant that science and philosophy began to dissolve these boundaries – at first in the abstract, then slowly through policies and politics, then even more slowly via the hearts and minds of citizens. But it takes many hundreds of years for revolutions in thought to become universally adopted. Democracy is a simple enough idea, but we still wrestle, hundreds of years after its installation in Great Britain, the US, and France, with its implementation.

Common humanity may take another 300 years to reach deeply and widely into our collective psyche. The 20th century saw some of the worst instances of difference-based hatreds which, coupled with 20th-century technology, produced humanitarian disasters on previously unseen scales. Given that spotted history – how parochial, selfish, bigoted, and nationalistic humans can be – it seems remarkable that we have things such as international aid and disaster relief, that the United Nations and countless charities do their best to help the neediest, and that the world developed the Universal Declaration of Human Rights that 48 countries have signed.

Altruism is **supererogatory,** a term that ethicists use to describe doing more than duty requires, more than the minimum, and more than is expected. Caring, protecting, and providing for one's family is, of course, virtuous. However important, it is instinctual and deeply grounded in our biology[90] and not supererogatory – it is expected. There is something uniquely human in going beyond what instinct calls upon us to do.

However, genetic hardware and cultural software arguments miss a finer point. We, as humans with sophisticated brains and moral intuition, get to **choose our behavior** – we can transcend our inherited tendencies, whether biological hardware or cultural software. We are **free to choose** altruism, not as a matter of biological or cultural inheritance, but as a purpose to which we can devote our work and our businesses. This is a constructivist approach, as we can construct corporate and personal purpose (as well as meaning) as we like – for self-oriented gain or for the benefit of humanity. From a leadership point of view, the latter intention is not just the noblest but the most motivational, the most inspiring, and the best way to attract talent. The next chapter makes the case that constructing altruistic purpose is the most effective way to lead organizations.

Freely choosing altruism as a narrative for humanity matters a great deal because the stories we tell ourselves about ourselves matter a great deal. Today's dominant narratives are that humans are greedy, malign, and competitive – ideas about original sin reinforce the idea that we are fallen. Some see religion as a necessary counterweight to those innately sinful tendencies. Others, like political philosopher Thomas Hobbes, thought humans were predisposed to "brutishness and misery" and that we need the State to protect us from each other. Finally, practitioners of the "dismal science" use the premise that "rational economic man" is self-interested above all and is driven to maximize personal utility.

---

[90] Some would say, controversially, protecting and caring for our kin is "in our genes" – more precisely that natural selection operates at the kinship and group level.

What thinkers like these and followers of Ayn Rand's objectivism fail to grasp is that such stories create reality more than describe it. When a physicist describes a star, the behavior of the star is unchanged. However, this is never true in psychology. When an economist or psychologist makes such a pronouncement, that view affects (infects) human behavior – such is the nature of the social sciences. The economist's narrative of humans as short-term profit-maximizers finds its way not just into the human psyche but into institutions and policies. Behaviorist psychology of the 20th century found its way into workplace rewards, the justice system, and parenting practices. Books on happiness, as we saw, shift our view of what matters and how to get it.

If we treat human nature more flexibly – as less hardwired and more a function of stories we tell each other, we have more choice. For example, the view of humans as selfish and inclined to violence is a story about our neighbors – next door, the next tribe, or the next country. Taking this dim, mistrustful view of one's neighbors compels the building of walls and armaments. Your neighbor, gazing at your walls and weapons, views you with mistrust and suspicion, so they acquire their own. And so it goes. This misanthropic narrative self-perpetuates. A dim view of human nature creates societies armed to the teeth, but then government's "rational" response to escalate and create more fear. And so it goes.

LEADING PURPOSE

"The purpose of human life is to serve, and to show compassion and the will to help others."
ALBERT SCHWEITZER

As with most of the treatments in this book, Goodness and the other Transcendentals that might guide purpose are about choice and the narratives we create. Your purpose might be infused with all three, but perhaps one inspires you more than the others. I value a life surrounded by such richness, the arts for Beauty, science and philosophy for Truth, and my politics for Goodness. Without one of these stool legs, I feel an emptiness. But again, you do you. Balance them as you will but consider them as you reflect on your purpose.

The Transcendentals are independent of spiritual tradition – different traditions will have different approaches to Truth, but Truth matters; we have different ideas of beauty, but it matters; we have different conceptions of goodness, but goodness matters. Regardless of specific conceptions of Truth, Beauty, and Goodness, we need to teach our coming generations to venerate those over, wealth, happiness, and conquest – expecting that a life so dedicated will be more rewarding.

There is much more to say about goodness and business purpose. Mostly, it will await volume II (*Culture, Capitalism, Sustainability*) which, you could say, is entirely devoted to the idea of "good business" – how spiritual and philosophical ideas guide conversations about capitalism, employer brand, culture, values, and personal ethics. The ethos of that second volume may be summed up as:

Purposeful people in a purposeless organization is unworkable – the onus is on businesses to provide a way to harness the "will to purpose."

Re-orienting our lives and the world in these directions takes **leadership** – the ability to articulate purpose and move people beyond their self-interest toward a common purpose. The next chapter's idea of spiritual leadership offers a perspective and some tools for leaders to create common purpose and to support people finding meaning, goodness, and connectedness in their work.

CHAPTER

Spiritualty and leadership

Covered in this chapter:

CHAPTER 9

SPIRITUALITY AND LEADERSHIP

"A man with strong passions lives them; a man with weak passions is lived by them; weak passions paralyze the will, strong passions urge man to action."

PROFESSOR AND POET, MIGUEL DE UNAMUNO

A LEADERSHIP CRISIS

My favorite leadership theorist, Professor Jeffrey Pfeffer from Stanford, wonders why, "when medical science has made significant strides in treating many diseases, leadership as it is practiced daily all over the world has continued to produce a lot of disengaged, dissatisfied, and disaffected employees."[91] We could add to this deficit a list of business' eye-watering ethical disasters such as Wells Fargo, Enron, VW, Theranos, and *ad* – seemingly – *infinitum*. Either the theories of leadership experts suck, or practitioners ignore them – either way, we experts are doing a terrible job.

I have a theory. Philosopher Karl Popper said, "science proceeds from rectification of error." Rectification of error necessitates vigorous debate and critique, largely absent in leadership change,

---

[91] Pfeffer, J., *Leadership BS, Fixing our Workplaces and Careers One Truth at a Time*, Harper Business, 2015

culture, and management. By my count, twenty of the best-selling business books of all time are about leadership. By Amazon's count, there are 57,136 (!) books with leadership in the title, and over a thousand are published yearly. How much do most help? Consider some great leaders from forty years ago, perhaps Reagan, if you lean that way or Carter if you lean the other. Perhaps Havel, King, or Mandela are your cup of leadership tea? Had they read any of those fifty-seven thousand books? Were those leaders "naturals" whose lessons are found in the books but which we mortals are too dense to learn? How useful does that make the books? I'd also hazard a guess that you know someone who seems to have read all 57,000 and is still a pretty awful leader.

Leadership theory, in my view and in Pfeffer's, has merely inched forward since the 1960s, proceeding at a glacial pace compared to science, technology, and health, usually each time by putting a new adjective in front of "leadership" (X-leadership) and then listing its attributes which differ very little from the "X"s of years prior.[92]

There are hundreds of different "X"s, a few examples being authentic, level 5, embodied, responsible, digital, sustainable, democratic, visionary, transactional, cultural, cross-cultural, global, situational, VUCA, strategic, agile, 4-H, inspirational, dynamic, values-based, purpose-driven, and so on. When we choose between them, it seems often a matter of fashion and fad rather than based on side-by-side evaluation or rational debate and critique as we see in science.

The world of spiritual leadership, which we are about to dive into, is already awash with terms that people would like to equate it with. Some of those are conscious leadership, integral leadership, servant leadership, authentic leadership, systemic leadership, stewardship, inner leadership, transpersonal leadership, faith-based leadership, ethical leadership, and transformational leadership.

---

[92] If you doubt that, check out *The Human Side of Enterprise*, published in 1960, or James MacGregor Burns transformational leadership model from 1978.

Does spiritual leadership add value to this messy array of leadership theories to distinguish it from the other fads that end up shelved with all the X-leaderships of decades prior? Will we resolve the crisis in leadership ideas by merely adding a new "X" to the list?

This chapter offers some unique ideas on leadership and proposes a new "X" – spiritual leadership – based upon our definition of spirituality. Here we tie spiritual leadership to our definition of spirituality and ask: if purpose matters, what does it mean to **lead purpose**, and what tools might a leader use in doing so?

However, first, I have an additional worry about the concept of spiritual leadership specifically, even though I will advocate for our version of it.

Spiritual leadership – Necessary, nice to have, wishful thinking, or only sometimes?

If spirituality is **necessary** for good leadership, that means all good leaders have to be spiritual. Do they? Though we haven't defined spiritual leadership yet, the term might include values such as humility, self-awareness, care, devotion, piety, sacredness, faith, mindfulness, love, altruism, compassion, and so on. So, are those qualities **necessary** for good leadership? Do those surround us in the business and political worlds?

We must ask ourselves whether spirituality is necessary for leadership **generally**, or whether spiritual leadership is only a particular kind of leadership, or whether it is only useful in a specific kind of organization and not, for example, in a culture that values swagger and aggression (some financial services companies and certainly my old home Wall Street).

Moreover, we need to be careful, because while we **would like** the leaders we follow to have spiritual values, we must wonder whether they are necessary. You can undoubtedly think of contemporary and historical political and business leaders who possess **none** of the above virtues. In talking about spirituality and leadership, are we guilty of wishful thinking, talking about seldom-realized ideals or naturally occurring qualities that only certain leaders possess – a leadership type that is useful in only a few contexts?

Since the turn of the millennium, nearly two dozen countries have elected leaders reminiscent of 1930's style "strong man" leadership – in other words, heading away from the concepts and ideas of this chapter and which I presume you'd favor. That suggests that in the parts of the world where elections happen, more than half the voters prefer an authoritarian style.[93] It is a fascinating disconnect, like the young lover who yearns for deep romantic long-term relationship but ends up fatally attracted to miscreant bad boys (or women).

Could this be a tussle between our evolutionary biological instincts, where we want the biggest, meanest "alpha" protecting the troop or pride, and our more evolved instincts to want more empathetic, cerebral, spiritual leadership? I will leave the reader who is sympathetic to the ideas of spiritual leadership to mull over this puzzling disconnect as we close this chapter with a discussion of using spiritual leadership development ideas in Global-100 multinationals.

As you read on in this section, continue to ask yourself whether these leadership ideas are necessary, aspirational, and/or idealistic. If they are ideals worth embracing, how do we know they would make leaders more effective? In which contexts would such traits be desirable? I challenge you to challenge me on my conclusions.

---

[93] This excludes countries, such as Byelorussia, North Korea and parts of Africa where "free" elections produce 99% majorities for the Supreme Leader. Such "tough guy" countries include Poland, Hungary, Brazil, Turkey, the Philippines, Russia, Brazil, and the United States. Such leaders may enjoy an immense popularity.

DEFINING SPIRITUAL LEADERSHIP DISTINC-TIVELY AND UNIVERSALLY

As you may recall from Chapter II, 21st-century spirituality, **we define spirituality as growing and striving for meaning, purpose, goodness, and connectedness.** That definition of spirituality is based on common ground between people of faith and non-faith traditions. It is grounded in what people say spirituality means to them and what scholars such as theologians, philosophers, psychologists, and sociologists think it should be.

This definition, in our context, has thus far applied only to individuals. But **how does a leader support growing and striving across an entire team or business? How do they lead and scale meaning, purpose, goodness, and connectedness?** Does "scaling meaning" consist of making shared, collective meaning out of personal meaning? Should "scaling goodness" mean using the power of big organizations to benefit humanity?

Let's consider how our definition translates to the collective, organizational level, shown in Figure IX – 1.

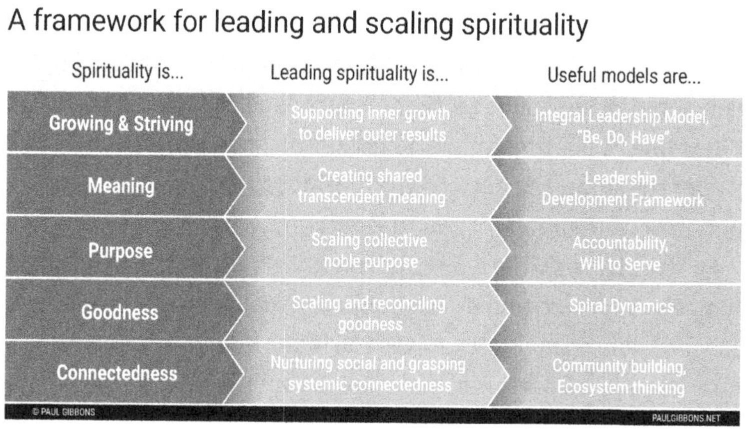

A framework for leading and scaling spirituality

Spirituality is...	Leading spirituality is...	Useful models are...
Growing & Striving	Supporting inner growth to deliver outer results	Integral Leadership Model, "Be, Do, Have"
Meaning	Creating shared transcendent meaning	Leadership Development Framework
Purpose	Scaling collective noble purpose	Accountability, Will to Serve
Goodness	Scaling and reconciling goodness	Spiral Dynamics
Connectedness	Nurturing social and grasping systemic connectedness	Community building, Ecosystem thinking

© PAUL GIBBONS · PAULGIBBONS.NET

Figure IX-1: Spiritual leadership should lean hard on a definition of spirituality to be distinctive, valuable, and useful.

In the leftmost column of the image is our working definition of spirituality; the middle column shows what leaders should do to "scale and lead" that dimension, and the rightmost column contains the examples of models (incomplete, there are many more) that are explained in the rest of the chapter. If you are a leadership expert, you will already know some of the models, but this chapter's mapping of them onto our definition of spirituality might provide you with deeper insight into the "why" of models you already know. If you are a work-a-day business leader, this may seem like model soup – but stretch yourself to map them onto your personal knowledge of leaders you admire and don't, and historical leaders and their traits.

SCALING AND LEADING SPIRITUAL GROWTH

"The fault, dear Brutus, is not in our stars, but in ourselves."
CASSIUS, JULIUS CAESAR, ACT I, SCENE 3

In an earlier book (*The Science of Organizational Change*), I suggested how Carol Dweck's idea of growth mindset might be applied **at scale** in a business to create a **growth culture.** Picture a graph of time (x-axis) versus capability (y-axis) for all the people in your team or business – I suggest that leaders need to focus on the **slope of that line** as opposed to the height of their current capability. The steeper the slope, the better. Why (besides the obvious that people get better at their jobs)? Two reasons.

First, cultures where people constantly stretch and improve themselves are exciting places to work – that growth in capability, self-confidence, and skills makes the highs higher, creates a much more engaged workforce, and makes the business more future-proof. Second, your strategy is accelerated (so to speak) "from below." This isn't abstract. No lesser a CEO than Satya Nadella has made "growth culture" a priority.

Even if you accept that though, where does spirituality fit in? Isn't

spiritual growth what pastors, spiritual directors, gurus, and priests do? Why would an executive meddle in that territory? If spirituality is to be applied "in the temple of life," a lot of that life happens at work. Without donning a frock or saffron robe, (can you picture "Zuck" doing so?), what can a leader do to promote spiritual growth?

If we agree that spiritual growth matters in general – that is that growing meaning, purpose, goodness, and connectedness matters – then we agree that it matters in business — a tremendous amount of the "general." And if spiritual growth matters in business, then leaders (and leadership development experts) must embrace the opportunity to make growth holistic in terms of developing their people and organizations. But, how do you lead spiritual growing and striving?

Below are two tools that help make sense of the opportunity that holistic leadership development presents: **The Integral Leadership Model** and the **"Be, Do, Have" Model.**

The integral leadership model (systemic holism)

Although the idea of **holism** is not unique to spirituality, holism is a feature of many spiritual leadership models. Those models try to understand leadership in a **non-reductive** way (not through a single factor such as strengths indicators or emotional intelligence.) The Integral Leadership Model (ILM) may seem complex at first look, but leadership is an extremely complex social phenomenon, and despite its complexity, the ILM remains simpler than the real thing!

In the **Integral Leadership Model**[94] (shown in Figure IX- 2 below), the top two quadrants are **individual** aspects of leadership. The bottom quadrants are **collective** aspects (such as culture, more on

---

[94] This model appeared first in a chapter of mine in an early academic reader on workplace spirituality titled *Work and Spirit: A Reader of New Spiritual Paradigms for Organizations,* first written in 1997 and published in 2000. Since then endless refor- mulations have appeared.

which later.) The quadrants on the right contain **objective**, "exterior," and visible aspects of leadership (for example, behaviors.) The leftmost quadrants have "soft," subjective, interior stuff. (You can't measure from the outside, you have to "get inside" by inquiring and listening to people to uncover, for example, their vision and beliefs.)

Integral Leadership Model (Gibbons, 1997)

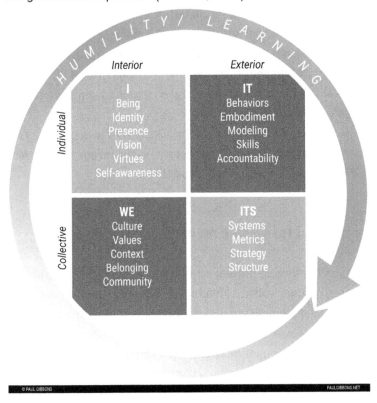

Diagram IX – 2: Integral leadership circa 1997: hard-to-measure leadership attributes get insufficient attention. (This was the metamodel upon which my 2001 consultancy was founded.)

One simple way to understand the model is through the I, WE, IT, ITS labels of each quadrant. "I" is the subjective stuff about the leader, "WE" the subjective stuff about the team or organization. "IT" are measureable aspects of the leader, and "ITS" are visible aspects of the leadership system (such as how the team is structured.)

In more detail, the top-right "exterior" quadrant includes behaviors, embodiment, modeling, performance, skills, and role—these are the more measurable (objective) attributes of a leader. The majority of leadership development activities occur in this quadrant, for example, all the skills training programs that abound (such as, performance management, negotiation, or influencing skills)

The model gets more interesting in the leftmost column (subjective, "interior"). The features in the top-left quadrant (being, identity, presence, vision, virtues, and self-awareness) are **subjective**, hard to measure, hard to manage, and **easy to overlook in leadership development**. As an executive coach, I've helped leaders develop these more ephemeral (some spiritual) characteristics, starting with helping them become more aware of how they "show up." If you examine that list of features, you can see how important such features are to building trust, and at the end of this chapter, we talk about how those can be the focus on a leadership development program.

The bottom-right quadrant shows **collective** aspects of leadership such as systems, metrics, strategy, and structure. You may say, "those aren't leadership." However, you are missing a trick. The collective and individual levels act reciprocally upon each other – for example, the structure of a team and its reward systems will affect an individual leader's behavior and performance. Likewise, the skillset of an individual helps determine how a team needs to be structured; the structure of a team will limit or enhance a leader's effectiveness.

Finally, in the bottom-left quadrant, we find culture, values, context, belonging, and community. These bottom-left collective attributes are reciprocal: leadership shapes culture, but culture also determines what kind of leadership will succeed. (Try being directive in a university culture!) Leaders build community, but reciprocally, communities are the soil from which leaders grow.

Again, the rightmost aspects of the model are easier to measure and manage than the leftmost. Ergo, succession planning, KPIs, people analytics, recruitment strategy, and skills development get a lot of attention. You will remember Peter Drucker's cliché "what gets measured gets managed." It was always nonsense because **not all that can be measured matters, and not all that matters can be measured**. Furthermore, it implies a corollary: **what doesn't get measured may get overlooked**. Models like this help avoid that trap.

I appreciate that the model is very abstract. We could make it more so by discussing the different epistemologies of the left and right columns or the metaphysics of collective versus individual lenses. Rather than do that (and have you reach for the sick bag), here are three practical examples that make it more concrete.

Examples of the Integral Leadership Model in action

The OG integral theorist, Ken Wilber described the following scenario:

> *"A malformation—a pathology, a 'sickness'—in any quadrant will reverberate through all four quadrants, such as slave wages and dehumanizing labor conditions [a bottom-right structural issue.] This may reflect in low self-esteem for laborers [an upper-left "interior" phenomenon,] and an out-of-whack brain chemistry ([an upper-right, empirical, objective phenomenon] that might, for example, institutionalize alcohol abuse as self-medication, ... a cultural phenomenon [bottom-left.]"*

We saw such reverberation in 2020's COVID-19 crisis, when attitudes (lower left) from politics and culture affected herd behaviors (lower right) such as mask usage and distancing which affected disease incidence in individuals (upper right), placed demands on systems and healthcare structures (lower right) and affected people's mental health (upper left). When policymakers tried to lower the incidence of disease by structural means such as lockdowns, there was a backlash in the cultural quadrant, and in the mental costs of isolation. A leader needs to consider all four quadrants when making decisions in a complex system to be maximally effective and to avoid unintended consequences – that is what the ILM approach to holistic leadership allows.

Finally, let's consider a signature leadership skill such as influencing. Influencing behaviors are visible and measurable, but features such as intention, integrity, and authenticity affect the results those behaviors produce. A people developer can teach influencing skills until the cows come home, but if the wannabe influencer cringes in team meetings or appears inauthentic or lacks presence (weaknesses in the upper left quadrant,) they will be ineffective. Influencing also happens in cultures, and what counts as a good influencing strategy in one culture, say a Trump rally, might not fly at the American Association for the Advancement of Science (and vice versa.)

The leadership influencer may wish to shift culture and create new policies and systems that affect the inner lives and behaviors of followers. Such a leader making use of the ILM will appreciate that inner qualities are reflected in outer behaviors that affect structure and strategy and culture. But also, that causality works in the opposite direction. Structure and strategy affect mindset, behaviors, and culture. Think about a **creating growth culture** – all four quadrants have to pull together or else the weakest link, be it rewards, mindset, culture, or behaviors will block progress.

What makes this model a useful development tool besides its holism is its focus on **inner work**—you can't develop presence, vision, virtues, and self-awareness without taking leaders well out of their comfort zones and challenging them to shift their deeply held patterns. **Too much development focuses on areas that are easy to develop rather than interventions that provide highest leverage**, just like a driver looking for car keys under a lamppost not because they are lost there, but because that is where there is the most light. It is easy to "check a box" with a 3-day executive education program, but how many of those produce real the shifts in leadership capabilities that we are looking for? How many are just convenient options?

HOLISM – THE SYMBIOSIS OF INNER GROWTH AND OUTER RESULTS

All spiritual ideas on leadership embrace some kind of holism, and that is what unites the dozen or so ideas that follow. However, not even the ideas here describe an entirely holistic approach. One kind of holism we find is a symbiosis of **inner growth** producing **outer results.** Inner work includes appreciation of the Jungian idea of shadow – hard-to-see, darker aspects of even good leaders. For example, an enthusiastic, charismatic leader's shadow might be their difficulty with hearing bad news or empathizing with struggling followers. Leaders with unresolved insecurity issues may unknowingly attract only sycophantic followers. Shadow can be pernicious because **weaknesses are often overplayed strengths**. I had a client who became CFO because of a reputation for prudence and risk-aversion – but when being considered for a CEO position, that "default setting" that had produced 30 years of outstanding career success became a liability. It is axiomatic with big role changes and promotions that **what got you where you are won't get you where you are going.**

Developing leaders also requires **personal development**, whatever your model of that may be, from "head, heart, hands, soul" to "mind, body, spirit" or broader.[95] In one program, my consulting team used the "Be, Do, Have" model as seen in Figure IX-3.

---

[95] This idea is called Integral Transformative Practice or Integral Life Practice developed by George Leonard and Michael Murphy.

Self/fundamentals	Learning Themes	Results
• Centered Presence	• Speaking powerfully	• Outstanding financial results
• Authenticity	• Making assessments	• Deeper client relationships
• Integrity	• Declaring a future	• Powerful presence and impact in
• Vitality	• Using the voice and body	communication
• Self-awareness	• The power of enrolment	• Greater accountability
• Personal learning	• Managing moods	• self
	• Building trust in relationships	• team
	• Creating and co-ordination of action	• KPMG
BE	DO	HAVE

Figure IX-3: Leadership development should link spiritual development, skills development, and business results. (from a 2004 program)

Participants set "being" goals (self/fundamentals), "doing" goals (skills), and "having" goals (results). In this way, we created a link in their minds between business results, the skills they required, and the deep personal change needed. To reinforce the emphasis on deep personal change for investment bankers in that program, we began each day of our leadership programs with fifteen minutes Qi Gong and Yoga, followed by a thirty-minute run, followed by a twenty-minute meditation.

Great leaders of organizations always keep the focus on their own development, their own learning, their own motivations, and their own "shadow." Only then can they expect to lead teams where learning, development, motivation, and authenticity are important. Only then can they better know themselves, understand the perspective from which they view the world, and thus change their thinking and behavior. Only through such self-mastery can they achieve social mastery.

While no leader (business, education, politics, or wherever) can supplant the role of professional spiritual support, you could say that part of caring for employees is caring for their souls. That is, caring that they have meaning and purpose and caring that they are able to grow and strive. As someone who has run leadership programs along these lines for decades, I have never used the word "spirituality" with clients simply because it is too laden with specific connotations from specific traditions that might alienate my audiences. Nevertheless, programs developed using these principles have been run in the most orthodox and conservative businesses in the world, and by our definition of "spirituality," those programs do contain spiritual elements.

FROM INDIVIDUAL MEANING TO COLLECTIVE MEANING

When it comes to the meaning dimension of spirituality, we must revisit what we mean by "meaning." Ten employees can attend the same meeting, and each takes away ten different meanings – meaning-making is deeply personal. Imagine that two people are doing identical tasks, for instance jointly developing the same software. One of these people may find meaning in one aspect of the task, perhaps to do with their love of software engineering, while the other may find meaning in the software's functionality (perhaps because it provides an improved user experience).

This leads us to the question of what a leader can do to create collective meaning from individual meaning along with what they can do to "raise the stakes," helping followers to seek deeper meaning in their work. Meaning-making must begin with the leader who creates her own narratives of meaning – they can only invite depth of reflection from followers when they do so themselves.[96]

Meaning-making will always be deeply personal. Meaning-making is therefore facilitative; it is more about the questions than about the answers. In the context of work, you may ask yourself the following questions (among others) to develop your own meanings. Questions that embrace such depth are:

---

[96] I am grateful to my collaborator Ro Gorell for some of her insights here.

- What do you see as your personal legacy and the legacy you'd like to leave to our organization?
- Which values are most important to you?
- Which of those are expressed in your work here?
- How does this job fit with your view of your career and long-term goals?
- What that we do here makes you most proud?

Leaders can help followers take a larger view of their place in the world, a bigger perspective of the organization or systems to which they belong, or on a longer timescale than they are naturally inclined to consider. One of the best leadership development models for this is the Leadership Development Framework ("LDF," below) which is based on pioneering research by Harvard psychologist Robert Kegan and made practical by Bill Torbert, Suzanne Cooke-Greuter, and David Rooke.[97] The LDF takes a developmental perspective. In this framework, leaders make decisions using various "action-logics"— from the **opportunist** (embraces short-term outlook, externalizes blame, and exhibits limited self-control) through the results-oriented, driven **achiever**, to the **alchemist** who creates positive-sum games, understands complexity theory, and addresses problems from a systemic perspective.

For the **Opportunist**, impulses rule – think of a child or juvenile adult with no self-control and a short-term focus. At the second level – **Diplomat** – rules, norms, and identity replace impulses as drivers of behavior. Then at the third level – **Expert** – we become more rational, but it is a limited rationality that only sees its own perspective.

Then, at the **Achiever** level, more personal responsibility for creating goals and shaping a future takes hold. At the next level, **Redefining**, we make a big jump to being able to question our

---

[97] "The Seven Transformations of Leadership", David Rooke and William Torbert, Harvard Business Review, April 2005

Leadership Development Framwork

Opportunist	Short-term horizon; focuses on concrete things; rejects feedback; externalizes blame; fragile self-control; treats what they can get away with as legitimate.
Diplomat	Overseas protocol; works to group standards; conforms; seeks membership and loyalty; attends to social affairs of group and avoids hurting others; face saving essential.
Expert	Regards their way of seeing things and their reality as the only valid reality. Interested in problem solving, chooses efficiency over effectiveness. May be dogmatic; critical of self and others, values decisions based on " incontrovertible facts".
Achiever	Feels like an initiator, not a pawn; mid-term goals; future is vivid and motivating; effectiveness and result orientated. Adopts rather than creates goals; welcomes feedback, blind to own shadow.
Redefining	Increasingly questions own assumptions. Increased understanding of complexity, paradox and working through relationships. Attracted by change and difference more than stability and similarity. Increasingly aware of own assumptions and shadows.
Transforming	Recognizes importance of principle, contract, theory and judgment - not just rules and custom. Creative on conflict resolution, aware that what one sees depends on one´s world view. Able to identify unique market niches.
Alchemist	Creator of events and reframes situation to see new opportunities. Blends opposites, create positive sum gaines, researches interplay of institution, thought, action and effects on outside world. Involved in spiritual quest and helps others in their life quest.

© PAUL GIBBONS   PAULGIBBONS.NET

Diagram IX-4: The leadership development framework links adult development and leadership

assumptions, to seeing ourselves seeing, and working with complexity. (We can pause here – how many leaders do you know operate at this level?) At level six – **Transforming** – we can integrate multiple perspectives masterfully. Finally, the **Alchemist level is characterized by** reframing, zero-sum games, combining intuition with rational judgment, and seeking a higher good.[98]

To better understand the LDF, take each level and identify a leader you know, from your company or from public life. Does it feel to you as if this truly is a developmental model of leadership and that the levels are correctly ordered? How does it fit alongside your

---

[98] Paraphrased from, What's Integral about Leadership? A Reflection on Leadership and Integral Theory Jonathan Reams, The Integral Review, 1, 2005

own ideas of leadership and how leaders develop? Would you rather work for an alchemist (bottom tier) or a leader from an earlier tier?

The next dimension of spirituality that a leader can learn from and make use of is nurturing and growing organizational purpose.

THE POWER OF PURPOSE – ACCOUNTABILITY

Accountability is not a spiritual concept, but it is an important leadership concept – in my view, it is one of the signature **differences between management and leadership**.[99] Spirituality, though, contributes to higher levels of accountability, which, enables a more powerful inspirational leadership. Let's explore how.

Consider the **Leadership Accountability Model** shown in Figure IX– 5. At the lower levels you are accountable only to yourself, your own life, and your results. As you grow in your career, you become accountable for the results of the team you lead. Then, as you mature as a leader, you become accountable for the results of your team of peers, then for the entire business. However, the final level of accountability – to a supra-organizational ideal, standard, or purpose – is rare. The model proposes that to progress from **manager to leader to transformational leader**, the leader must grow their accountability.

Growing your accountability isn't easy. It is all too common for bad leaders to blame their bad results on circumstances or on others. In this worst case, they don't even get on the pyramid, to be **accountable for themselves**, much like a teenager who isn't yet accountable for their room, grades, or choices. In business, there are some leaders who let the buck bounce off them rather than the buck "stopping here." These types of leaders take credit for the good stuff and make sure others take blame for bad stuff; this is what I call "anti-accountability." As a thought experiment, picture

---

[99] See "Accountability – the difference between management and leadership" at https://paulgibbons.net/accountability-difference-management-leadership.

The Leadership Accountability Model (Gibbons, 2001)

Diagram IX-5: Declaring yourself accountable for a transcendent purpose is a source of power.

a corporate or political leader who blames everyone around them – their staff, the competition, the market, or China.

As managers grow, they progressively take ownership of their followers' results, seeing their followers' failures as a function principally of their lack of effectiveness. If you blame crappy followers, guess whose job it was to develop and get the best from them! Good managers are accountable for what happens in teams they manage, but it is at the next, higher level of accountability where position power matters much less and leadership really begins.

In school, we don't normally see ourselves as accountable for everyone else's homework or exam results. (Imagine a teenager saying, "I see you are struggling, but with my support, I think you can get an 'A.'") But at the next level of accountability, this is what is required. Everywhere in business, the individualistic mindset, inherited no doubt from our educational experience, persists.

On **high-functioning teams**, each team member is accountable for the other team members' results. Sports teams are a good functional example of this. But in business, the story is more typically: "my group is producing, but I wish the others would sort themselves out." Or worse, the "team" members actually compete with one another for resources and sometimes (absurdly) foil each other's plans. Rather than a culture in which team members support and challenge one another to deliver excellence, they embrace the absurd "stay in your lane" mentality which suggests collaboration is unwanted.

How can leaders take accountability for a whole organization? The best of them do, irrespective of their position in the pecking order. I recall a 25-year-old at PwC whose vision was to turn that behemoth company into a force for good in the area of sustainability 25 years ago. His sense of purpose got him on the chairman's radar. Pause for a second. How many 20-somethings at JP Morgan have the ear of Jamie Dimon and talk to him about JP Morgan's role in the world? This young man did that at PwC and birthed a bevy of firmwide initiatives sponsored by the chairman. (The now not-so-young man, called the Honorable James Shaw, is now the co-leader of the New Zealand Green Party and is a cabinet minister.)

At the highest level of accountability, leaders declare themselves accountable for an abstract ideal: democracy, freedom, equality, goodness, or peace. Charismatic preachers do this – they aren't preaching about themselves or even the country, but something larger. How can you do that as a business leader (or school or community leader?) You begin by saying it, then by living it, then by enrolling others in your vision.

When Gandhi began to stand for the **freedom** of India, he had none of the traditional sources of power such as wealth or political influence. Martin Luther King Jr. stood for **equality** as a Black man in a part of the United States where Black people were legally and culturally treated as second-class citizens. Both men stood for something far beyond their reach and far beyond their political power, yet their **taking a stand for something greater than**

Figure IX-6: Would these leaders have been as powerful if they had "played smaller" - by taking on big things, they made themselves bigger.

themselves became a source of their power. See other examples of this phenomenon in Figure IX-6.

Consider, via a thought experiment, other great political and spiritual leaders. Many of these leaders seem to have powerful ideological or ethical stances that most organizational leadership models do not capture. Exemplary leaders, as in the accountability model, seem to stand for ideals and ideas – e.g., Tony Blair for "third-way" politics, Ronald Reagan for small government, Elon Musk for an interplanetary civilization, Greta Thunberg for a carbon-free future, Paul Polman of Unilever for sustainability, Malala Yousafzai for human rights, and Martin Luther King Jr. and Nelson Mandela for human dignity and racial equality. (Even despotic leadership, with misshapen ideals, may harness purpose to effect – for instance, the notion of *Das Tausendjähriges Reich* galvanized a people to horrific effect.)

Again, it is leaders standing for something greater than themselves that **provides power and mobilization.** Thunberg, improbably, is a 17-year-old student "on the spectrum." All of these leaders, as she did, began with a very small reach, but "spiritual accountability" to higher purposes propelled their influence and eventual greatness. Ask yourself whether Thunberg standing for something less visionary would have propelled her so quickly into a global role – an inspiration to her generation and to ours. Would SpaceX be inspirational if Musk were committed to putting a few satellites in orbit and making fat stacks by doing so?

For our purposes, accountability reveals the **power of purpose** – followers respond to leaders who take accountable stances. The bigger the leader's stance, the more power they have to effect change.

Can businesses really put this to use? Would it be weird if a corporate leader started talking about peace? Many of the above examples are from politics, but this insight can be used in business if done so carefully. Generally, most businesses are far too short-sighted and "secular" in the purposes they choose – not nearly ambitious or visionary enough.

There is a debate among purpose authors. Some believe corporate purpose (on which much more in Volume II) should be as abstract as possible, as in "improving the welfare of humankind." I think, differently, that business should link their bold purpose statements to their corporate strategy. Nike and Starbucks get their statements of purpose right, balancing abstraction and inspiration with the concrete day-to-day of their business:

Nike: To bring inspiration and innovation to every athlete*
in the world. (*If you have a body, you are an athlete.)

Starbucks: To inspire and nurture the human spirit – one
person, one cup and one neighborhood at a time.

We have seen that **self-awareness** and **inner work** paired with **accountability** for something greater than the individual are powerful leadership phenomena. One further spiritual idea that couples leadership with purpose is the idea of **servant leadership.**

Purpose and the Will to Serve

*"I slept and I dreamed that life is all joy. I woke and I saw
that life is all service. I served and I saw that service is joy."*

KHALIL GIBRAN

One of the most enduring ideas on spirituality and leadership dates back to 1970: **servant-leadership**. This concept's originator, Robert Greenleaf, got his inspiration from Swiss novelist, Hermann Hesse, whose timeless fictions, such as *Siddhartha*, explore spirituality and our search for authenticity and meaning. Thus inspired by Eastern spirituality, servant leadership proposes "serving others—including employees, customers and community—as the number one priority ... [it] also emphasizes a holistic approach to work, promoting a sense of community, and the sharing of power in decision making."[100] In a world where the half-life of management fads is measured in months, we rarely see a fifty-year-old business idea that is still as widely accepted and used.

Servant leadership prompts us to overcome our dysfunctional psychological impulses to attempt to control and dominate. Instinctively, humans may try to control the environment to make certain the uncertain and ease anxieties about the future, and they may try to control relationships through domination to protect from their messiness and the pain they can cause. The **Will to Control** is a neurobiological impulse rooted in fight or flight responses from the limbic system. To transcend those impulses requires higher cognitive faculties to "own" their vulnerability and uncertainty and realize when instinctual responses are unhelpful.

Leaders can create structures, rules, and hierarchies as an expression of this Will to Control.[101] **The Will to Serve** operates

---

[100] From www.greenleaf.org

[101] This sounds like Nietzsche and the inspiration did come from him, but his Will to Power is misunderstood – it is not a desire to dominate but rather a desire for self-improvement and self-overcoming – much healthier.

Will to Control versus Will to Serve

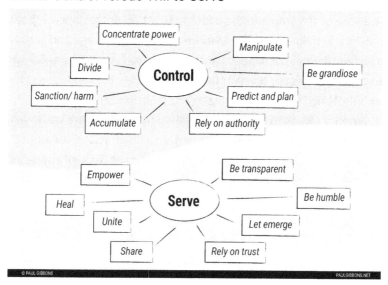

Figure IX – 7: The Will to Control versus the Will to Serve
(Based loosely on the philosophy of Friedrich Nietzsche.)

oppositely, as table IX – 7 illustrates.

Again, as a thought experiment, try the Will to Serve model on for size – can you visualize corporate and political leaders whose tendencies might fit into either category? Most lists of servant leaders select the usual suspects: Mother Theresa, Martin Luther King, and Albert Schweitzer. We need more role models in the corporate sector – unless you think servant leadership should be confined to politics and religion. Examples sometimes offered are Herb Kelleher of Southwest Airlines, Warren Buffett of Berkshire Hathaway, President Jimmy Carter of the Carter Center, Angelina Jolie in her work on behalf of refugees, Paul Polman of Unilever, and Peter Diamandis of X-Prize fame.

However, we really do not want to restrict our concept of servant leadership to just the biggest business names; the idea should infuse leadership behavior down to the captain of the high school tennis team, community leaders, and entry-level business leaders when first charged with leading a team. Abandoning the need to control (in order to feel more emotionally secure) takes sufficient self-awareness to be aware of the trap and the courage to let go of that need – great maturity. Yet while we'd like insecurity to wane with age and accomplishment, it does not happen inevitably. I've worked with many C-level execs who at deeper levels retain some of their teenage insecurity – about fitting in, being recognized, or being "found out."

When it comes to leading and scaling purpose, where we began, accountability gives followers something inspirational to aim at – noble ends. The Will to Serve provides the means. To lead and scale purpose, both are required.

SCALING GOODNESS – MAKING A BIGGER DIFFERENCE

"One of the criticisms I've faced over the years is that I'm not aggressive enough or assertive enough, or maybe somehow, because I'm empathetic, I'm weak. I totally rebel against that. I refuse to believe that you cannot be both compassionate and strong."
PRIME MINISTER JACINDA ARDERN

Part of what business allows us to do is make a bigger difference than we could make alone and to use the scale of business to create more value for more people. With business, we can take on and conquer greater challenges to grow the grandness of the world, and with that ability to have impact comes the potential to do more good.

If goodness is a spiritual thing, and as we've defined it, it surely must be, then scaling goodness must be among the noblest purposes of business.

In a pluralistic world where notions of what constitutes goodness fiercely diverge, and in which (notwithstanding ideology) people have multiple real-life perspectives (worker, union leader, manager, executive, shareholder, activist,) we have a tinder box for conflict. Most happy-clappy writing on business talks about the culture or purpose of a company the same way people talk about "Western culture," or "Walmart's culture," **as if culture and purpose were homogenous**. This view, ridiculously, presumes an untroublesome alignment of interests and values between stakeholders.

Even in a simpler time, it was difficult enough to align a team of engineers from Tulsa dressed in identically pressed khakis and golf shirts around a shared conception of goodness (perhaps as in Figure IX – 8). Leaders today operate in more complex systems with social diversity (thankfully) and multiple stakeholders: partnerships, suppliers, regulators, communities, JVs, activists, and different regional cultures. Hydraulic fracturing or the operation of water and power utilities are two classic examples where stakeholders have different ideologies and perspectives and, from a leader's point of view, power to torpedo their ambitions.

Figure IX – 8: Aligning workers was difficult enough when teams were homogenous rows of male engineers in white shirts with pocket protectors.

To lead in this pluralistic world, the leader must **integrate** values, stakeholders, and communities in those **complex systems** and get them to make nice. Those thorny problems are sometimes called "wicked messes": problems with deep technical and social complexity. I recommend the writings of Adam Kahane, *Solving Tough Problems*, for the best practical tools in leading in complex systems. There is an entire section on leading in complex systems in *The Science of Organizational Change*[102].

So, how can a leader successfully navigate "wicked" organizational "messes" as described above? Our job here is to offer one more set of insights and a tool. The next model, Spiral Dynamics, shown in the Diagram IX-9, is an abstract model of leadership that helps leaders work with such diverse values and needs and is of extreme practical value.

While there is no magic bullet for understanding values diversity, Spiral Dynamics has a useful take on the subject. Each of the model's levels represents a system of values that, as humans started evolving about ten thousand years ago, helped them adapt to changing life conditions. As conditions became more complex through the ages, different values and **leadership styles, organizational or otherwise,** became better suited for society's prosperity and survival. The key point is that these different worldviews were effective in moving humanity forward at the time they dominated. When we talked about proto religions (pantheism, polytheism, shamanism), we saw they were unifying forces that allowed communities to form deeper bonds. We were, in Spiral Dynamics terms, describing "purple" – the Magical Animistic level. When we talked about the pre-modern, pre-Enlightenment era, Truth and authority were vested in Scripture, the Church, and the Monarchy – the "blue" Purposeful-Authoritarian level. The center of gravity in today's world is spread between "Green" and "Orange" – sort of, very roughly, between modernism and postmodernism.

---

[102] There is a fascinating ethical leadership challenge in the book Defining Moments: When Managers Must Choose Between Right and Right, where a pharmaceutical CEO had several governments, several activist groups, differences within his own board, and technical challenges with the release of a new drug to surmount.

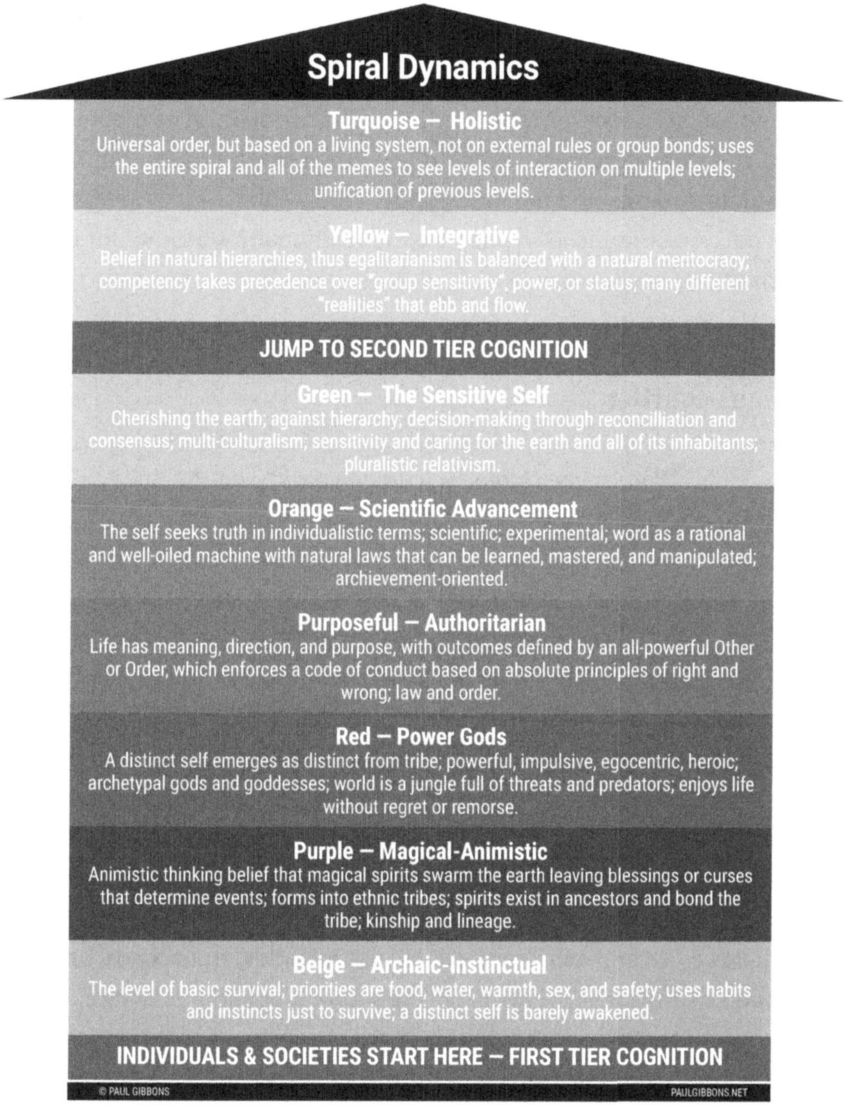

Figure IX-9 Spiral Dynamics has been used successfully in business and on wicked social programs for three decades.

Look closely at the table and map it to your understanding of human cultural evolution, from hunter-gatherers, to tribes, to warlords, to kingdoms, to religion, to capitalism and the industrial revolution, to the green revolution. Think also about which leaders today are representative of each of those tiers. (Let me help. Kim Jung-un – Red. Where would you put Jacinda Ardern, Nelson Mandela, Charles and David Koch, Ayatollah Khomeini, Elon Musk, Bill Gates, Marianne Williamson, or Jane Goodall? Which might be second-tier in your view?)

Values conflict

> *"Values are things we can only fight about."*
> ISAIAH BERLIN – PHILOSOPHER, SOCIAL THEORIST

Is Berlin (above) right, or can "evolved" leaders do better? The bottom six "first-tier" levels may mistrust and actively "war" with each other. Consider today's culture wars between traditionalists (blue), capitalism and science (orange), and egalitarian environmentalists (green). The model captures some of the tensions we see in multi-stakeholder systems between, say, indigenous value systems (purple) and industrial society and between, for example, fundamentalist strains such as Sharia law (blue) and European modernity (orange).

Leadership in complex systems, claims the Spiral Dynamics model, requires a "second-tier" perspective that **includes, transcends, and respects** earlier levels. Leading in the second tier requires a systemic perspective that **uses the valuable aspects of the earlier tiers and facilitates collaboration and integration of perspectives to deal with today's complexity**. Science has its place, as do free enterprise, social justice, the Rule of Law, egalitarianism, tribe and tradition, environmentalism, and individual drive and ego. When those worldviews can collide, we can get a hot mess. But second-tier leadership can effect change by finding common purpose in diverse groups.

An example of second-tier leadership would be if a natural resources company sat down with indigenous communities (Purple), environmentalists (Green), governments (Blue and Orange), and geologists (Orange) to hammer out a solution where all might prosper and without one side resorting to force or coercion.

Again, spiritual leadership should want to scale goodness, and we will not achieve all of spiritual leadership's benefits unless we engage people and take them with us. Consider climate change. It is no longer only a scientific problem but also an ideological, political, and behavioral one. Just how does one change the behavior of 7 billion people and adapt their institutions appropriately? A first-tier leader might see climate change as a science problem, or as a legal-regulation problem, or as an ecology problem, or in terms of its unequal human costs, or as a threat to their position. So scientists yell, "look at the science!" and ecologists yell, "look at the biosphere!" and industrialists yell, "our business needs energy and natural resources!" And after all that yelling, not much happens.

The world isn't about to get any simpler, so we need tools that help us harness the power of diversity, even the sort of diversity that at first seems intractable.

This is the biggest spiritual challenge of our time
– our world is irreversibly connected economically,
informationally, and geographically. All our systems are
also connected to the biosphere. However, the world is not
connected ideologically or culturally. That is a shear point,
a "clash of civilizations" as it has been put.

Spiral Dynamics is a practical way of understanding and empathizing with ideological difference. [103] It may seem abstract, but it has been used all over the world to help tackle complex social problems where

---

[103] There are now so many resources on Spiral Dynamics and different takes than mine. For further reading on business and Spiral Dynamics, try *Reinventing Organizations*, by Frederic Laloux.

stakeholder groups view the world in wildly different ways and have different objectives along with different understandings of the same problems. My consulting firm began to use Spiral Dynamics with clients to help them with thorny stakeholder issues, and we used it on ourselves (so to speak) twenty years ago. Mostly our work was with "extractive" industries like oil and mining because when they wade ungracefully into communities, huge political problems ensue. In the US for example, there are constant tensions between native communities, corporations, and environmentalists, over fracking, the Keystone Pipeline, and Arctic National Wildlife Refuge. When inter-stakeholder dialog is absent, such things become political footballs as different governments force through their view. Then they lose power and another forces through its view. From the corporation's (purely commercial) point of view, that creates an unstable and financially risky environment for eleven- and twelve-figure investments.

Scaling goodness, making a bigger difference, and using the power of large organizational structures to do more good requires this ability to manage different interests and engage external and varied communities – something that (mostly) business is terrible at.

LEADING CONNECTION – COMMUNITY AND ECOSYSTEMS

"Power corresponds with the human ability not just to act, but to act together."
HANNAH ARENDT

As you'll recall, our definition of spirituality includes connectedness. What does it mean to lead and scale connection? We have seen one example of this as we explored connecting people with **deeper purpose**. There are two other important examples to note, **one social and one systemic**. By social, we mean connecting people in community, a much deeper network of connections than just a group. By systemic, we mean the connectedness suggested by complexity theory and ecosystems, including business ecosystems. So how does a leader lead social and systems connectedness?

Creating community

"Humility isn't thinking less of yourself; it's about thinking of yourself less."
CS LEWIS

If we leave aside metaphysical explanations, there is something religion functionally provides perhaps better than any other institution — **community**. Religion's efficacy in building community may correlate with its ability to improve mental (and physical) health as we saw in Chapter VII. Community meets our interest in spirituality because it creates a sense of connectedness, a feeling of being part of a larger whole. Part of leading spiritually is creating a context in which communities emerge spontaneously and where groups and teams become operationally community-like.

We can start, ironically, with a quote from Brian Greene, an atheist, physicist, and mathematician who nevertheless realizes how religion delivers a profound sense of community:

"There are many others who recognize that the value of religion is found in its capacity to provide a sense of community, to allow us to see our lives within a larger context, to connect us through ritual to our forebears, to alleviate anxiety in the face of mortality, among other thoroughly subjective benefits. When I'm looking to understand myself as a human, and how I fit in to the long chain of human culture that reaches back thousands of years, religion is a deeply valuable part of that story."

Despite its ubiquity, the word "community" is often used loosely and badly, sometimes by realtors to mean that a neighborhood has a special closeness and vibe but in fact merely consists of a bunch of identical houses whose residents never talk to each other. People use the word "community" in place of "group" or even talk about their entire organization as a community despite its lack of connectedness. In organizational leadership and learning circles, the term "community" should embody much deeper meaning than it currently does, but even people who should know better continue to use it to describe loosely associated groups.

A better definition of workplace community (admittedly my own) is:

> "... a group who shares a common purpose and
> passion, one that intentionally creates connections
> that promote learning and growth, and one that
> intentionally builds trust and deeper relationships
> while empowering the individuals within."

We want to build that community as leaders because "relationships" matter, and communities nurture those. The Harvard Health Study that began studying teenagers in the 1930s who are now approaching 100 found that participants' **quality of relationships** and **social ties** were consistently among the most **significant predictors of their well-being, health, and longevity**. "The benefit of friends, family, and even colleagues turns out to be just as good for long-term survival as giving up a 15-cigarette-a-day smoking habit!!"[104]

> Building community is therefore a principal way that
> leaders nurture followers and their wellness.

---

[104] Harmon, Katherine, Scientific American, "Social Ties Boost Survival by 50 Percent," July, 28 2010

Workplaces should be a vital source of community. They are already so, but only in a loose, accidental sense of the word and **not by design**, and therefore **insufficiently so.** The right question might not be whether organizations intentionally create community, but rather whether they unintentionally destroy it.

Workplaces, sadly, are going in the opposite direction and have become **less** community-like for a variety of reasons including virtual working, the gig economy, faster career changes, pressure on productivity, and internal competition for reward. An effect of this is that we no longer make as many close friends at work. Research on how much we socialize or vacation with colleagues proves that workplace socialization is declining. In 1985, almost 50% of Americans reported that they had a close friend at work. Three decades later, this proportion dropped to 30%.[105] Prominent Harvard scholar Robert Putnam said in *Bowling Alone: America's Declining Social Capital* that "Americans are right that the bonds of our communities have withered, and we are right to fear that this transformation has very real costs." [106]

As someone who has run conferences, strategy sessions, offsites, training programs, and other corporate events for many decades, I have been astonished (and a little disappointed) that after-event feedback **always** includes "spending time with colleagues" as one of the events' most-valued aspects. People like to hang out together and bond. However, note again that social interaction is usually an **unintentional benefit** of events like these – workplaces could do much more to **design community intentionally**, and not just as an unintended benefit of throwing people in a room together. It seems to me that Google gets this right. When I gave a talk there recently, it felt different. I cannot speak to worker experience, but the place had fun places to work collaboratively, attractive spaces to hang

---

[105] See Friends at Work? Not So Much, by Adam Grant, *The New York Times*, Sept. 4, 2015, for a longer, thoughtful treatment of this subject.

[106] Putnam, Robert D. "Bowling Alone: America's Declining Social Capital." Journal of Democracy, vol. 6 no. 1, 1995, p. 65-78.

out, and (of course) technology-enabled knowledge sharing. These seemed to enable a greater sense of camaraderie than I've seen in other organizations.

There are some very practical strategies that companies can undertake to intentionally build community. At PwC in the mid-1990s, we founded a learning community using a weird hippie tech called the internet. "The Kraken" shared knowledge and best practice but was entirely peer-to-peer (in the way many systems such as Slack operate today.) The ethos of that community, its dedication to learning and personal excellence, was unlike anything I've felt since. Other companies have created onboarding programs, used enterprise social networks, encouraged "water cooler" interactions (by making the water cooler cooler), made more time for company recreation, designed office spaces with community in mind, and initiated more town-hall style communications.

When it comes to building community, we find that leadership behaviors make the biggest difference, bigger than the structural stuff from Google and PwC. An MIT study published in 2019 listed 27 pro-community leadership behaviors in the domains of trust, purpose, and "energy" generation. Those included taking time to explain what work means (the "why"), showing appreciation for others, generously offering their time to others, managing conflict synergistically, and maximizing diverse involvement in discussions.[107] Thus we have a link between scaling meaning and building community because shared meaning just won't happen in loosely connected groups, especially if those connections happened accidentally.

Leading connectedness, though, isn't just about social connectedness and community – part of the leader's role in connection is systemic. Though that sounds abstract, when the media ask me

---

[107] Cross, R., et al, "A Noble Purpose Alone Won't Transform Your Company", Sloan Management Review, December 2019

their stock question, "what one thing would you teach leaders if you could teach nothing else?" systems thinking and the complexity ideas that follow always come to mind.

Leading systems

When it comes to connectedness, we can say "everything is connected," but that statement can be profoundly meaningful or profoundly trivial depending on the context. As a thought experiment, consider that argon is an inert gas in the air we breathe, and it is statistically probable that you have breathed an atom of argon that Jesus or Socrates breathed. That same argon was made inside a star more than 5 billion years ago – so yes, the world is profoundly connected. Moreover, the **feeling** of being connected to everything is profound and can deeply influence your worldview, your relationship to others, and your views of and relationship to the universe.[108]

We also see evidence of connectedness in historical events. The COVID-19 crisis of 2020 showed us the interdependence of human systems – how the transportation, political, economic, hospital, public health, pharmaceutical, treasury, and public health systems affect outcomes such as our health, wealth, and much more. These systems causally affect each other, and those respective outcomes feedback on each other. "Leading goodness" in such a Gordian knot of cause and effect takes a more advanced kind of thinking – systems thinking – that allows seeing and acting **holistically, globally, creatively, and wisely**.

What does systems thinking have to do with our interest in spiritual leadership? If we value **spiritual outcomes** (our conceptions of purpose and goodness) in complex systems such as the organizations and ecosystems in which we operate, we need the wisdom

---

[108] In other books, I have lengthy treatments of systems thinking, holistic thinking, creative thinking, and critical thinking.

that systems thinking affords. Ethical disasters such as the Deepwater Horizon, the Wall Street crisis of 2008, and leadership failures during 2020's pandemic arose from leaders' failure to consider ethics and an abandonment of systems thinking. More simply, that means that key actors simply failed to think through the unintended consequences or multiplicative effects of their decisions.

When we act small-mindedly without considering our effect on systems, we create sometimes grave unintended consequences, for instance as we fix symptoms while worsening underlying problems or even creating new ones. Taking strong pain medicine for your back gets you through the day but can get in the way of long-term solutions (such as yoga) and might get you addicted. Quick-fix management solutions offered by consultants rarely consider long-term effects or unintended consequences.

Narrow thinking (linear, mono-causal, and "small picture") allows businesses to disregard communities and the environment. It allows consumers to fill shopping carts with thirty single-use plastic bags and disregard their carbon footprint when choosing a car, a home, or a holiday. It creates win-lose dialogues between couples, families, communities, businesses, and nations. Such zero-sum dialogues are the cause of considerable suffering.

The move toward systems thinking is sometimes called a paradigm shift, from **egosystem** to **ecosystem**[109] leadership as illustrated in Figure IX – 10.

The diagram explains the organizational imperatives for today's businesses. They aim at networked, open-source, partnership innovation structures; the embrace ideas such as sustainability and the circular economy; they take a global perspective but are sensitive to local conditions; they use dialog and an agile, adaptive mindset to innovate and lead change.

---

[109] Although the table and any errors are mine, the term was introduced by Otto Scharmer of MIT who is also known for "theory-U," an approach to change that arguably has spiritual principles embedded.

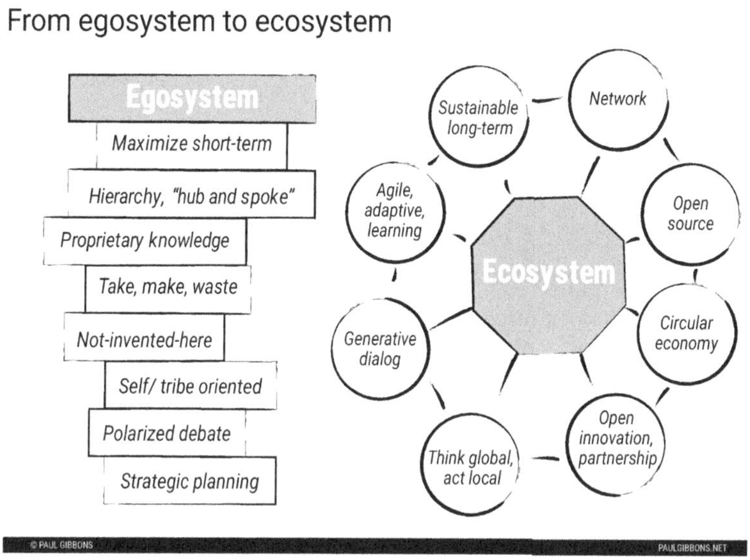

From egosystem to ecosystem

Figure IX-10: Leadership is about thinking in wholes and about self-transcendence (Model based roughly on the moral psychology of Lawrence Kohlberg.)

Leaders need to lead the interconnectedness that is a physical property of our world. That is, the non-linearity, virality, long chains of causality, feedback loops, and unintended consequences. We talked about the spiritual attitude "everything is connected." That can sound very woo, but that attitude, when it drives thinking about the world and how to be effective in it is powerful in terms of hard results.

The key point in leading interconnectedness is one of integration. We want our very human ability to reason in complex systems and our highest rational faculties **integrated** with our sense of purpose and our highest values and principles. Reason and spirituality, as Pope John Paul II put it, should not be distinct and disconnected. *Fides et ratio,* faith **and** reason, need to work in concert: faith without reason is superstition, and reason without faith is unguided. We have talked a lot in this book about the *fides*, we also need some good *ratio*. Systems thinking allows us to realize our values and noblest ambitions – to lead the connectedness that leaders in our century require.

CONCLUSION

We began this chapter with words of caution. There are likely 100 varieties of "X"-leaderships already, so we have to ask ourselves whether spiritual leadership is distinctive and to what extent it adds value to existing leadership theories. Our second caution was in wondering whether **spirituality is necessary for leadership generally**, or whether it depends on the context. We'd all, I imagine, prefer to work for someone who is spiritually inclined (by our definition), who prefers the will to serve over the will to control, who thinks in ecosystems, and who leads at the higher reaches of the Leadership Development Framework. Those are, I believe, our highest intentions and do the most good for businesses and the planet. While a good case might be made that business CEOs of today can increasingly lean in that direction, voters of the world have different ideas exposing a puzzling gap between, in my view, our highest intentions when we think about the desirable traits of leaders and the leaders we actually choose. I feel this tension in myself, wanting leaders with humanistic values, but also those that can kick some ass. Was Jimmy Carter, perhaps the most spiritual US president in the 20th century, too "soft" to effectively operate in a political culture where deceit, manipulations, and ass-kicking are the norm – perhaps even required?

If rising interest in "business meets spirituality" means business leaders focus more on inner work and ethical norms, rather than purely material and monetary ones, the consequences could be far-reaching. Business is sewn through the fabric of human existence, providing us with livelihoods and (when well run) an essential source of meaning, joy, and purpose. I do not think its importance as an ethical actor can be understated – that is to say, its ethics affect individual lives and the future of humanity.

As businesses make up a vast portion of our life on earth, to make life better – more spiritual or at least more just – we need to think of improving our work and leadership spiritually. Even if readers still reject the term "spiritual," business needs to embrace the definition's meaning – what we propose in this book – if businesses are to maximize their potential to do good in the world.

LEADERSHIP EPILOGUE: CREATING "SPIRITUAL" LEADERSHIP PROGRAMS IN GLOBAL-100 COMPANIES

"Better leaders for better businesses for a better world"
(FUTURE CONSIDERATIONS' MISSION CIRCA 2003)

Starting in the 1990s, I began to wonder whether these ideas on leadership could be put to good use in leadership development work with the world's biggest companies. I wanted to empower business and political leaders to see beyond the urgent and who, when they say "the next quarter," sometimes mean the next quarter-century. We need to build more cathedrals – monuments that will dignify our age – and that will require a level of vision and foresight lacking from all but a very few leaders.

In 2001, I founded a firm Future Considerations. Our mission was "better leaders, for better businesses, for a better world." Our leadership and change methodologies came from deep within the personal growth and spiritual development traditions, but our aim was to help businesses become more sustainable. At the time, business sustainability, although much discussed, was light-years from a boardroom priority.

We were shooting at both levels of workplace spirituality, the personal **and** the organizational. We would do the inner work with leaders to produce outer results of value to the world. We were not the only consulting firm advising on sustainability, business and human rights, corporate social responsibility, and carbon neutrality, nor were we the only one who did transformational leadership development. What was novel in 2001 was that we sought to do both, to bring those progressive forces together—that is, uniting the worlds of leadership development, organizational development, organizational change, and sustainability to produce organizations fit for the 21st century.

Our mission to create the "next generation" of business leaders was based around the premise, widely accepted now, that leadership development and personal development are sides of a coin—leadership development requires deep personal development. We used mindfulness meditation in all our programs, although we kept that quiet at the proposal stage! (Mindfulness was considered pretty "woo" two decades ago.) "Under the hood" were developmental models such as the ones above, and systems models also from the integral stable. Part of our methodology was also from the embodiment (somatics) stable. This was risky because even now the jargon associated with these ideas makes then seem obscure and not just a little "out there." (If you aren't a leadership development person already familiar with such ideas, the above may seem like a word salad.)

My ambition was to empower people to bring their "whole selves" to work so that they would not feel as if they had to wear a mask or conceal part of themselves in the workplace. This transparency applied also to policies, as we experimented from the get-go with an open-book salary policy and highly participative decision making. As we grew, our sense of purpose grew, and (albeit with growing pains) began to translate that purpose into strategy and eventually into a fully democratic, staff-owned consulting firm[110]. At our firm we felt we could not espouse models, ideas, practices, or policies with clients that we were unwilling to use on ourselves and on occasion that was difficult and painful.

Would companies buy deep personal development work? The

---

[10] We started on this "second-tier" journey in 2001 and in Volume II, I will describe many of the high-highs and low-lows along that path. In 2016, Frédéric Laloux chronicled the attempts of many larger organizations to organize themselves thus in his

leadership development world has thousands of competitors, from big universities, Harvard, Duke, and Oxford, to Big Four consulting firms, to global specialist firms such as the Center for Creative Leadership, to the leadership practices of big headhunters such as Korn Ferry. Then there are hundreds of small firms, and then thousands of individual coaches with their own practices. How was our tiddler start-up to compete?

Companies bought. The methodologies and models described above became differentiators – suggesting to me that even two decades ago, there was a tremendous hunger for purpose, meaning, and goodness in the world's most admired companies.

In the mid-2000s, clients were the world's biggest non-Chinese bank (HSBC), the fourth biggest consumer goods company (Unilever), the second and fourth biggest professional services firms (PwC and KPMG), the fifth and seventh biggest oil companies (BP and Shell), and the seventh biggest mining firm (Anglo-American.) After I left the firm, Phillips, Bayer, Zappos, and Microsoft became clients. For a firm started just a few years prior in my living room, this was exciting stuff.

Our signature program of that era was to take high-potential bankers from HSBC and take them on a seven-month personal development journey that included fieldwork in the world's most needy areas, for example, rural India or indigenous communities in Brazil. This raised the bankers' consciousness of global issues such as deforestation and poverty and gave them a sense of gratitude not often found in the boardrooms of the world's then-largest bank. They used their finance, leadership, and strategy skills on development problems. We gave them tools such as mindfulness, creative problem-solving, leading multi-country teams, cross-cultural leadership, and multi-stakeholder dialogue that they could take back and use in the business upon return from the field. The work was recognized in both HBR and the Financial Times. Said the bank's Chairman, Stephen Green, "These high-ROI innovations mean the program pays for itself many times over. The elegance of its design means that strong financial returns, talent development, and the creation of social value coexist. The mutual reinforcement and harmony between these goals is precisely the bank's ambition — for frequently these are seen as tradeoffs: do-good or make money, drive efficiency or develop people."

In another program of that era, we ran a development program for investment bankers specifically aimed at increasing sales, revenue per partner, and number of landmark deals. The goal was for them to go toe-to-toe in the market versus Goldman Sachs, and my old employer Crédit Suisse. The partners worked on presence, gravitas, leading with values, creating and sharing vision, and having greater "impact" with clients (challenging them harder.) Over two years revenue doubled, and they went from the lowest revenue per partner in the firm to the highest.

Our programs "worked" for individuals in our programs, that is, to the benefit of the participants as well as their firms. Yes, some of our participants decided to "follow their bliss" elsewhere—they self-actualized their way out the door. Some clients found the deeper personal work threatening and rejected it out of hand (talking about emotions, vision, and values was not sufficiently business-like). Of those that stuck around, many prospered. One client went from running a tiny part of a business (a few hundred staff) to running the whole 20,000-person organization in just a few years.

In summary, very "soft" leadership development programs produced very hard results for clients. The inner work produced outer results – as we had hoped.

Post-script/ spoiler

However, lets this sound like a story of unqualified success and a "humble brag," there is a darker side to this tale. In Volume II (*Culture, Sustainability, Capitalism,*) when we discuss values and values conflict, I describe how our little firm nearly self-immolated because of "spiritual conflict" which may trace back to my idealistic notion of "bringing your whole self to work."

CHAPTER 10

Love in the Time of Covid: A Spiritual Case Study

Covered in this chapter:

Collaboration and Connectedness

Systems, Causality, and Blame

Connecting Science and Spirituality

Compassion and Altruism

Change, Innovation, and Learning

Global Community

LOVE IN THE TIME OF COVID: A SPIRITUAL CASE STUDY

"When it is dark enough, you can see the stars."
RALPH WALDO EMERSON

As this book landed at the end of 2020, the world was in the midst of a once-in-a-century health and economic crisis that was a paradigmatic case for the abstract VUCA (Volatile, Uncertain, Complex, and Ambiguous) [111] notion. Within the first 90 days of the COVID-19 pandemic, a "butterfly flapping its wings" in a place nobody could find on a map had upended the lives of 7.4 billion people. In February 2020, the US crashed out of what economists call the eleven-year "Obama boom," the longest economic expansion in post-war history and a near-tripling of the Dow Jones kicked off by the Recovery Act of 2009. When the party ended, unemployment claims increased **33-fold** to 6.6 million. Air travel dropped from about 4 billion passengers a year to merely a few percent of that. The trillion-dollar events industry was shut down. The billion-dollar corporate conferences industry likewise. Staycations, the norm in summer 2020, crippled economies that depend on tourism.

Lest the economist in me get carried away, the loss of lives to Coronavirus was worse than its economic impacts. COVID-19 killed

---

[111] A common term in consultant-land that was coined by the US military. See *The Science of Organizational Change* for a long treatment of VUCA and leadership.

just over a million people in 2020, and treatment protocols for the very ill required complete isolation. Most families were unable to visit their dying loved ones during the last weeks of their lives with nurses holding up phones so patients could hear their families' goodbyes – a cruel twist of the knife into society's already gaping wounds.

We, because of the internet, travel, and globalization are more connected than before: local becomes global, and global quickly becomes local. Now, "thanks" to COVID-19, we see luridly how events on the other side of the world can affect our lives, and that our connectedness came with a cost. That cost arose principally because government and public health authorities are **less connected** than other systems, lacking the systemic mindset described in this book, the foresight, and institutions for a global response.

It is said that adversity tests the "mettle of a man," but it also tests the mettle of a civilization. The adversities of 2020 put humankind to the test – would wise heads prevail? From our point of view, would that wisdom include **spiritual values and principles** we have explored in this book? Has Coronavirus brought out the best in us? Has it made us more human? Has it provided insight into our highest values? Has it strengthened our institutions? Has it driven us to compete or collaborate? Have we found ways to remain compassionate even when we are most afraid? Have we embraced or shunned one another? Did we stay connected, or retreat behind walls? Did we permanently adapt, or yearn to rush back to how things were? Did we strengthen the global community, or let it fall asunder?

We saw that spirituality in its myriad forms helped bind small communities and even nation-states. Could it, in the 21st-century, promote a sense of global community and unite rather than divide us as it now does? (Or, are diverse conceptions of spirituality, as with religion in the 20th century, solely a source of division and strife?)

In this conclusion, I'd like to visit those questions and some of the themes found in this book to see perhaps whether Tolkien was right that, "Courage is found in unlikely places." As you read, consider our definition of spirituality, "meaning, purpose, goodness, and connectedness" and consider also, as suggested in Chapter III, whether we, as a world and individually, lived our highest values and grew spiritually during this time.

COLLABORATION AND CONNECTEDNESS

"Remember your humanity, forget the rest..."
BERTRAND RUSSELL, 20TH-CENTURY PHILOSOPHER

Collaboration separates us from the rest of the animal kingdom — it is humanity's superpower. To quote Yuval Harari, "A coronavirus in China and a coronavirus in the US cannot swap tips about how to infect us more effectively." But humans did exactly that. What a doctor in Seoul discovered in the morning saved French lives in the afternoon.

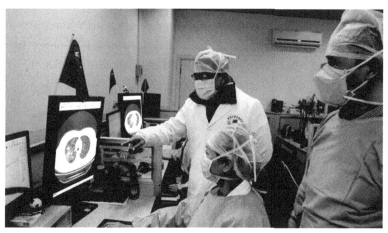

Figure X-1: COVID has ushered in an unprecedented level of scientific collaboration while political collaboration was scarcer.

In contrast to the political sphere, the pandemic saw global scientific collaboration as never before. Within two weeks of the WHO sounding the alarm, China had shared the SARS-CoV-2 sequence with the rest of the world. Treatment protocols were as quickly tested and shared, scientific research exchanged without paywalls, raw data published to help others' research, drug candidates moved quickly into human trials, and vaccine development has never been faster.

In an instant, most of us became used to mask-wearing, isolation, and social distancing. Those are collaborative behaviors by the billions that **protect the herd** more than they protect us individually. (In the absence of herd immunity, masks and social distancing are a good proxy.)

This rising above self and tribe is another human virtue; compassion and empathy are the superpowers that enable collaboration and community. We saw how this arose through cultural selection – **spirituality guided pro-social behaviors** that allowed human communities to prosper. During the pandemic, most individuals rose to the sacrifice and became part of the solution, not part of the problem.

But individual virtue, in a complex world, is not nearly enough. Leaders need to harness individual proclivities to do good and to build institutions and communities to serve that good. Although the individuals who make up society by and large showed collaborative and altruistic behaviors through COVID-19 pandemic (I'd give them a B), world leaders collaborated far less (I'd give them a D-).

Politically speaking, the crisis saw a retreat, not an advance in global thinking and collaboration. Most leaders, some under political pressure at home, told the world to "stay in its lane." Help was not offered, and expert advice usually not well received.

The growth of global institutions post World War II anticipated this hyper-connected future in which we now live. The possibility of global war required global diplomacy and problem solving. Financial interconnectedness required the IMF and World Bank, and the importance of human rights gave us the Universal Declaration of Human Rights, midwifed by Eleanor Roosevelt. From the pandemic's birth, the WHO acted swiftly in announcing the global health threat on January 13th. On the 14th, my family ordered 100 face masks and a gallon of hand sanitizer – but people can react more surefootedly than highly politicized democratic governments. Health experts knew what was afoot but piercing through the denial of many world leaders proved impossible. If this had been the Titanic, some leaders did not react when they saw the iceberg, but waited until they felt the icy waters around their loins.

According to balanced analysis, the WHO "deployed scientific skills, epidemiological expertise, medical know-how, outbreak-response capacities, and global networks in helping fight the disease."[112] However, the WHO also showed it had more fur than fangs in confronting countries about their public health practices and arguably tiptoed around US and Chinese political sensitivities – unwilling to confront the original epicenter or the eventual one. To my mind, this speaks to the need to **strengthen** our ability to fight global problems by **strengthening global institutions** that were birthed with those problems in mind – to make them more effective rather than further defang them. Bizarrely, the US decided to abandon the WHO rather than strengthen it at the very peak of the pandemic – a symbolically puzzling act in the eyes of the world, particularly as their efforts were laudable if not perfect.

If spirituality is partly about our ability to **think big picture and to use our species' superpower, collaboration,** then we still have much to learn about doing that on a global scale. If it is about putting aside self-interest and parochialism in favor of what is good for humanity, leaders got a D minus.

For our future, say there was a problem on which we agree, or a nobler goal, could we move in concert? (Say there was an even more virulent disease, or natural disaster on a new scale, or a nuclear superpower abandoned deterrence for aggression.) Perhaps not yet. Our short-term and nationalistic thinking remain too much of a liability.

---

[112] https://www.thinkglobalhealth.org/article/world-health-organization-and-pandemic-politics

I've playfully graded humanity and its leadership **as a whole** in this conclusion, glossing over the sometimes-huge differences between how countries, communities, and leaders performed. Partly I'd like to give some leaders an F and some an A, but that is the sort of attitude I criticized in the chapter on accountability. If you remember the schoolroom analogy, teenagers are only judged by how **they** did on the test, and no teenager worries about the whole class achieving. But when global problems (or opportunities) rear their head, the whole "team" of global leaders should get a grade - individual grades matter less. If little Johnny in the back row gets an 'F', the whole team suffers. Except that kind of team accountability thinking was nowhere to be found.

KAIROS, LOGOS, PATHOS, AND ETHOS

To the contrary, perhaps excluding the EU *senza* Britain, the world Balkanized. Global leaders didn't say, "The disease in rampant in Brazil but if Brazil and its economy tank, our chance of eradicating the disease and recovering global prosperity are diminished. How can we as a global community help Brazil?" Leaders' attitudes were more like, "Lets make sure we get that PPE from China before those Brazilians get their dirty mitts on it and keep those damn Brazilians out of our country."

The failure of Balkanized thinking applied also within the United States which has an exceptionally long history of according the fifty states great autonomy. This resulted in a patchwork of policies with varying effects. State governors in the US insisted upon their auton-omy (say from mask or lock-down requirements) and sometimes that autonomy cost lives. A patchwork response to the disease made suppression challenging because no matter how effective state or local leaders were, a Louisiana hot spot did not stay in Louisiana for long. There was even brief talk about regional restrictions on travel – proposing that New Yorkers could not travel to Florida, or vice versa when New York flattened the curve and Florida became the hottest hot-spot.

States have considerable autonomy in the US federal system and the culture is fiercely individualistic. The US, famous for its national solidarity in tough times, struggled because of its failure to act swiftly and lack of central coordination of response. This (in part) made the US the world's epicenter with the highest number of cases and among the highest deaths per capita but initially among the lowest testing rates and weakest contact tracing despite its economic resources. The world has a history of looking toward the US for leadership, and historically the US has often provided that. For the US to become the world's sick child during the pandemic rather than lead the world out of it was a new page in modern history.

The interesting question for our age, while perhaps unlikely to be solved in our lifetimes, is whether a connected world requires connected leadership and governance. Is it possible, even in theory? Within the last century, globalization thrust connectedness quickly upon us, and technological innovation accelerated that connectedness during recent decades. But how we think, lead, and govern still lingers in the 19th century, as competing nation-states remain unwilling to seek bigger picture solutions. We have found ways to race ahead technologically while leaving a gap between the connectedness of the world and the disconnectedness of our mindsets and politics. The world continues to suffer from an absence of spiritual wisdom, empathy, holism, compassion, and shared purpose, that would allow us to work together to solve problems. We must continue to ask ourselves the hardest question of all – **what do we owe to fellow humans as citizens of the same planet?**

SYSTEMS, CAUSALITY, AND BLAME

"The world is a complex, interconnected, finite, ecological–
social–psychological–economic system. We treat it
as if it were not, as if it were divisible, separable,
simple, and infinite. Our persistent, intractable
global problems arise directly from this mismatch."
DONELLA MEADOWS, BIOPHYSICIST AND ENVIRONMENTAL SCIENTIST

If I could magically change just one deficit in the way humans think about problems, it would be their notions of monocausality. In complex systems, be they businesses, countries, or the world, there never is a single cause. Think about the statement, "the spark caused the fire." Even in this trivial instance, the fire required oxygen, flammable material, and lack of a fire suppression system. COVID-19's disruption of the world required a virus, vectors, human susceptibility (we weren't immune as with measles), social connectivity, global transportation systems, slow government responses, human denial, inexpertise in dealing with global challenges, the economic pressure to keep economic systems working, inadequate testing, and lack of PPE or effective treatments. To say "X caused the pandemic," (China being the favorite X-culprit) is naïve.

The global system described above was the flammable tinder, lack of a timely response was the oxygen, and the absence of a national and global fire suppression capability disabled us from successfully preventing the spread. From a systems point of view, we want to study cause and effect so we can devise prevention strategies, but that isn't the same as lashing out emotionally with blame. Crises require expert, instant decisions to save lives, whether the "spark" (i.e. patient zero) came from Wuhan, Washington, or Waziristan is a side show. We needed concerted, accountable action followed by rigorous causal and systemic analysis - not scapegoating.

The Buddha said, "if there is an arrow in your heart, don't worry about who shot it. Get the damn thing out." (Or something like that.)

Casting around for one entity to blame is dim – it allows leaders to play the victim card rather than look at the system in all its complexity to identify the parts of that system that they have the power to influence.

We saw in the Integral Leadership Model (shown below) that a dysfunction or weakness in any quadrant caused a dysfunction in the whole system. To contain the spread and mitigate the economic collapse and to successfully lead the world through this pandemic with systems thinking, we would have needed to get right mindset, cultural norms, behaviors, measurement, and systems. Few global leaders got anywhere close. Here are a few of the right questions they should have asked: What behaviors are mandatory? How do we model those? How do we create behavioral nudges? How do we create cultural norms around prevention? What mindset will help slow disease progress? How do we accurately measure progress? How do we create systems (say testing or contract tracing) that arrest progression?

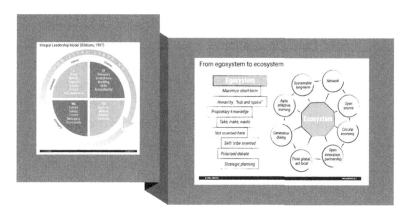

Figure X-2: Systems thinking was absent from COVID-19 leadership

We also suffered from the weaknesses of egosystem thinking (above.) We made tribal thinking and polarized debate the norm. Leaders wanted to get economies moving quickly to minimize short-term damage, but the cost was a resurgence in infection rates. This led to zig-zagging policies and caused consumers and businesses further uncertainty that continued to delay their comeback. For example, if you were considering a family vacation, you might demur thinking the easing of restrictions is another false dawn. This is the case with business investment and rehiring workers – short-term, zig-zagging policies affect the risk of decisions so economies that rushed to open, and then reclosed, damaged the business and consumer confidence which is essential to recovery.

The internet became a blessing and a curse, simultaneously connecting us while spreading disinformation and conspiracy as quickly as valid information. On a positive note, the world's healthcare and drug development systems shifted to a more open source model – scientific papers were shared in draft form to speed collaboration. (Although, a draft paper in the hands of a keyboard warrior is a dangerous thing!) A dispersed, networked system of collaboration meant health care professionals learned more quickly how to save lives.

Leaders who think in systems are rare. Many leaders have a hammer and see a lot of nails, some fail to take multiple views on complex systemic problems, others resist challenge, and still others do not understand (or care) about diverse stakeholders.

> *The answer would seem to lie partially in the spiritual*
> *realm, joining as Pope John Paul II said, fides et*
> *ratio – values and reason. In our scheme, "fides"*
> *is growing and striving for meaning, purpose,*
> *goodness, and connectedness. "Ratio" includes*
> *systems and ecosystem thinking as we explored.*

CONNECTING SCIENCE AND SPIRITUALITY FOR HUMANKIND

In the NOMA world (from Chapter I) where science deals with the world of fact and spirituality with the world of morals and meaning,

COVID-19 would have been a straightforward problem. The morality was straightforward, we want a disease-free world and a recovering global economy. The facts, though evolving, said: we have a highly infectious disease, transmitted through exhaled droplets, that requires hospitalization in about 15% of cases and has around a .5-1% IFR (Infection Fatality Rate.)[113]

If only things were so simple! For science to work, it must change behaviors: e.g. if there is a vaccine, people must get vaccinated. Pre-vaccine, they should stay apart. Scientific knowledge must interact with a culture that may or may not trust and value it. Institutions that recommend policy and the media who communicate the science rely on that trust. If we look again at the Integral Leadership Model, you can visualize the science (top-right) requiring a shift in mindset, behaviors, systems, and culture. Without those cultural elements in place, it does not matter how correct the science is or how loudly the facts are trumpeted on CNN.

As we see with long-term problems such as climate change and plastics, issues often masquerade as purely scientific. "If only people would listen to scientists!" becomes the cry. That, too, is narrow-minded – and scientists and experts are as guilty as politicians in how they frame these debates. Few people take accountability for the whole system – the level of scientific knowledge in the population, the level of trust in institutions, and variations in culture (individualism versus collectivism.)

COVID-19 science was fluid. That is a feature of science, not a bug. Science admits error and revises itself. But in the mindset of a scared populace (or one that is politicized) that leaves people not knowing whom to trust – that is a systemic problem, not a science problem. Today's problems were worsened because lots of people tried to make a fast buck: hydroxychloroquine, miracle cures, sunlight, Vitamin D, and bleach. The US FDA warns against over one

---

[113] Mallapatty, S.,"How deadly is the coronavirus? Scientists are close to an answer," Nature, 16 June 2020

hundred of these, but those are a few that were blessed by senior leaders. This is all made even worse by a surge in what psychologists call motivated reasoning "I don't want to wear a mask, ergo, masks are useless." (People don't actually say that, but the motivation not to wear a mask demands they make up reasons why.) We should trust scientists, not because they are perfect demi-gods, but because when it comes to epidemiology, there ain't nuthin' better – certainly not your buddy Fred who saw an article on www.clickbait-whatdodoctorsknowanyhow.com.

That may seem like more science than spirituality, but leading change that is guided by scientific knowledge requires trust and empathy. Empathy, showing that you care, creates trust. Trust in you, as a leader, is essential to effecting the results the world needs. Leading change guided by science requires enough humility to not pretend to be more knowledgeable than the scientists because that undermines **trust in the science you would like people to follow.** At the same time, leading change requires big picture systems thinking and accountability – two things rarely found during our crisis.

In the fight between politics, ideology, culture, and science, people died. Nobody was thinking deeply enough about the interaction between those different spheres – nobody was accountable.

As the world becomes more complex scientifically, we are going to need a synthesis of science and spirituality to achieve all we might.

However, there were brighter spots than those cultural and institutional weaknesses. Humanity did "ace" some aspects of the pandemic. Let's look first at the compassion and altruism we have seen in recent times.

COMPASSION AND ALTRUISM

"The world is not comprehensible, but it is embraceable:
through the embracing of one of its beings."
MARTIN BUBER, AUSTRIAN PHILOSOPHER

Solving problems collaboratively and globally requires trust and empathy — **seeing other as brother**. When the health crisis began, there were outbreaks of compassion. Said the New York Times, "Some landlords are waiving or lowering rent. Volunteers are buying groceries for their neighbors, cities are starting programs to feed the homeless, and stores are offering exclusive hours for older shoppers. In Kansas, after schools were closed for the rest of the academic year, six tents were set up around Kansas City where students could pick up breakfast and lunch, school officials said."

That altruism extended to vaccine trials which usually require huge populations and long incubation periods as researchers wait to see if the vaccinated group avoids infection. A "human challenge" study infects thousands of volunteers deliberately who risk getting terribly ill — it is quick, conclusive, and dangerous. Yet thousands of people volunteered for such a study.

We created new standards of businesses caring for their employees. Clever businesses found clever new ways to serve customers. The usual practice in a recession, culling employees to protect sacrosanct executive salaries and dividends was delayed or reduced — employees got paid, and executives and sharehold-ers took pay cuts — perhaps setting a new standard for ethical business behavior.

Politicians, even the worst of them, at least briefly, put citizen health before economic growth, realizing for the first time that the former matters more and that the latter depends upon the former. "When pushed," said Mark Carney, former governor of the Bank of England, "societies prioritized health first and foremost and then looked to deal with the economic consequences.... the values of

Figure X – 3: Unemployment lines longer than ever before, but shorter than they might have been had business culled workers.

economic dynamism and efficiency was joined by those of solidarity, fairness, responsibility, and compassion."

For all the failures in the political realm, business arguably embraced more human-centered principles and lessened or at least delayed the economic sting that many families would have felt. But Harvard philosopher Michael Sandel poses an uncomfortable question, lest we become too pleased with ourselves:

> "What kind of economy will emerge from the crisis? Will it be one that continues to create inequalities that poison our politics and undermine any sense of national community? Or will it be one that honors the dignity of work, rewards contributions to the real economy, gives workers a meaningful voice and shares the risks of ill health and hard times? "

CHANGE, INNOVATION, AND LEARNING

"There are two kinds of pain in this world; pain that hurts,
and pain that alters. Today you get to choose."
DENZEL WASHINGTON, IN "THE EQUALIZER"

If an animal's habitat changes dramatically for the worse, the best they can do is flee. Humans, in contrast, have yet another super-power: learning. We can transcend our instincts, alter our behaviors, and modify our habitats.

We quickly learned how much of what we consume we can forgo: flying, restaurants, theater, movies, and sporting events. Although nobody enjoys missing such things, we made do without proms, pic-nics, parties, and weddings. As we isolated from cherished friends and family, especially vulnerable grandparents, those relationships seemed more precious. The overnight adaptations in our personal lives were remarkable – not just working from home, but changes to shopping, viewing, hygiene, parenting, grooming, and exercising behaviors. Social isolation imposed a psychological toll, but it also reminded us of the importance of relationships. We became more **grateful** for the daily bounty of our lives.

Crises fast forward historical processes
of change, innovation, and learning.

Trends that were proceeding glacially, such as remote working, virtual conferencing, online parties, video fitness, and telemedicine became instantly normal. Now that the Band-Aid is ripped off, we will not return completely to the *status quo ante*, and that will be exceptionally good for the planet — if also terrible for airlines, commercial property, the conference industry, and those of us who pound the speaking circuit.

The list of business innovations is a mile long, even without counting pharmaceutical and medical advances. It includes robot cleaning and deliveries, drone monitoring of population health from above, streaming portals for music events such as AllDayIStream. com, contact tracing apps, lights out manufacturing, rapid retooling to make sanitizers, ventilators, and masks, smart city innovations, and increased use of additive manufacturing to augment disrupted supply chains.

Figure X-4: Robot innovation and adoption have taken off.

The crisis became a test of business' ability to respond to human needs — companies found themselves judged by "what they did during the war." For the most part, business rose splendidly to the occasion. (Coming from a business ethicist, this is no faint praise.)

To return to Emmerson, "when it is dark enough, you can see the stars." I began to see glimmers of global solidarity and community that give me hope.

GLOBAL COMMUNITY

"Andrà tutto bene!" (It will all be good.)
(ITALIAN EXPRESSION THAT WENT VIRAL IN 2020 DURING THE CRISIS
TO PROVIDE REASSURANCE AND COMFORT.)

It is wise to remember that pre-crisis "normal" was a crisis for many humans. Children starving to death, particularly in rich countries is a crisis; 2 billion people without clean water is a crisis; 150 million metric tons of plastic in the oceans is a crisis.

It is also wise amid disaster to remember how much worse COVID could have been. According to the journal Nature, as of mid-year, tens of millions of infections and millions of deaths were prevented in Europe alone.[114] This counter-factual, "what-if" type analysis may be cold comfort to people who lost loved ones or are suffering economic hardship. However, our science and the willingness of most people to comply with public health directives saved millions. The only examples that match this scale are the roughly two to three million lives saved each year by vaccination. The only thing that might exceed it is providing sanitation to the 4.5 billion people who lack it. (Imagine world leaders getting behind something as simple and cheap as a toilet to save the lives of roughly half a million children under five per year.)

Toilets and sanitation ain't high-tech. Therefore, it isn't science, but spirituality – compassion, care, purpose, goodness, and ethics that would make the biggest difference to the lives of those billions of children's lives.

COVID-19 left many feeling powerless, as people say they feel in the face of global challenges such as climate change, plastics, and

---

[114] Bhatt, S., et al., Estimating the effects of non-pharmaceutical interventions on COVID-19 in Europe, Nature volume 584, pages 257-261(2020)

hunger. "What can I, alone, possibly do? "If a billion plastic bags and a trillion plastic straws are the problem, what difference will this one make?" Political philosophers and game theorists call that a **collective action problem**. In this dilemma, people know they ought to do the right thing but feel **powerless** as individuals or remain guided by self-interest.

The feeling of individual powerlessness only subsides with feelings of solidarity and community; only then do we lose that sense of isolation and find our collective power. In those communities, we can find shared purpose and meaning. We can work toward goodness that sits above ideology – human welfare, prosperity, and peace.

The great leaders of this crisis harnessed this shared struggle to **connect us** so we could take collective action to **protect** and **heal** one another. They connected us by creating common vision and purpose inside communities to support the collaboration and innovation so essential in our time of need. Other leaders have used this to blame and divide: China versus the US, the media versus the government, public health authorities versus freedom, global organizations versus national interest, and science versus "common sense."

Figure X-5: Great leadership during COVID made a huge difference to the number of deaths in some countries – leaders who have been effective have seen their reputations soar.

To return to Carl Sagan's beatiful homily to the Earth, "The Earth is the only world known so far to harbor life. There is nowhere else, at least in the near future, to which our species could migrate. Visit, yes. Settle, not yet. Like it or not, for the moment the Earth is where we make our stand." This is the only chance we will get - it would be wise to take our best shot. There are no Cosmic do-overs.

The health and economic crisis of 2020 has shown us how imper-manent our world is. It is a reminder that we are not bullet-proof and our existence here is fragile. In the long run, this harbinger of vulnerability may help us find humility and resolve in the fight against climate change and habitat destruction.

With concern for others, collective thinking, and collective action we have demonstrated how powerful we can be when we act together. The crisis increased our **collective self-efficacy,** the belief in our collective agency, and power — what we do can make a difference.

*This sense of **collective** power may sow the seeds of a new global conscience and willingness to tackle challenges that before seemed too great.*

We flattened the COVID curve, now can we flatten some other curves such as the climate curve and the plastics curve? Imagine, for an instant, if we felt the same solidarity and urgency around plastic use and billions of us were to cease using single-use plastics quickly!

Our challenging times reminded us that we are members of a global community built on a foundation of compassion, connection, collaboration, and learning. We learned that we thought was normal was in fact a crisis, and in the crisis, we found aspects of our selves we would like to become normal.

We have been reminded of what we are capable. While many world leaders failed to promote collaboration and lead systemically through COVID-19, humanity at large proved its enormous potential for altruism, innovation, and community-mindedness.

This crisis has shown us the potential we have for progress. We (mostly) agree that climate, habitat destruction, child poverty, human rights, economic welfare, clean water and air, domestic violence, and bloody war are threats. Can a sense of shared destiny, as a species, help us fight them? We saw that spirituality supported collective action in small groups. Could it work for us in the complex societies and world of the 21st century?

For humanity, change is inevitable, but whether it constitutes progress is up to us humans.

PREVIEW OF VOLUME II (CULTURE, CAPITALISM, SUSTAINABILITY)

At the end of a long book, there is still much left unsaid. The astute reader will wonder:

- What about ethics, surely spirituality and philosophy inform that?
- Can humanizing business ever become more than just feel-good words?
- What about purposeful businesses, not just purposeful people? Are there case studies of purposeful businesses?
- What about spiritual conflict? Could that be worsened as more people bring their "whole selves" to work?
- Is capitalism evolving? How does spirituality affect ideas on how to do that?
- To make our business more human using principles from this book, we need to change culture. How do we do that?
- Are values statements a useful leadership tool – do they add any value?
- Is "conscious capitalism" a step in the right direction, or "lip-stick on a pig?"
- What about attracting and retaining talent, is there a "spiritual employer" brand?

- What have been the foremost efforts to reform capitalism from within? Are they working?
- What is the difference between sustainability, CSR, and the circular economy?
- What would human-centered capitalism look like?

These are the right questions, as necessary or moreso than the ones we have explored. What we don't know (at all) is—what are "spiritual people" like to work with? (What is the evidence?) Are they more helpful, less nasty, or better bosses? As spirituality is a journey beyond self-interest, does it manifest itself in outcomes that matter to colleagues, workplaces, and society?

When we try to scale spirituality organizationally, we run into a new set of problems discussed in Volume II. For the spiritually inclined, there are tools for finding purpose and meaning – that can be a private affair – and unarguably a good thing. If an individual finds that "centering themselves" through prayer, meditation, or yoga during a work-break helps them to be more productive or happier, or more considerate at work, then it is to be encouraged.

However, as workplace spirituality becomes less private, perhaps extending itself into small group activity, or perhaps as individuals become more vocal about their spiritual beliefs, organizations will have to take an interest. Boundaries and guidelines will have to be established to prevent infringement of the rights of spiritual minorities or the non-spiritual. How do leaders balance freedom of expression with protections for workers?

Perhaps this isn't attractive? Could business leaders be creating a rod for their own backs? Afterall, if our workers decide they want purposeful, meaningful work, will they be unhappy when they don't get it? Might they purpose themselves out the door?

Then there are more significant questions. Can spiritual businesses compete for capital and talent? If as a leader, I implement a series of human-centered policy reforms making my business kinder to workers, does that put me at a cost disadvantage, and therefore risk the disfavor of Wall Street whose eagle eyes demand efficient use of financial capital. If I, as a leader, redirect my business toward other stakeholders, communities, and human welfare, will I suffer financially? How, again, will Wall Street look upon a business that eschews highly profitable endeavors because by human-centered metrics, not just money, they do not measure up?

Then there are bigger questions still. In centuries past, people commissioned great works of art and architecture that would take a century to build – notably the great cathedrals. What, dear humanity, cathedrals should we be building today? What are we attempting today that will take a quarter-century to achieve, yet which is of even greater human value than a cathedral? Orthodox religion inspired those – what will inspire us to do even more?

ORGANIZATION SCIENCE RESEARCH ON SPIRITUALITY

Organizational behavior and organizational psychology study the relationship between various "spiritual variables" and variables such as job involvement, organizational identification, organizational commitment, job satisfaction, customer experience, work overload, productivity, organizational citizenship behaviors, learning, and innovation behaviors. However, most of the research is non-experimental—that is, based upon **correlations** between two variables. You ask people about their spiritual beliefs and practices and about the attitudes above. You look for correlations, but correlations don't answer chicken-and-egg questions about causality. Imagine you have an amazing job. Your job satisfaction will be super high. Might you not experience, meaning, purpose, and connectedness **as a result** of having a great job? You might. We want to understand, in many instances, whether spirituality is causal – for example, does teaching people to meditate **cause** an increase in focus, executive function, and creativity? We want to know whether people who seek meaning and purpose at work are happier as a result of that search.

Furthermore, there is often considerable overlap between spiritual measures and outcomes such as job satisfaction, researchers are often asking the same question a different way, so correlations are unsurprising. For example, a spiritual question might be, "I am inspired by my work." To assess job satisfaction, you might ask something like, "I enjoy my work most of the time." The researcher should not be surprised to find a positive correlation!

Another problem, common to much psychological research, is the use of self-report questionnaires. "Being spiritual" has a substantial amount of **social desirability**. There is always a gap between what people say and what they do, what they espouse and what they practice. People, being smart cookies, know what the "right" answer is when asked about spiritual attitudes such as compassion. (Who, when asked if they are compassionate, says "hell no?") If religious people are asked whether "I have a deep belief in God," the legit response is skewed toward the affirmative.

The first version of this book, although unrecognizable as such now, presented a lot of that research. My aim was to survey the subject's empirical research base (as it was in 1999.) Today because of the "overlap issue" and the others referred to above, I'm less convinced that research of that kind helps us as much I thought it would in 1999.

However, for the interested reader, there are a few good academic overviews. Notably, *The Handbook of Workplace Spirituality and Organizational Performance*[115] offers a comprehensive overview written by dozens of scholars over 500 pages. The earlier *Spiritual of Audit of Corporate America*[116] took a case study approach to the same.

You might ask, why measure spirituality at all? Afterall, there is enough phenomenological and anecdotal evidence that people find it important to their lives, and that it helps them think through vocation choice and find meaning and purpose in what they do. People also say that their spirituality or religion provides them with a moral compass, a "true north" in their dealings with others, and in the ethical dilemmas that a manager faces.

---

[115] Giacalone, RA, and Jurkiewicz, CL, *The Handbook of Workplace Spirituality and Organizational Performance*, ME Sharpe (2003)

[116] Mitroff, I, and Denton, E, *A Spiritual Audit of Corporate America,* Jossey Bass (1999)

There is a case for doing so. In Chapter VII, we surveyed some of the research: Are "spiritual people" happier? Is their mental health better? Is their task performance on the job better? Does organizational spirituality motivate workers to stay, or to perform? In the same chapter, we saw that beliefs matter much less than factors such as "spiritual striving" and "centrality."

To answer those questions, we relied upon spirituality measurements without saying too much about them. Here are some of the measures and some (more) of the problems.

To measure spirituality, believer/ non-believer distinction seems an easy place to start. You could measure belief versus, say, satisfaction at work. This simple idea turns out not to work in practice. Why? The "do you believe?" question means different things to different people. For some, the transcendent is real, immanent, omnipresent, and material; for some, it infuses all living things; for others, it is impersonal and less concrete. We find that even answering so a seemingly simple question produces different meanings – and **what the concept means** will determine its effect.

There are hundreds of scales for measuring religion from the Psychology of Religion. They distinguish between **typologies, single-trait,** and **multi-traits**.

- Some **typologies** might be denominational, Catholic or Protestant, religions or non-religious. Other typologies seek to distinguish according to the ontology of religious beliefs: **Realist, Existential, Pragmatist, or Idealist**.
- **Single-trait** approaches measure **specific beliefs,** values, and attitudes such as centrality, orthodoxy, and scriptural literalism.
- Multi-trait approaches might simultaneously measure the **ideological, intellectual, ritualistic, experiential, and consequential aspects** of an individual's religion. (In simpler words, the books, beliefs, behaviors, experiences, and "results" of religion.) This echoes a framework from

Hinduism, *hatha* (the body), *raja* (the being or mind), *bhakti* (the emotional and experiential), *jnana* (the intellectual or metaphysical), *kriya* (purification), and *karma* (selfless behaviors.)

Just as finding a definition of spirituality with which most people agree is difficult, likewise finding a measure that is **broad enough to encompass contemporary pluralism**, and yet **specific enough** so it is asking **only** about spirituality is extremely difficult.

Early measures of spirituality were deeply flawed. Here, for example, is one from 1985.

Web model of spiritual well-being

Relationship dimensions	Temporal dimensions
Belief in, and relationship with a Supreme Being	Past experiences: parental influences, formal belief systems, cultural legacy
Deep, supportive relationships with family and friends	Present integration: finding meaning and purpose in life situations, and a sense of congruence between one's values and behavior
Relationship with self: self-satisfaction and acceptance, positive attitude, and self-determination	Future hopes: afterlife, ability to achieve goals, attaining fuller integration, continuing the search for meaning and purpose
© PAUL GIBBONS	PAULGIBBONS.NET

Table XII-1: Web Model of Spiritual Well-being[117]

As you can see, the questionnaire includes terms such as "Supreme Being" and "afterlife" neither of which is, according to our definition and the way the term spirituality is currently used, essential.

Nevertheless, this "two-dimensional" approach is commonplace. The "vertical" dimension measuring relationship to a transcendent (a **meaning dimension**), and the "horizontal" dimension relating to purpose in life (a **purpose dimension**.)

---

[117] Hungelmann JA, Kenkel-Rossi E, Klassen L, Stollenwerk RM. Spiritual well-being in older adults: Harmonious interconnectedness. Journal of Religion and Health. 1985; 24:147–153.

Another scale, the SAS[118] (Spirituality Assessment Scale) has four dimensions (subscales) 1) Purpose and Meaning in Life, 2) Interconnectedness (connectedness to others and to the environment), 3) Innerness (inner peace and inner strength in times of difficulties) and 4) Transcendence. This measure is much closer to the definition that we used and encompasses more of what people mean by spirituality today.

Other scales measure spiritual experience, for example, the Daily Spirituality Experience Scale and others are multi-dimensional, for example, the Brief Multidimensional Measure of Religiousness/Spirituality developed by the Fetzer Institute. Yet others focus on Humanistic spirituality. Two of the most common of these are shown in the table below. While there is overlap between the two measures, for example, meaning and values, the Fetzer Institutes scale leans toward traditional religion, while Elkin's is Humanistic.

Two common measures of spirituality used in spiritualty at work research

Elkin's humanistic-phenomenological (1988)	Fetzer Institute (1999)
Transcendent	Daily spiritual experiences
Meaning and purpose	Meaning
Mission	Values
Sacredness	Beliefs
Spiritual values	Forgiveness
Altruism	Private religious practices
Idealism	Spiritual coping
Awareness	Support
Benefits	Spiritual history
	Commitment
	Organizational religiousness
	Religious preference

© PAUL GIBBONS · PAULGIBBONS.NET

Table XIII - 2: Two common measures of spirituality used in spirituality at work research

---

[118] Howden, J. W. (1992). Development and psychometric characteristics of the spirituality assessment scale. Ann Arbor: Texas Woman's University, UMI Dissertation Services.

It is my view, shared by many other scholars, that most of these measures are still fairly weak because a) many still use religious terms, b) they lack "convergent validity" (that is to say that the items on the scale "agree" with one another, or converge, c) they frequently overlap (tautologically) with the items we want to compare spirituality with (for example, motivation, well-being, commitment, health, or life satisfaction.)

Nevertheless, these are topics we need to understand more deeply. In meditation research, we found a change in valuable outcomes for new meditators – people taught to meditate. That tells us something about cause and effect. We want to understand links between beliefs and behaviors – for example, are people who believe in a deity more ethical actors in the world? Given how quickly the spiritual landscape has changed, it is challenging for researchers to keep up – but the prize is promising.

ACKNOWLEDGEMENTS

Thanks to my father, Professor William Gibbons, who taught me to love science, ideas and learning while I was still a tot; and to my mother, Moira Donnelly, who passed on her voracious appetite for knowledge. We were a Catholic family, and my time with the Jesuits deepened my love for scholarship and science, as well as mystery and wonder.

My colleagues at Future Considerations, The Hon. James Shaw, Cari Caldwell, Mark Young, Arjan Overwater, Peter Hamill, and Kate Larsen were inspirational – I get credit for founding the business, but it might still be in my living room if not for the extraordinary talents of above. It was their curiosity and interest in these topics that introduced many of the methods and tools found in this book to clients.

This book was first written as a thesis. My advisor, Professor Rob Briner, now at Queen Mary College, University of London, encouraged me even though the topic might then have seemed off-piste. Price-waterhouseCoopers sponsored this research and allowed me to take a sabbatical leave, attend a half dozen conferences, and to purchase hundreds of books. Most of the original research was done while a Visiting Fellow at the University of Wisconsin – Madison. Dean R.D. Nair's support made available the superb research facilities of the Business School. Professor Ray Aldag provided friendship, encouragement, and feedback, and Professor Laura Hartman offered direction in business ethics.

Drafts of various chapters received challenging reviews from both friends and subject experts. Those included Ro Gorell, David Bennett, Prof. Don Mayer, Dr. Dan Sweeney, Dr. Robin Wood, Maureen Metcalf, Aíne Watkins, Cari Caldwell, Prof. Denis Collins, Prof. Robert Giaccalone, Dr. Judi Neal, Dr. Andrew Taggart, Arjan Overwater, Kate Larsen, Anita Cochrane, Adam Gold, Charles O'Malley, and Tremaine du Preez. The errors that remain are all mine.

I'd like to thank Cory Emberson, Dania Zafar, Kelli Collins, and Andrés Goldstein for their superb assistance with production and editing.

BIBLIOGRAPHY

Allport, G. & J. Ross. "Personal Religious Orientation and Prejudice." Journal of Personality and Social Psychology, 5 (1967): 432–443.

Allport, Gordon. *The Individual and His Religion*. New York: Macmillan, 1950.

Austin, N. "Does Spirituality at Work Work?" Working Woman, March 1995.

Barrett, Richard. *Liberating the Corporate Soul: Building a Visionary Organization*, Boston: Butterworth-Heinemann, 1998.

Barrett, Richard. *The New Leadership Paradigm*, Lulu, 2011.

Bauman, Zygmunt. "Postmodern religion?" In Heelas, Paul (Ed.), Religion, Modernity and Postmodernity, Oxford: Wiley-Blackwell, 1998.

Beazley, Hamilton. "Meaning and Measurement of Spirituality in Organizational Settings: Development of a Spirituality Assessment Scale." Ph.D. dissertation, George Washington University, 1997.

Beck, D., & Cowan, C. *Spiral Dynamics: Mastering Values, Leadership, and Change*, Blackwell, 2005.

Berger, Peter L. and Thomas Luckmann. *The Social Construction of Reality*, New York: Doubleday, 1966.

Blackwood, Larry. "Social Change and Commitment to the Work Ethic." In Wuthnow, Robert (Ed.), The Religious Dimension: New Directions in Quantitative Research, New York: Academic, 1979.

Bloch, Deborah P. and Lee J. Richmond. *Connections between Work and Spirit in Career Development: New approaches and practical perspectives*, Palo Alto: Davies-Black, 1997.

Block, Peter. *Stewardship: Choosing Service over Self-Interest*, San Francisco: Berrett-Koehler Publishers, 1993.

Blond, Phillip. "The primacy of theology and the question of perception," In Heelas, Paul (Ed.), *Religion, Modernity and Postmodernity*, Oxford: Wiley-Blackwell, 1998.

Bolman, Lee G. and Terrance E. Deal. *Leading with Soul: An Uncommon Journey of Spirit*, San Francisco: Jossey-Bass, 1995.

Boldt, Laurence G. *Zen and the Art of Making a Living: A Practical Guide to Creative Career Design*, New York: Arkana-Penguin, 1991.

Bowles, Nellie. "God is Dead. So Is the Office. These People Want to Save Both," The New York Times, August 28, 2020.

Brief, Arthur P. *Attitudes in and Around Organizations*, California: Sage Publishing, 1998.

Briskin, Alan. *The Stirring of Soul in the Workplace*, San Francisco: Berrett-Koehler Publishers, 1998.

Carson, Rachel. *Silent Spring*, Houghton Mifflin, 1962.

Chödrön, P. *The places that scare you: A guide to fearlessness in difficult times.* Boston: Shamabala. 2007.

Christian, David. *Maps of Time: An Introduction to Big History*, University of California Press, 2004

Creedon, Jeremiah. "God with a Million Faces," Utne Reader, July–August (1998): 42–48.

Cousins, Lance. "Buddhism," in Hinnells, John R. (Ed.), *A New Handbook of Living Religions*, London: Penguin, 1997.

Csikszentmihalyi, Mihaly. *Flow: The Psychology of Happiness*, London: Rider, 1992.

Dewey, John. *A Common Faith*, New Haven: Yale University Press, 1934.

Diener, Ed. "Subjective Well-Being," Psychological Bulletin 95 (1984): 542–575.

Elkins, D., J. Hedstrom, L. Hughes, A. Leaf, and C. Saunders. "Toward a Humanistic Phenomenological Spirituality: Definition, Description, and Measurement," Journal of Humanistic Psychology 28, no. 4 (1988): 8–15.

Emmons, R.A., C. Cheung, and K. Tehrani. "Assessing Spirituality Through Personal Goals: Implications for Research on Religion and Subjective Well-Being," Social Indicators Research 45 (1998): 391–422.

Emmons, Robert A. and Cheryl Crumpler. "Religion and Spirituality? The Roles of Sanctification and the Concept of God," The International Journal for the Psychology of Religion 9, no. 1 (1999): 17–24.

Emmons, Robert A. and Raymond F. Paloutzian. Annual Review of Psychology 54 (2003):377–402. doi: 10.1146/annurev.psych.54.101601.145024

Fetzer Institute. "Multidimensional Measurement of Religiousness/Spirituality for Use in Health Research," Jan. 1999.

Fields, R., P. Taylor, R. Weyler, and R. Ingrasci. "To Work Is to Pray," in Whitmeyer, C. (Ed.), *Mindfulness and Meaningful Work*, Berkeley" Parallax Press, 1994.

Fitchett, G. "Screening for Spiritual Risks: A Guide to Selected Resources," Chicago: Center for Spirituality and Health, 1997.

Frankl, Viktor E. *Man's Search for Meaning*, New York: Washington Square Press, 1959.

Fowler, James W. *Stages of Faith: The Psychology of Human Development and the Quest for Meaning*, HarperCollins College Division, 1981.

Fox, M. *The Reinvention of Work: A New Vision of Livelihood for Our Time*, San Francisco: HarperCollins, 1994.

Fromm, Erich. *To Have or To Be*? New York: Harper & Row, 1976.

Gaus, Gerald. *The Order of Public Reason: A Theory of Freedom and Morality in a Diverse and Bounded World*, Cambridge: Cambridge University Press, 2011.

Giacalone, Robert A. and Carole L. Jurkiewicz. *Handbook of Workplace Spirituality and Organizational Performance*. New York: M.E. Sharpe, 2003.

Gibbons, Paul, *The Science of Organizational Change: How Leaders Set Strategy, Change Behavior, and Create an Agile Culture*, Phronesis Media, 2019 (2nd Edition.)

Gibbons, Paul, *Impact, 21st-century Change Management, Behavioral Science, Digital Transformation and the Future of Work*, Phronesis Media, 2019.

Gibbons, Paul and Ragan, Tim. *Reboot Your Career: A Blueprint for Finding Your Calling, Marketing Yourself, and Landing Great Gigs*, Phronesis Media, 2016.

Gibbons, Paul. Spirituality at Work: Definitions, Measures, and Validity Claims, in *Work & Spirit: A Reader of New Spiritual Paradigms for Organizations,* Biberman, Jerry (Ed.) and Michael D. Whitty (Ed.). University of Scranton Press, 2000. (74th Edition, April 30, 2005)

Glock, Charles Y. "On the Study of Religious Commitment," Religious Education Research Supplement 57 (4) (1962): 98–110.

Grayling, A.C., *Meditations for the Humanist, Ethics for a Secular Age*, Oxford, 2002

Grayling, A.C., *The God Argument, The Case Against Religion and for Humanism*, Bloomsbury, 2013.

Greanleaf, Robert. "Servant Leadership," in Spears, L. (Ed.), *Insights on Leadership: Service, Stewardship, Spirit, and Servant-Leadership*, New York: Wiley, 1996.

Greene, Yvonne and Bryan Hiebart. "A Comparison of Mindfulness Meditation and Cognitive Self-Observation," Canadian Journal of Counselling 22 (1) (1988) 25–34.

Habermas, Jürgen. *Knowledge and Human Interests*, Boston: Beacon, 1971.

Harari, Yuval, *Sapiens: A Brief History of Humankind*, Harper, 2015.

Harari, Yuval, *Homo Deus: A Brief History of Tomorrow*, Harper, 2017.

Harman, W. "21st Century Business: A Background for Dialogue," in Renesch, J. (Ed.) *New Traditions in Business: Spirit and Leadership in the 21st Century*, San Francisco: Berrett-Koehler, 1992.

Heelas, Paul. "On Differentiation and De-differentiation," *Religion, Modernity, and Post-modernity*, Oxford: Blackwell, 1998.

Heelas, Paul and Linda Woodhead. *The Spiritual Revolution. Why Religion is Giving Way to Spirituality.* Oxford: Blackwell, 2005.

Danièle Hervieu-Léger. "The Role of Religion in Establishing Social Cohesion," 2006. http://www.eurozine.com/articles/2006-08-17-hervieuleger-en.html.

H.H. the Dalai Lama and Howard C. Cutler. *The Art of Happiness*, New York: Penguin, 1998.

Hood, Ralph. "Sin and Guilt in Faith Traditions: Issues for Self-Esteem," in Schumaker (Ed.) *Religion and Mental Health*, Oxford: Oxford University Press, 1992.

Hunglemann, JoAnn, Eileen Kenkel-Rossi, Loretta Klassen, and Ruth Stollenwerk. "Spiritual Well-Being in Older Adults: Harmonious Interconnectedness," Journal of Religion and Health 24 (2) (1985): 147–153.

Isen, A.M., and R.A. Baron. "Positive Affect as a Factor in Organizational Behavior," Research in Organizational Behavior 13 (1991): 1–53.

James, William. *The Varieties of Religious Experience*, New York: Penguin, 1902.

Jung, Carl. *Modern Man in Search of a Soul*, New York: Doubleday, 1974.

Kahane, Adam. *Solving Tough Problems: An Open Way of Talking, Listening, and Creating New Realities.* San Francisco: Berrett-Koehler, 2007.

Kanfer, R. "Motivation Theory in Industrial and Organizational Psychology," in Dunnette, M. (Ed.), *Handbook of Industrial and Organizational Psychology,* Volume 1. Chicago: Rand-McNally, 1990.

Kanungo, R. and M. Mendonca. "What Leaders Cannot Do Without: The Spiritual Dimensions of Leadership," in Conger, J. (Ed.) *Spirit at Work: Discovering the Spirit in Leadership,* San Francisco: Jossey-Bass, 1994.

Kegan, R. *The Evolving Self: Problem and Process in Human Development*, Harvard, 1982.

Kets de Vries, Manfred and Danny Miller. *The Neurotic Organization*, San Francisco: Jossey-Bass, 1984.

King, Ursula. "Spirituality," in Hinnells, John (Ed.) *A New Handbook of Living Religions*, London: Penguin, 1997.

Kurtz, Ernest and Katherine Ketcham. *The Spirituality of Imperfection*, New York: Bantam, 1992.

Laloux, Frederic. *Reinventing Organizations: A Guide to Creating Organizations Inspired by the Next Stage in Human Consciousness*, Nelson Parker, 2014.

Larsson, G. "Routinization of Mental Training in Organizations: Effects on Performance and Well-Being," Journal of Applied Psychology 72 (1) (1987): 88–96.

Lips-Wiersma, Marjolein and Lani Morris. *The Map of Meaningful Work*, Abingdon: Routledge, 2018.

Mackey, John and Rajendra Sisodia. *Conscious Capitalism: Liberating the Heroic Spirit of Business*, Boston: Harvard Business School Publishing Corporation, 2014.

Maslow, Abraham. *Religions, Values, and Peak Experiences*, New York: Penguin, 1970.

Masters, K. and A. Bergin. "Religious Orientation and Mental Health" in Schumaker, J. (Ed.), Religion and Mental Health, Oxford: Oxford University Press, 1992.

May, Gerald. *Will and Spirit: A Contemplative Psychology*, San Francisco: Harper-Collins, 1982.

May, Gerald. *Addiction and Grace: Love and Spirituality in the Healing of Addictions*, New York: Harper-Collins, 1988.

Meadows, Donella. *Thinking in Systems*, Chelsea Green. 2008.

Morgan, Gareth. *Images of Organization*, California: Sage Publications, 1986.

Neal, J., B. Lichtenstein, D. Banner. "Spiritual perspectives on individual, organizational, and societal transformation," Journal of Organizational Change Management 12 (3) (1999).

Neck, Christopher P. and John F. Milliman. "Thought Self-Leadership: Finding Spiritual Fulfilment in Organizational Life," Journal of Managerial Psychology 9 (6) (1994): 9–16.

Nietszche, F. *A Nietzsche Reader*, London: Penguin. 1977.

Nietszche, F. *Ecce Homo: How One Becomes What One Is*, CreateSpace. 2018.

Nietszche, F. *The Will to Power*, CreateSpace 2017

NIV Study Bible, The. London: Hodder & Stoughton, 1973.

Norager, T., "Metapsychology and Discourse: A Note of Some Neglected Issues in the Psychology of Religion," International Journal for the Psychology of Religion 6 (3) (1999).

Novak, M., *Business as a Calling*, New York: Free Press, 1996.

Oldham, J. "Amen at the Top." The Los Angeles Times, June 4, 1998.

Palmer, Parker. "Leading from Within: Out of the Shadow, into the Light," in Conger, Jay (Ed.), *Spirit at Work: Discovering the Spirituality in Leadership*, San Francisco: Jossey-Bass, 1994.

Pargament, Kenneth I. "The Psychology of Religion and Spirituality? Yes and No," The International Journal for the Psychology of Religion 9 (1) (1999): 3–16.

Pargament, Kenneth I., Forrest B. Tyler, and Robert E. Steele. "Is fit it? The relationship between the church/synagogue member fit and the psychosocial competence of the member," Journal of Community Psychology 7 (1979).

Peck, M. Scott. *The Road Less Traveled: A New Psychology of Love, Traditional Values, and Spiritual Growth*, New York: Simon & Schuster, 1978.

Peck, M. Scott. *Further Along the Road Less Travelled: The Unending Journey Towards Spiritual Growth*, New York: Touchstone, 1998.

Perez, S., Religious and Non-Religious Aspects of Spirituality and Their Relation to Myers-Briggs Personality Typology, Doctoral Dissertation: Georgia State University (1998).

Pigliucci, Massimo. *How to Be a Stoic: Using Ancient Philosophy to Live a Modern Life* Paperback, Basic Books, 2018.

Pinker, S., *Enlightenment Now, The Case for Reason, Science, Humanism, and Progress*, Viking, 2017

Pfeffer, Jeffrey. *Leadership BS, Fixing our Workplaces and Careers One Truth at a Time*, Harper Business, 2015.

Poggi, Gianfranco. *Calvinism and the Capitalist Spirit: Max Weber's Protestant Ethic*, London: MacMillan, 1983.

Poloma, Margaret M. and Brian F. Pendleton. "Religious Domains and General Well-Being," Social Indicators Research 22 (1990).

Putnam, Robert. *Bowling Alone: The Collapse and Revival of American Community*, New York: Simon & Schuster, 2001.

Ray, Paul. *The Integral Culture Survey: A Study of the Emergence of Transformational Values in America*, Sausalito: Institute of Noetic Sciences (IONS), 1996.

Rafaeli, Anat and Robert I. Sutton. "The Expression of Emotion in Organizational Life," Research in Organizational Behavior 11 (1989): 1–42.

Renesch, John (Ed.) and Bill DeFoore (Ed.). *The New Bottom Line: Bringing Heart and Soul to Business*, Pleasanton, California: New Leaders Press, 1998.

Richards, Dick. *Artful Work: Awakening Joy, Meaning, and Commitment in the Workplace*, San Francisco: Berrett-Koehler Publishers, 1995.

Rivers, Stephen M. and Nicholas P. Spanos. "Personality Variables Prediction of Participation in and Attrition from a Meditation Program," Psychological Reports 49 (3) (1981).

Roberts, K., "The sociology of work entry and occupation choice," in Watts, Super, and Kidd (Eds.), *Career Development in Britain*, Cambridge: Hobson's Press, 1981.

Rodgers, D., *The Work Ethic in Industrial America*, 1850–1920, Chicago: University of Chicago Press, 1974.

Roof, Wade Clark. *A Generation of Seekers: The Spiritual Journeys of the Baby Boom Generation*, San Francisco: HarperCollins, 1993.

Sandel, Michael. *Justice – What is the Right Thing to Do?* Farrar, Straus & Giroux, 2010.

Sandel, Michael, *Public Philosophy: Essays on Morality and Politics*, Harvard, 2006.

Sandelands, Lloyd E. and Georgette C. Buckner. "Of Art and Work: Aesthetic Experience and the Psychology of Work Feelings, Research in Organizational Behavior 11 (1989): 105–131.

Scharmer, Otto & Senge, Peter, *Theory U: Leading from the Future as It Emerges*, Berrett Koehler, 2016.

Schmidt-Wilk, Jane, Charles N. Alexander, and Gerald C. Swanson. "Developing

Consciousness in Organizations: The Transcendental Meditation Program in Business," Journal of Business and Psychology 10 (4) (1996): 429–444.

Schlossberg, Herbert, Vinay Samuel, and Ronald Sider, *Christianity and Economics in the Post-Cold War Era: The Oxford Declaration and Beyond*, Grand Rapids: Eerdmans, 1994.

Schumaker, J., *Religion and Mental Health*, Oxford: Oxford University Press, 1992.

Senge, Peter, Richard Ross, Art Kleiner, Charlotte Roberts, Bryan Smith, *The Fifth Discipline Fieldbook*, London: Nicholas Brealey, 1994.

Sharfman, Mark. "The Effects of Managerial Values on Social Issues Evaluation: An Empirical Examination," Academy of Management Review, Best Papers, 1997.

Shaver, P., M. Lenauer, and S. Sadd. "Religiousness, Conversion, and Subjective Well-Being: The "healthy-minded" religion of modern American women," American Journal of Psychiatry 137 (1980): 1563–68.

Sims, Ronald. *Ethics and Organizational Decision Making: A Call for Renewal*, Westport: Quorum, 1994.

Spilka, Bernard, Ralph Hood, and Richard Gorsuch. *The Psychology of Religion: An Empirical Approach*, New Jersey: Prentice Hall, 1985.

Swinburne, Richard. *The Evolution of the Soul*, Oxford: Clarendon Press, 1997.

Terkel, Studs. *Working*, New York: The New Press, 1972.

Tillich, Paul. *What Is Religion?* New York: Harper & Row, 1969.

Tillich, Paul. *Dynamics of Faith*, New York: Harper & Row, 1957.

Toms, Justine Willis and Michael Toms. *True Work: The Sacred Dimension of Earning a Living*, New York: Bell Tower, 1998.

Torbert, W. *Action Inquiry: The Secret of Timely and Transforming Leadership*, Berrett-Koehler, 2004.

Trott, David Crooker. Spiritual Well-Being of Workers, Doctoral dissertation, University of Texas – Austin (1996).

Underhill, Evelyn. *The Spiritual Life*, London: Hodder & Stoughton, 1937.

Vergote, Antoine. *The Religious Man: A Psychological Study of Religious Attitudes*, Dublin: Gill and MacMillan, 1969.

Walls, Andrew. "Christianity" in Hinnells, J. (Ed.), *A New Handbook of Living Religions*, London: Penguin, 1997.

Walsh, Roger. "Meditation Practice and Research," Journal of HumanisticPsychology 23 (1) (1983): 18–50.

Watts, Anthony. "Socio-political Ideologies in Guidance," in Watts et al. (Eds.), *Rethinking Careers Education and Guidance: Theory, Policy and Practice*, London: Routledge, 1996.

Weber, Max. *The Protestant Work Ethic and the Spirit of Capitalism*, New York: Scribners, 1930.

Weick, Karl. *Sensemaking in Organizations*, California: Sage, 1995.

Weightman, Simon. "Hinduism," in Hinnells, J. (Ed.), *A New Handbook of Living Religions*, London, Penguin, 1997.

Weisbord, Marvin. *Productive Workplaces: Managing for Dignity, Meaning, and Community*, San Francisco: Jossey-Bass, 1990.

Wheatley, Margaret. *Leadership and the New Science: Discovering Order in a Chaotic World*, San Francisco: Berrett-Koehler, 2006.

Whitmyer, Claude. *Mindfulness and Meaningful Work*, Berkeley: Parallax Press, 1994.

Whyte, David. *The Heart Aroused: Poetry and the Preservation of the Soul in Corporate America*, New York: Doubleday, 1994.

Wigglesworth, Cindy. *SQ21: The Twenty-One Skills of Spiritual Intelligence*, Select Books. 2014

Wilber, Ken. *Integral Psychology: Consciousness, Spirit, Psychology, Therapy*. Boston: Shambhala Publications, 2000.

Wilber, Ken. *Sex, Ecology, Spirituality: The Story of Evolution*, Boston: Shambhala Publications, 1995.

Wilber, K., *The Marriage of Sense and Soul: Integrating Science and Religion,* New York: Random House, 1998.

Witter, R., W. Stock, M. Okun, and M. Haring. "Religion and Subjective Well-Being in Adulthood: A Quantitative Synthesis," Review of Religious Research 26 (1985): 332–342.

Wood, RL. *A Leaders Guide to ThriveAbility: A Multi-Capital Operating System for a Regenerative Inclusive Economy* AuthorHouse. 2015.

Wright, T. A., and R. Cropanzano, R. "Psychological well-being and job satisfaction as predictors of job performance," Journal of Occupational Health Psychology 5 (1) (2000): 84–94.

INDEX

Made in the USA
Monee, IL
31 October 2020